TALES FROM NOWHERE
EDITED BY DON GEORGE

LONELY PLANET PUBLICATIONS

Melbourne • Oakland • London

Tales From Nowhere: Unexpected Stories From Unexpected Places

Published by Lonely Planet Publications

Head Office:
90 Maribyrnong Street, Footscray, Vic 3011, Australia
Locked Bag 1, Footscray, Vic 3011, Australia

Branches:
150 Linden Street, Oakland CA 94607, USA
2nd floor, 186 City Rd, London, EC1V 2NT, UK

First published 2006
This edition published 2011
Printed in China

10 9 8 7 6 5 4 3 2 1

Copy edited by Martine Lleonart
Designed by Mark Adams
Cover design by Roberto de Vicq de Cumptich

National Library of Australia Cataloguing-in-Publication entry

Tales from nowhere : unexpected stories from unexpected places / edited by
Don George.

2nd ed.

ISBN 978 1 74179 520 2 (pbk.)

1. Travelers' writings. 2. Voyages and travels.

910.4

CONTENTS

There are people everywhere who form a Fourth World, or a diaspora of their own. They are the lordly ones! They come in all colours. They can be Christians or Hindus or Muslims or Jews or pagans or atheists. They can be young or old, men or women, soldiers or pacifists, rich or poor. They may be patriots, but they are never chauvinists. They share with each other, across all the nations, common values of humour and understanding. When you are among them you know you will not be mocked or resented, because they will not care about your race, your faith, your sex or your nationality, and they suffer fools if not gladly, at least sympathetically. They laugh easily. They are easily grateful. They are never mean. They are not inhibited by fashion, public opinion, or political correctness. They are exiles in their own communities, because they are always in a minority, but they form a mighty nation, if they only knew it. It is the nation of nowhere.

– Jan Morris

INTRODUCTION –
NOWHERE, EVERYWHERE

BY DON GEORGE

We've all been to Nowhere. It might have been in the middle of
Mongolia or Manhattan. It might have been at a Zen monastery,
a no-man's-land border outpost, or a six-palm island in an
endless sea. You may have found Nowhere on a sultry summer
night in Paris when you'd spent your last euro and had no place
to sleep; or on a midnight jeep safari in the Tanzanian bush
after you'd blown your last spare tyre, with your campsite a
distant pinprick of light; or in the comforting cocoon of an all-
night train compartment, sharing soul-secrets with a total
stranger. Nowhere is a setting, a situation and a state of mind.
It's not on any map, but you know it when you're there.

Nine months ago, when Lonely Planet announced the theme
of this year's literary anthology, *Tales from Nowhere*, I
embarked on my own journey to Nowhere, an editorial
expedition into uncharted wilderness. There were no
guidebooks or landmarks; no compass or map. Where is
Nowhere? And how do you create a book about it?

As with many great journeys, setting out was simultaneously
exhilarating and unsettling. Fortunately, compiling two
previous Lonely Planet anthologies, *The Kindness of Strangers*
and *By the Seat of My Pants*, had taught me to trust this

process: to trust the theme, because it resonated with my own travel lessons and those of other travellers; to trust the journey, because when you open yourself to the world, the world always responds with grace; and to trust the untapped tales that awaited in the wilderness.

And what tales awaited! In the months after we announced this theme, hundreds and hundreds of stories arrived by digital camel, bus, túk-túk and canoe. The range and quality of submissions astonished and delighted me – tales that I never could have imagined, and that expanded the characteristics and boundaries of Nowhere day by day.

In the end, choosing the stories for this collection was an extremely arduous and edifying task. The thirty-one pieces presented herein are exceptional not just for their literary qualities but for their life qualities as well. Full of passion, surprise, wonder, curiosity and revelation, these real-life tales compose a kaleidoscopic portrait of the many Nowheres we visit – and the many roads we take to get there – in our lives.

In some of these stories, the authors intentionally journey to Nowhere, but with unintended consequences. Simon Winchester wings off on assignment to cover the worst country in the world – and brings back an all-too-dramatic souvenir; Pico Iyer searches for nothingness on Easter Island, and finds it in greater abundance than he'd hoped for; Laura Resau unwittingly bonds with Mexican villagers through a succession of mysterious Maya rites; Angie Chuang pursues a pulse-pounding pilgrimage into the heart of Afghanistan; Christopher Cox confronts lethal mines and memories en route to Pol Pot's Cambodian hideout; and Stanley Stewart ventures upriver beyond the last human settlement in Sarawak.

In other stories, the authors stumble upon Nowhere by accident, and recount the adventures, encounters and illuminations that ensue. Marooned at a dusty nondestination in Malawi, Judy Tierney learns to revel in everyday riches; Lisa

Alpine tumbles into an oasis of tranquillity in war-torn Israel; James Hamilton is transported by a symphony of art and nature in Death Valley; Conor Grennan skids into an unforgettable encounter in rural Sri Lanka; and Rolf Potts gains a new worldly perspective in a rural Kansas town.

Other authors enter the gates of Nowhere via circumstance and serendipity. Danny Wallace's condemnation to airport-lounge limbo is commuted by an unlikely angel; Karla Zimmerman's country-road collision on a Vietnamese bus builds impromptu bridges; Don Meredith's spontaneous detour to join an old friend on an African engine safari ends in a celebration of Shakespeare, Tuskers beer and the simple bounties of the bush; and Pam Houston's odyssey into the wilds of Australia introduces her to a character named Cool Beans and the wonders of Western Australia.

Finally, some of these tales travel rare, rugged roads to unexpected Nowheres, as in Davi Walders' deeply moving discovery of a place – and its courageous witness – that almost ceased to exist; Joshua Clark's extraordinary excavation and evocation of an obliterated neighbourhood and its indomitable denizens; Karl Taro Greenfeld's gripping depiction of doggedly tracking an interminable trail into a deadly territory; and Jason Elliot's deliciously eye-opening account of a journey to a place where cultures clash and coalesce.

o o o o o o o o o

Re-reading these tales and reflecting on my three decades of travel, I realise that my own adventures have taken me to Nowhere almost everywhere: when I left the comfortable Connecticut countryside for the widening wilds of college, when I left college for Paris, when I left Paris for Athens. All these were excursions to Nowhere. I recall the initial intimidations and later illuminations of Princeton, literature and writing classes and teachers that deepened and directed my life. I recall my first fledgling forays in Paris – *le jeune américain* slipping on identities like overcoats, trying to fashion a new life in a new language in a new city, drunk on art and architecture and history, wandering in the footsteps of Hemingway and Baudelaire. In Athens I recall out-of-time afternoons at a no-name seaside café with an alluring, elusive expat who embodied all the clarities and confusions of Greece for me; an off-limits border town called Pythion, where I missed the connection for the Istanbul-bound train and had to linger for twelve hours in the rail station with only a suspicious policeman and my journal for company; and most hauntingly the Palace of Knossos on Crete, where past-life intimations plucked me around every corner.

A year later I found myself – or lost myself – in Japan: among the mesmerising moss-pocked rocks and meticulously raked sands of Kyoto's Ryoanji Temple rock garden, an exquisite enigma designed so the viewer cannot see the entire garden from any vantage – but must 'see' it, complete it, in the mind; under the soft and softly scented pink petal fall of cherry blossoms in spring, efflorescent affirmations of evanescence and eternity; and on the idyllic island of Shikoku, site of a sacred pilgrims' path, where my own heart's pilgrimage culminated in a Shinto wedding ceremony in my wife's village home.

In the ensuing decades I have visited Nowhere around the globe: in the simple, time-fusing touch of hand to holy water at Notre Dame cathedral in Paris; in watching sunrise fire up the pulsing, breathing earth energy of Uluru, in Australia's Outback; in scrunch-scrunch-scrunching along Pakistan's Karakoram Highway, a momentary mote among the aged implacable peaks; in swimming among sea lions and bounding among blue-footed boobies in the raw, rooting wonder-world of the Galápagos; in adrenaline-pulling past a momentary glimpse of oblivion on a sheer slippery ascent of Yosemite's Half Dome.

Whether setting, situation, or state of mind (or usually, some conjunction of all three), what all these Nowheres share is the quality of disorientedness. For a moment you lose your bearings, there are no coordinates, all sense of the familiar is gone: you're Nowhere. Then you settle into your neo-Gothic dormitory room, assemble an identity at the Musée d'Orsay and the local café, you reach the Karakoram guesthouse, flop back onto the Galápagos ship, hug your wife and kids on Half Dome's glinting peak. Your jagged edges snap back into the global picture-puzzle.

But for a moment that you will never forget, you were a disconnected piece in another puzzle: Nowhere.

o o o o o o o o o

The pieces in these pages map the geographical reaches of Nowhere, from Tuscany to Timbuktu, Antarctica to Yap, and the emotional reaches too: delight and despair, remorse and reconciliation, humour and heartache, loss and longing and love.

As I survey this map now, five interwoven lessons seem to stand out in relief.

The first is that Nowhere, like beauty, is in the eye of the beholder. One person's Nowhere is another person's Everywhere. The most unimaginably remote outpost is someone's everyday world – and means the world to that person. Everything is relative, and we would all do well to heed this humble, humbling lesson.

A second, corollary lesson is that we are always, everywhere, surrounded by riches. If we assess a place as Nowhere because it is impoverished or dull or boring, that is because we are impoverished in attention and appreciation. Virtually wherever we are, if we can slow down, focus and absorb the Nowhere around us, we will be astounded by its intricate depths and riches.

The third, linked lesson is that the size of the world is not fixed. It is as big as our experiences and our imaginations; it grows as we grow. This is true for all humans, whether in steel-and-glass city skyscrapers or branch-and-mud jungle treehouses, stony highland castles or goatskin desert tents. In this sense, too, every Nowhere is a Somewhere: every excursion to Nowhere expands the dimensions of our world.

The fourth lesson is that humans are a remarkably resourceful and resilient species: we confront unimagined challenges and overcome them. If we can embrace and embody the qualities Jan Morris ascribes to Nowhere in the epigraph to this collection – courage and compassion, humour and humility, tolerance and understanding – our potentials are infinite.

The fifth lesson is a simple truth the tales within these pages abundantly illuminate and celebrate: The world has an inexhaustible ability to surprise us, and grace us, with revelations. If we embark on each adventure with an open heart and an open mind, trusting in the journey, travel will take us places we never planned to go, and enrich and enlighten us in ways we never otherwise would have known.

And so it is with this adventure, for my own *Tales from Nowhere* journey has led me to one final revelatory surprise: Nowhere is not, as I had believed, an isolated outpost of disorientation; Nowhere is an everyday human hub of intertwining roads, where life-changing connections, revelations and resolutions are bestowed.

As the end approaches, I want to thank the countless fellow travellers who have helped me on this trail: in particular, the hundreds of writers who submitted their tales to this collection; my Lonely Planet colleagues, who embraced and supported this journey every step of the way; and my family, who anchor and answer my own life's journey, day by day.

Now I hand this adventure over to you. Here's the map, and a simple prayer: May it lead you Nowhere, everywhere.

Middlebury-Piedmont
April 2006

FOREWORD –
THE ROAD TO FLOWBEE
BY TIM CAHILL

HERE'S HOW I broke my right big toe. I can tell you from experience that there is never a perfectly peachy time to break a toe, but such an injury, for me, at this moment, was a catastrophe. I was doomed.

It was a late winter day in Wisconsin, I was a senior in high school, and in three days the state swimming meet would be held, a competition in which I had every chance of winning both the 50- and 100-yard freestyle sprints. I had already registered the best times in the state that year, and had beaten my nearest competitors every time we raced. The win – the state title – would likely earn me an athletic scholarship at any number of colleges. This was a matter of some financial consequence to my parents and one that would have a rather large effect on the next several years of my life.

So there I was, less than a week before the meet, when I was attacked fiercely by late-night hunger pangs, as teenagers often are. I recall strolling barefoot into the family kitchen and opening the freezer, which was located about head height at the top of the refrigerator. A ball of frozen hamburger, wrapped in foil, rolled out of the freezer compartment. Later examination showed that it was larger than a softball, though not nearly so big as a cantaloupe. It weighed a little over three pounds, and dropped directly on my right big toe.

When I limped into the pool the next day for practice, the coach learned of the perfidious nature of balled ground beef. I suspect he might have laughed, except for the fact that our team was very good, and we were the favourites in the state meet. My injury put our chances of victory in deep jeopardy.

I was given the remaining practices off, and ordered to stay off my feet and to be good and damn ready for the meet in two days. And then I was at the meet and I recall standing on the blocks waiting for the starting gun. My entire psyche was somewhere else that day – it was, I now realise, in a Nowhere place.

I didn't feel any pain: not when I wrapped my toes over the block, not when I dove, not when I flip-turned and exploded off the wall, once in the fifty, three times in the 100. I don't recall much except looking over to the other lanes and seeing no-one there. My arms pulled me through the water with no thought at all. The techniques I'd practised since I was ten years old took over from my conscious mind. Things seemed to move unbearably slowly: I felt my hands entering the water smoothly, without a splash; these hands that hardly seemed to belong to me were 'feeling' the water, pushing against it with efficiency and power. There was an agreeable muscular beating pressure on my chest and shoulders and thighs. Simultaneously – and this was a paradox – things also seemed to be happening very fast indeed. The temporal world felt as if it had skipped a beat. The starting gun had only just sounded but in what seemed like moments, I was done and watching the others beside me come in and touch the wall. Slow and fast at the same time, as in kung fu movies or certain television series of decades ago – *The Six Million Dollar Man*, for example – where fast actions were expressed in slow motion. That's what it was like. The other sprinters were only tenths of seconds behind me, but I could have written a novel in the time it took them to finish, or so I sensed.

I won. Our team won.

We didn't use the word back in those days, but I was in what athletes now routinely call the 'zone'. So totally absorbed was I in the contests of that day, I never acknowledged the pain in my foot. I might not even have been aware that it existed.

I didn't know it at the time, but I had been to Flowbee.

Now, there are numerous Nowheres in the pages of this excellent and inspiring collection, but there is nowhere as literally Nowhere as the place I want to talk about here. Flowbee does not appear on any map, and it has no GPS coordinates to track, but it is as important to me – and I would hazard to guess, to the other writer-adventurers in this book – as any actual place on this planet.

How do you get to Flowbee? Let me tell you what I've learned in my own staggeringly roundabout research.

I didn't always recognise Flowbee for what it was – for years I'd only felt it – but I knew this state of physical and mental absorption existed. I had experienced it several times, not just in swimming, but in other sports and certain intellectual endeavours. There seemed to be a number of paths to this place, but nobody got a free ticket. I had, for instance, spent eight years of my life working on my swimming and basically attempting to turn myself into an outboard motor. For this reason I thought early on that maybe you had to suffer – or at least work a lot harder than you really wanted to – to reach Flowbee, but now I think that's only part of the picture.

A couple of dozen years ago, I found myself intrigued with the concept of risk: At the time, this was an all-encompassing notion that on various occasions had left me hanging from my fingertips high on rock walls and paddling rivers that ate up my raft and sent me whirling underwater and unable to surface. (River-runners call this unfortunate state of affairs being maytagged – the sense that one is trapped for an unseemly amount of time inside a washing machine, an appliance from which one will eventually emerge, defunct but well scrubbed.)

Another time, for reasons I was never able to explain even to myself, I copiloted a hot-air balloon over Pikes Peak, despite the fact that the most experienced pilot in my group felt the stunt was deadly on this particular day. He was convinced that whirling gusts of invisible winds called rotors existed just over the summit, and that the balloon would be caught in those rotors where it – and consequently its pilots – would be dashed onto the rocks below. Fly the thing, he said, and we were, in effect, dead. He sensibly backed out. But I had spent weeks learning to fly the craft and thought it could be done. The copilot and I would assess the winds aloft by feel, I told myself. So we threw fire into the throat of the balloon and rose up into an unpromising pearlescent sky. We felt some turbulence near the summit and we rose over it at one point, then decided to drop into and under it at another. It was tricky flying and we navigated the sky without much in the way of what one might call conscious thought. But the balloon survived, and when we landed a strange sensation coursed through my brain, such as it was. I thought: this was all over too quick.

It always seemed to happen this way. Another example: A traverse of Pigeon Mountain cave in Georgia took me eighteen hours, including an initial rappel of over 400 feet and a final climb up a rope of another 440 feet – yet those eighteen hours felt like a brief afternoon's caving.

What inexplicable mental tick threw me into these potentially deadly activities? I crashed and burned a number of times learning paragliding – the senseless but exhilarating process of running real fast down steep hills and hoping that the parachute laid on the hillside behind you will, in fact, inflate so that your descent will be something less than a freefall. The chute inflated every time, though I still have scars from inept landings. I climbed up and rappelled down El

Capitan in Yosemite on a rope. I flew any number of hang-gliders headfirst into sand dunes or sometimes grassy hillsides. I was good at bloody noses.

But in my own defence, I wasn't a complete fool. I trained hard for each and every one of these moronic exploits and believed them feasible. The process was always the same. There was an initial dread, a minor terror that went a bit beyond butterflies in the stomach and into something more like a giant horde of vampire bats ripping at the intestines. And then the baneful event commenced, and I was lost in the execution, the performance, the seemingly unconscious and intuitive understanding of what was at stake and how, most precisely, to survive. It was a state free of consciousness, of brooding, or even thinking in the ordinary sense. If you had to ask yourself 'Am I there?' – you weren't. The writer Diane Ackerman, commenting on this phenomenon, has used the word 'creatural'. I quite agree: it's not instinctive; it's 'creatural'.

Not surprisingly, there was always a euphoria associated with a risk taken and safety attained. I wondered, at the time, if that was what drew me to fear, to risk: was it the resultant sense of euphoria that could be achieved in no other way? Maybe I lacked something others had as a matter of course. As the Scots say, 'Some men are born two drinks short of par.' Maybe I had been born deficient in the euphoria department: could it be that other people felt just hunky-dory and totally immersed in their lives at all times? Why did I have to jump off big damn cliffs just to get some small hit of beatitude?

So, I thought, maybe I was using risk to mix up my own biological cocktails: instead of whisky it was adrenaline and dopamine and serotonin and noradrenaline. Bang! Euphoria.

Risk, I discovered, was addictive in its way. I can't recall the number of times I've uttered the eternal prayer: 'Just get me out of this one and I'll never…' And then, two weeks later, there I'd be, in the water diving with great white sharks. Later, I'd find myself sharing the resultant euphoria with my fellow shark divers, all of whom were, no doubt, born two drinks short of par, or at least several cans short of a six pack.

I'm not talking about pleasure here. Pleasure was something else: sex, seeing a fine movie, eating a good dinner. I like pleasure, of course – who doesn't? But euphoria was something else altogether. In a recent book, *The Happiness Hypothesis*, Jonathan Haidt, a professor of psychology at the University of Virginia, cites studies by psychologist Milhaly Csikzentmihalyi, who has found that people are most content when they are experiencing what he calls 'the flow', which Haidt defines as 'the state of total immersion in a task that is challenging yet closely matched to one's abilities'.

Csikzentmihalyi has been working on this idea for thirty years. For his doctoral thesis, in the 1970s, he studied artists, taking pictures of painters at work every three minutes. He was, he wrote, 'struck by how deeply they were involved in work, forgetting everything else'.

'That state,' he continued, 'seemed so intriguing that I started also looking for it in chess players, in rock climbers, in dancers and in musicians. I expected to find substantial differences in all their activities, but people reported very similar accounts of how they felt. Then I started looking at professions like surgery and found the same elements there: a challenge which provides clear, high goals and immediate feedback…They forget themselves, the time, their problems.'

OK. But if Csikzentmihalyi is right, if I could have found Flowbee via chess or the cello, why was I so addicted to life-threatening situations?

A writer named Douglas Eby quotes the doctor as saying: 'Some flow experiences involve low danger, like reading a good book. But certain people are disposed to respond to risk, and their flow will depend on it more than somebody else's. Danger is the hook. But their descriptions are not that different from, say, a Thai woman's description of weaving a rug. The qualities of concentration, forgetfulness, involvement, control are similar.'

The flow – Csikzentmihalyi is careful to call it a metaphor – is similar in its various descriptions to Eastern meditative states. That is to say, some people can get there sitting cross-legged in a room while others of us need a harder bump. Athletes in the 'zone' are, in my opinion, tapping into the flow: Flowbee.

It's worth pointing out that a person cannot find this place I call Flowbee without some prior training or experience. A neurologist may feel that a five-hour operation took a mere ten minutes. But someone untrained in medicine performing the same procedure will not find happiness or euphoria, and neither will his patient. Conversely you won't get to Flowbee if the task at hand is less than challenging. A world-class rock climber isn't going to experience the flow climbing a flight of stairs. Those hordes of bats have to be tearing at your guts before you begin the activity that will put you in the flow.

So how does an artist enter the flow? Where's the challenge? Recently I was chatting with Robert Stone, one of America's premier novelists, and he said that every time he starts a book, he fears that it will finally expose him 'as a fraud'. That's the sound of a man who's felt the bats ripping at his guts. That's why Robert Stone routinely writes books critics hail as 'another masterpiece'.

And though I seldom pursue risk for risk's sake anymore, I do find myself entering that felicitous flow on certain occasions when I am writing. But here's a further paradox: Since this journey to the Nowhere I call Flowbee results in euphoria, why on earth don't I write easily and enthusiastically every day of my life, skipping joyfully to my desk each morning?

I think the essential element is fear. Dr Csiksczentmihalyi has noted eight components necessary to enter the flow – concentration, a task that we have a chance of completing, time distortion, and immediate feedback are among them – but I feel he gives short shrift to fear. What is the fear in creating art? What generates that horde of eutherian mammals in the gut sack?

Perhaps, for painters or dancers or writers or sculptors, it is, in fact, survival: if this piece isn't good enough, I don't get paid. Consequently, the mortgage doesn't get paid, the house gets sold at auction, my spouse leaves me and I'm out on the street, just another has-been, exposed for the fraudulent poseur I've always been. (Artists boast in public and agonise in private.)

It's always that way for me: I've been writing for a living for over thirty years, and the fear at the beginning of any project feels precisely similar to the familiar terror of preparing to climb a cliff wall or parachute out of a perfectly good airplane. In my experience, fear, whatever its cause, always feels the same. Which is the reason, I think, so many writers and artists are 'deadline junkies'. It is only when the fear becomes overwhelming that we commence our work.

And here's what happens. You spend half an hour or more, and nothing you've accomplished is any good at all. A writer of my acquaintance, Dick Wheeler, the author of more than fifty books, says the process is rather like pumping water out of a long unused well. The first fluid brought up is dark with dirt and rust. But keep pumping, and soon enough the water begins to flow clear.

So it is. On my best days, when I enter what for me is the flow, I get there in about forty-five minutes. Ideas I didn't know I had materialise on the page; humorous or dramatic situations arise and are documented. Connections I didn't know connected tie themselves up in neat little knots. I'm not aware of how this happens and have been able to tell writing students only that it seems to come from the great and physically nonexistent Kingdom of Flowbee. Three or four hours pass by in thirty minutes, or so it seems.

Then, all too soon, I've lost the connection. My mind is mush. I can proofread, or polish, or research, but I can't create anymore. A close reading of what poured out of the pump on a good Flowbee day generates a euphoria similar to the sensation of having just run a nasty Class Four rapid.

The next day is no different: fear, dreck and then, if I'm lucky, the flow – a place where I surprise myself with words I didn't know I needed to write. It is as if these sentences have come out of, well, Nowhere.

Which brings us back to this book, and its indelible collection of searching and illuminating – connecting – tales. In my experience one of the most important things you need to get to Flowbee is a sense of risk. The journey starts when you find yourself confronted by a feasible challenge that nevertheless scares you witless – and you take the plunge. As in that long-ago high-school pool, as in the tales that follow.

Dr Csikzentmihalyi would seem to concur. In an attempt to define the flow, he starts with risk of a sort: 'Imagine that you are skiing down a slope and your full attention is focused on the movements of your body, the position of the skis, the air whistling past your face, and the snow-shrouded trees running by. There is no room in your awareness for conflicts or contradictions; you know that a distracting thought or emotion might get you buried face down in the snow. The run is so perfect that you want it to last forever.'

But then the good doctor takes his definition a step further: 'If skiing does not mean much to you, this complete immersion in an experience could occur while you are singing in a choir, dancing, playing bridge, or reading a good book.' A good book, says Csikzentmihalyi: Well, you have one of those in your hands right now.

How do you get to Flowbee? The route can be via training, risk, fear, immersion; eventually, each person has to find his or her own way. But these stories can start you on the path and maybe even get you there. It's a much more pleasant road than the one that begins with a broken toe.

MEETING ECHO
BY DANNY WALLACE

ECHO CAME FROM a town near Guangdong and her father's name was Jing.

'I come from a town near Guangdong,' she said. 'My father's name is Jing.'

She looked at me, eagerly, awaiting my response. I didn't know quite what my response should be. This was the first thing she had said to me, on the first and last and only time we met, and I was confused. I didn't know who this girl was, I hadn't asked her where she was from, and I was fairly sure I wasn't wearing a T-shirt marked 'Tell Me Who Your Daddy Is'.

'I…er…I'm from England,' I tried, unsurely, putting my newspaper to my lap. 'And my father's name is Ian.'

There was a pause, and then Echo giggled. She was delighted. At the fact that I had responded in kind, I think, rather than at the fact that my father's name is Ian.

We were sitting on two chairs in Shanghai International Airport. My flights had been delayed by three hours. And then another four. And then another one. I was going nowhere, in a nowhere place.

'I have no pets,' said Echo. 'I would like to be a architect one day.'

I smiled.

'I have a cat,' I said. 'I would not make a very good architect.'

I didn't know quite where this conversation was going. It is rare that conversations begin with the name of your dad, your pet status and whether or not you'd be any good at building shopping centres. But I did know it was a welcome distraction. I'd been bored senseless. I had seen all there was to see in the airport. I had read most of my newspaper. I'd played the one thing I had on my Walkman to death. I now needed this conversation to work.

'I have two brothers,' Echo told me, brightly. 'Guangdong is warm in the summertime.'

'I have no brothers,' I replied. 'In London it often rains.'

At this – and I have no idea why – she laughed.

I was pleased that this odd connection had somehow sparked into life. Airports are a weird limbo – you're neither in the place you've been, nor in the place you're going. I, like you, have been in dozens of nowheres, nothing places like this. Spent probably days of my life wandering around their bland and manufactured worlds of the same shops, and the same bored people seeing the same boring things. And yet I remember virtually none of them. I know I was there, know I *must* have been there. It's just that they're never where you *want* to be, never where you're going to be. In the history of God's green earth, never has anyone gone to an airport just to go to an airport. And if they have, I'd like you to tell me their name, please, as someone should really alert the authorities.

But this time was different.

'I talk English with my aunt,' she said. 'My aunt name is Feng.'

'I talk English with…most people,' I said, and immediately wished that I hadn't, because if I had understood the rules of this conversation correctly, I would now have to name them all.

Echo was twenty, and I was twenty-two. Her English wasn't the best – as you may have worked out by now – but she said what she knew with enthusiasm and wide, pretty eyes, which smiled even when she didn't. She was as Westernised a girl as I'd seen in Shanghai – low-cut jeans and trainers and Marlboro Lights and a purse with a picture of James Dean on it.

For fifteen minutes or so we swapped simple, unrelated sentences, and we laughed. From what I could work out, Echo was on her way to Paris.

'I go to see my friend and the city,' she said. 'I am very excited.'

'I love Paris in the springtime,' I said. 'I love Paris in the fall.'

Echo raised her eyebrows.

'It's a song,' I said. 'It's about Paris.'

She nodded, but still didn't say anything.

'It's about someone who really loves Paris.'

Had I been in a film I daresay I would probably have stood up and sung it at this point, and the whole airport would have started singing too, and then Echo would have probably fallen in love with me. But I was not in a film and so I didn't. I simply said, 'Yep, they *really* love it.'

We both fell silent for a few moments. It seemed like perhaps we'd reached the end of our short conversation. I didn't know where to look; whether I should pick up my paper again and pretend to read. But I didn't want to. In some ways this had been a conversation about absolutely nothing, in a place that seemed absolutely nowhere. But in other ways, I'd actually learnt more about Echo than I knew about most people. I knew about her ambitions, her likes, her dislikes. I knew about her family. I knew where she went to school, who her best friend was, that she liked James Dean better than anyone. The most simple conversation made up of the most tiny details. But sometimes, those can be the most important.

Suddenly, she asked me about my cat.

'It is bigger than a car,' I said. 'And it looks like Mel Gibson.'

Echo looked shocked. I watched her try to work the

sentences out. And then, when she'd done it, she laughed. And she laughed again, and she reached for my hand and squeezed it. And quicker than I was expecting, she pointed upwards, and told me that her grandmother was a spaceman, and that she lived in the sky.

So I told her that my best friend was an apple and my shoes were made of water, and soon we were swapping sentences of such complete nonsense that the people around us must have assumed we were either simple or high.

But soon after, it was time for Echo to go.

'OK, Danny, I leave now,' she said, getting her things together, then smiling and standing up and kissing me once on the cheek. 'How are you, nice to meet you.'

I scribbled my email address on a napkin and gave it to her, and she said, 'Good, Danny!'

I smiled as she went. It was such a small thing, such a sliver of an event, but it turned a dozen hours in an airport into… well…something that I wouldn't just remember as a dozen hours in an airport. Nowhere was now somewhere – it was the place I met Echo. Thanks to her, a nothing was, for once, a something.

It's been years now. I still hope that one day I'll get an email.

Even if it *is* only to tell me that she still has no pets, or that she's from a town near Guangdong, and her father's name is Jing.

TIMBUKTU & BEYOND

BY ANTHONY SATTIN

THE NIGER RIVER was too low for the big ferries to run, so I went to Timbuktu in a local-style pirogue – a long, thin, wooden motorboat. Ibrahima, the owner, reckoned it would take us three days, but it could have taken three weeks for all I cared on that first morning, for I was wallowing in luxury. It wasn't that the pirogue was so very comfortable, though there was no hardship in its cushions and no sunburn beneath its woven roofing, the sides left open for the breeze. A couple of braziers in front of the engine served as a kitchen and a screened-off squat-hole at the very back accommodated life's other necessities. As for the service, Sylla, the boatman, laughed the entire way and Amadou, the cook, attended to our comforts. But the luxury I savoured most was the prospect of escape from phones and email, meetings and deadlines. I looked forward to seventy-two isolated hours stretched out on a bench, reading, sleeping, watching the world go by as we made the transition from the bustling port town of Mopti, now receding into the distance, to the Never-Never-Place that is Timbuktu. We were going nowhere and then I was continuing beyond it, to somewhere called Essekane, deep into the Sahara Desert.

But first there was the river, which wrapped us in its flat embrace and coloured the world with a limited palette: emerald green for the banks, blue for the sky, changing shades for the water – scattered with diamonds at dawn, dazzling at midday, mercurial in the evening, black at night. The sole reason for lowering a book and raising one's head from the cushion was either to look at a variation in this nature – a vulture overhead, a cluster of eucalyptus, a sunrise – or to admire the work of man, the casting of fishing nets, the pushing of immense pirogues, the construction of elaborate mudbrick mosques. We had encounters, too, with children on the shore, with friends of Sylla and Amadou and, before each lunch and dinner, with fishermen, Amadou picking through the flapping catch in their dugouts in search of something he hoped would satisfy us. Capitaine (*hamijeh* in Songhay, *salleh* in Bamana) was the fish of preference here, the Niger's most flavoursome and easily filleted; a six-pounder cost less than the price of a bag of fried potatoes in London. On that first day at noon, precisely, without a watch, with only the sun to guide him, Amadou served a lunch of grilled capitaine, pasta and tomato sauce.

The lunch and the heat sat heavily, so we dozed through that afternoon, only raising ourselves, much later, to visit a village, Wotaka, with Amadou acting as our guide and a group of children trumpeting us in with a fanfare of *'Bici, bidon, bonbon'* (pen, empty bottle, sweets). The village was small, quickly seen and easily enjoyed, particularly its extravagant mudbrick mosque. More enjoyable still were the elaborate rituals of greeting – in Bamana or Bozo, Dogon, Fulfulde, Soninké, Songhay, Tamasheq or any other of the thirty-odd languages current along the river – as we passed the mosque's imam, or a tattooed girl from the cattle-owning Peul tribe come to trade a calabash of milk for some fish, or the blacksmith, who doubled as village shaman, the propitiator of the river's spirits, and invoked their help to ensure our safe passage.

At the end of the day, the river reflected our torpor and lay like a mirror in which jumping fish, diving egrets and migrating flocks appeared. In the last of the light, Sylla tied up the pirogue, Amadou cooked pasta marinara and I put up gauzelike tents. We were camped on a rise across the water from the dry-season huts of Bozo fishermen. The kerosene lamp attracted such a variety of crawling and flying creatures that we spent the rest of the evening in moonless darkness, the stars showing off overhead. It may sound peaceful, but it wasn't. The evening started quiet enough, with Amadou singing a gentle delta blues, but before long something that sounded like a disco started up across the river and we could hear the Bozos singing and cheering. I have never been anywhere so remote that was so noisy.

The following night there were other noises. Amadou sang his blues again but this time accompanied by frog croak, cicada rhythm and mosquito whine. Still, there were no combustion engines, no electric generators – confirmation, if such a thing were needed, that we had passed into another world, an old world of foot, muscle and sail. There we found families of hippos, beady eyes and massive jaws emerging from the water line. Acacia, palm and eucalyptus broke the line of the sand banks; Peul farmers herded cattle on the shore; migrating flocks broke the skyline ahead. We would be in Timbuktu by nightfall, Sylla announced, and began to nurture plans to celebrate our arrival with a local girl and the tip he was expecting from me.

I didn't see whether his wish came true that night, because by then I was wrapped in wonder, in Timbuktu, with a smile on my face.

o o o o o o o o

'Is the rumour of thy Timbuctoo a dream as frail as those of ancient time?' So wrote the Victorian poet Alfred Tennyson, pointing up the fact that Timbuktu represents two very different things. On the one hand, it is a place in the Republic of Mali, caught between the river and the vast expanse of desert. On the other, it is the epitome of remoteness, shorthand for somewhere out of this world, an impression confirmed that evening by street corner fires, empty dirt tracks and a wide plain of sand and rock covered with low-rise mudbrick and breeze-block buildings, and the makeshift huts of the latest desert refugees. I celebrated my arrival at the heart of nowhere by dropping my bag in a hot room with a bare light bulb and immovable fan, in what passed for a hotel, and then by drinking a cold beer with my feet tucked into the Sahara.

Most visitors to Timbuktu agree with René Caillié, the Frenchman who broke the news to Europe in 1826 that the golden city of fable was nothing more than 'a mass of mud huts, surrounded by arid plains of jaundiced white sands'. But I sided with Gordon Laing, a Scottish explorer who reached Timbuktu before Caillié but was murdered on his way home. Laing wrote that the fabled city had completely met his expectations. I don't know what Laing was expecting, but I imagined somewhere dusty, a little drab and very exotic. And that was what I found.

In the morning, under a ruthless sun, I visited the shaded halls of the massive fourteenth-century mudbrick mosque, the modest houses of nineteenth-century explorers, including one that Laing is said to have occupied, a library of rare manuscripts and a room in the town hall that served as an Internet café. 'Come back next week,' the assistant suggested helpfully. 'We hope the lines will be reconnected by then.' But nowhere I visited that morning expressed the town's character better than the market, where I found traders from upriver Mali, downriver Nigeria, Algeria and Libya, and Touareg, the famous 'blue men', who knew better than anyone else how to live in the interior of the Sahara.

Most of these people were selling nothing more exotic than life's essentials, including rock salt cut far out in the desert, the old currency against which gold and slaves had been traded. As in the nineteenth century there was also plenty of cloth for sale. Mukhtar, a tall doe-eyed Wodaabe from Niger, asked if I was looking for a *chech*, a turban. He had one on his head. 'You will need it if you are going to Essekane,' he told me, pointing at the sun. He was happy to sell me his own for £5. I offered £4. 'I'll tell you what,' he concluded as he transferred the tightly wrapped metres of blue cotton from his head to mine, 'how about giving me three?' Even seasoned travellers need time to adjust to the strange ways of Timbuktu.

Like almost everyone in the market – and like me – Mukhtar was going to a weekend of music being staged far out in the sands, in Essekane. Now that he had earned enough to get there, he shook my hand and told me to look out for him in the crowd.

o o o o o o o o o

I had not thought much about what would happen beyond Timbuktu, but I suppose I was expecting to find myself in empty desert. The reality proved to be a little different: so many people were going to the festival that the lonely track had become a piste, and once on it, the journey became a rally that my driver was determined to win. For three hours he spun the wheel and we veered and jolted as jeeps and Landcruisers, big desert trucks and vans were lost in our dust trail. Then, suddenly, the landscape changed, we were in Essekane and I was facing another of those moments requiring adjustment because where I saw drifting white sand, my driver spotted a music festival.

Nowhere on earth can compare to the white dunes of Essekane as a festival site. At a makeshift gate, a man wrapped a band around my wrist to show I hadn't gate-crashed. Here? Beyond Timbuktu? In the middle of nowhere? 'You would be surprised what people will do to save money,' he explained. 'Even here.'

The site looked much as I imagined a trans-Saharan caravan camp must have looked in the days when people had no choice but to travel by camel: a mass of tents of varying shapes and sizes, arranged in some places in rows, in others in clusters. Here and there, a fire, food cooking, rugs spread out, a gathering and laughter and at the edge of all this humanity, the four-wheel drives and some camels.

In the middle of this sea of tents I spotted something you wouldn't have seen in those old camps: two concrete stages and a block of washrooms. These were the only permanent structures within sight, and around them the wind had lent a hand and carved a natural arena. Everything else had been brought from Timbuktu and beyond, every open-sided goatskin tent, every woven mat and sleeping bag, each microphone, cable and speaker, the many lights that flooded the stage at night and the technicians to work it all, the charcoal burned in braziers across the dunes to keep us warm, the copious meals of pasta and rice, mutton and vegetables, the water, the sweet, dark tea and warm beer, the necessities and souvenirs laid out in the shopping area – everything and everyone had been loaded into jeeps or onto trucks and camels and brought out into the desert for the festival. Everyone, that is, except the Touareg.

On that first evening, standing on the edge of a dune looking across a bowlful of people to the stage, I was so absorbed in the music I didn't notice anyone behind me. But when I turned around I saw that a group of Touareg men had ridden up on their camels. Their heads and faces were swathed in turbans and long swords hung by their sides. They were undoubtedly imposing and might also have been intimidating had they not been sharing their saddles with dancing, joking, joyous children.

The word Touareg means 'abandoned by the gods', but for a long time these people were also abandoned by man, herding along the borders of the Sahara and trading across the desert for centuries. They were, in other words, the leading citizens of nowhere. In the nineteenth century they were also notorious for raiding trans-Saharan caravans and being less than welcoming to outsiders. At the beginning of the twentieth century, when France sent an army to conquer this part of Africa, the Touareg tribes held out long after other native forces had been defeated. They have maintained this aura of untouchability and in the 1990s, when they came into armed conflict with the Malian government, they showed that they were still daunting adversaries. I looked behind me again at the group of camel riders only to find they had slipped soundlessly back into the desert night.

Later I tried the same trick, hoping to wander off and get some sleep, but a fire had been lit outside my tent and a group of people were warming themselves around it, among them several members of the Touareg band Tinariwen. Fifteen years ago these guys were in Libyan training camps preparing to fight for their rights to trade and travel freely across the Sahara. But now they were fighting with music, not with guns. 'Our music expresses the struggles facing Touaregs,' one of them explained in thickly accented French. 'It speaks of our suffering.' With its sweeping rhythms and laid-back beat, it also spoke volumes about the stark, seductive beauty of the landscape around us, which the musician called 'my cherished home'.

I stayed on the white dunes of Essekane for three days and wherever I went and whatever I did, whether I lay curled in a sleeping bag in a goatskin tent, sat cross-legged under a canvas shade to eat from a communal pot, bartered for drinks and crafts in the makeshift souq, watched camel races or listened to praise singers acknowledging the qualities of some worthy man, I was always in sight of Touareg, lounging in the sand beside a simmering teapot, or playing with their children, or sealing deals with the loud slap of a handshake, or doing one of the hundred other things that residents do in this 'cherished home'.

On the long drive back to Timbuktu I had time to chew over this idea, that one person's nowhere was someone else's home. The six of us in the car passed the time by playing a sort of I-Spy. Terrain, dune, desert, camel, acacia, Toyota, Touareg, tracks, sunset, dusk... We continued until night reduced the landscape to the narrow tunnel of sand caught in the headlights. And then silence. And then something unexpected happened: beyond the darkness, the horizon began to glow orange. What had we found? We made our guesses. A fire? A moonrise? An apocalypse?

We were all wrong. Long before we reached its limits, we were seeing the lights of Timbuktu. Only now it wasn't the place I had seen before, because everything is relative and because after those days of desert and Touareg, Timbuktu looked bright and unexpectedly bustling, a place of cold drinks and hot food, of hotels, phones and radio, a modern pivot between the Mali of the River Niger and the Touareg-inhabited desert. It had, in other words, been transformed and was now very much somewhere on the way to nowhere.

NORTH OF PERTH
BY PAM HOUSTON

I FIRST NOTICED we had officially entered Nowhere thirty kilometres after we left Northampton, a sweet-looking little town 450 kilometres north of Perth. We lost the farms first, then the power lines, then the fences, then all other traffic in either direction. We lost the *Nuytsia floribunda*, the Australian Christmas tree with its explosions of bright yellow and orange flowers. We lost the stunningly beautiful but slow-moving galah, grey-bodied cockatoos with rose-colored heads and fat cheeks, and the smaller, quicker bright-green budgies. Eventually we lost the line down the middle of the road.

The state of Western Australia covers one-third of the continent, is nearly four times the size of Texas, and has a smaller population than Nevada. Seventy-five per cent of those people live in Perth, the most geographically isolated city of its size in the world, and another handful live in the gorgeous Margaret River country to Perth's south. Everybody told me to go to Margaret River, but I found the big empty space on the map – the space the guidebook had labelled simply 'North of Perth' – more intriguing. My Nevadan friend Gary and I decided to drive a couple thousand kilometres up the wild coast, where almost nobody lives.

I live half the year in Creede, Colorado, and half the year in
Davis, California. The most likely commute between those two
('seventeen hours,' I always say, 'if you pee in a bottle') follows
US 50 across most of Utah and Nevada, a road that wears its
title, the Loneliest Road in America, with pride. Highway 1
(more commonly called the Brand Highway) in Western
Australia made the Loneliest Road in America feel more like the
New Jersey Turnpike.

It was mid-afternoon when we left Northampton and we had
300 kilometres to go. The friendly guy at the gas station (we
learned quickly never to pass up a gas station) had told us to
watch out for wildlife as dusk approached. What he didn't tell
us was that as soon as darkness fell we would be entering a
video game – *Need for Speed #2* meets *Cabela's Dangerous
Hunts* – populated with kangaroos (some with babies in their
pouches), several kinds of wallabies, emus, goannas (great big
lizards that lift their heads at danger, so even if you success-
fully straddle them they are goners), goats, sheep, horses, wild
burros, feral camels, bilbies (tiny endangered mice with see-
through ears), mallee fowl and echidna (an animal that
resembles a flattened porcupine, even before you flatten it).

We crawled along in the little blue Toyota Corolla, with eyes
like saucers, screeching to a halt every time a kangaroo
bounded into our path. Australians who live north of Perth
simply don't drive at night, and after that first night, we didn't
either. It took us three and a half hours to drive 150 kilometres
of pavement, 150 kilometres with not a single other car, not a
farm, not a shed, not a side road, not a radio tower – just a
couple dozen kangaroo carcasses, and the Billabong Roadhouse
with its red rotating sign that reads 'Serving Meals Now' that
you can see for fifty kilometres in all directions. We didn't stop
for meals. We didn't stop for anything. I came within inches of
a kangaroo only once, but he was a big one, and before it was
all over I had killed two rabbits and a goanna. I think Gary

035.

would back me up on this: both of those rabbits were trying to hit *me*.

We spent the next day seeing the sights of Shark Bay World Heritage and Marine Park: the friendly dolphins that come into shore in the morning to be fed; shell beach, a sixty-kilometre stretch made up entirely of cockle shells piled on top of each other to a depth of three metres; and the Hamelin Pool stromatolites, columns formed by cyanobacteria, the earliest life on earth. We went out on a racing sailboat that had once upon a time won the prestigious Sydney to Hobart yacht race with a guy named Captain Scottie who had long blonde dreadlocks and could scan the water, play guitar, and pick up whatever girl was handy, all while steering the eighteen-metre catamaran down six-foot rollers at twenty-one knots *with his feet*. Then we got back on the road for another 600-kilometre day, to the tip of the Exmouth Peninsula and the Ningaloo Reef Retreat.

Daytime travel was considerably easier. Once the punishing sun got high in the sky, nothing moved, and we flew up the empty roads. It was ten o'clock in the morning, and we hadn't seen an oncoming car since eight, when I sped past a cop who was hiding in the shade of a scruffy little boab tree on the side of the road.

'You've got to be kidding,' I said to Gary. I'd been going 130 kilometres an hour. The speed limit was 110.

He was a jolly cop, large and red-faced in the gathering heat. The first thing he did was make me take the first breathalyser test of my life.

'Breathe here, please,' he said, and we waited for the numbers to register in the box.

'Good on ya!' he said, and slapped my back when it came up all zeros. He gave us a rundown of everything there was to see at Ningaloo and a $100 ticket, which, he said, we could pay at any post office in Western Australia.

'Just Western Australia,' I said, 'or the whole country?'

'That I couldn't tell you,' he said. 'I've never been out of Western Australia in my life.'

o o o o o o o o o

A couple more hours of responsible driving later we came to the town of Carnarvon and found a little café that was serving fish and chips, and beef and beetroot sandwiches for lunch. I took a photo of a sign in the window: 'Lost: Kangaroo: Beloved Pet and Dogs Best Friend', with a phone number. Then we crossed the big, dry, red Gascoyne River Basin, and then the Tropic of Capricorn.

037.

The Ningaloo Reef Retreat is a tiny outcropping of blonde wall tents that sit slightly north of centre in the 260-kilometre stretch of coast that borders Ningaloo Marine Park along the west coast of the Exmouth Peninsula. Exmouth was the only town we'd seen since Perth that was showing any sign of growth – there was a big marina being built on the east side of town, and lots of cars wearing anti-resort bumper stickers – but emus still wandered between the houses and the coffee shops as if they owned the place, and when I went into the post office to pay my speeding ticket, all the women commiserated as if we were old friends.

We left town and entered Cape Range National Park, and drove sixty-five more kilometres to a parking lot, where we had been instructed to shove a few things into daypacks and walk the 800 metres into the retreat. A barefoot woman in khaki shorts and a wide-brimmed hat greeted us, mildly admonished us for being late (her email had recommended a 10am arrival), ushered us to our tent, showed us how to work the nature-loo, and promised to return shortly with a box of happy-hour snacks. In the five minutes she was with us, she used the expression 'cool beans' three times and 'cool bananas' twice, as in, 'You pump the water here, and push this lever here, right? Right! Cool bananas.'

Cool Beans was an expert on all the creatures that live on the reef, the largest fringing reef in Western Australia (or WA as she called it). She loved living in the park but hated the workload, and found ways to make us feel guilty every time we dirtied a plate. I got off to a bad start with her the first night when we cooked dinner (guests are encouraged to pitch in) and I added a teaspoon of red chilli flakes to a dish that she had the audacity to call Thai chicken curry. Spread around ten people's meals, the flakes left only the mildest suggestion of heat, but Cool Beans got so angry she threw her fork down and refused to eat it. Then she told all the other guests that I was banned from the kitchen.

(Thirteen hundred kilometres earlier, back in a town called Cervantes – a place we had thought of at the time as 'the middle of nowhere' but that now seemed like a suburb of Perth – we had bought the only bottle of Tabasco on the grocery store shelves, possibly the only bottle in Western Australia. It looked like it had been there for fourteen years and for some reason it cost $9 but it had been a lifesaver as a strategy for dealing with Western Australian cooking. Cool Beans may have been a pioneer chick living on the very edge of Australia and having 'no use for Sydney or any other city for that matter', but her stomach still belonged to the Queen.)

As a country, Australia is either completely relaxed or deeply in denial. 'No worries', Australians say, with the same frequency that Americans say 'yeah' and 'uh' and 'OK' and 'duh' combined. 'No worries', 'no problems', 'no dramas whatsoever', 'no catastrophes of any magnitude'. Well, I can say with confidence that the red pepper flakes in the Thai chicken curry were a catastrophe of the highest magnitude. I left the resort without having been forgiven, and I'm sure I haven't been forgiven to this day.

Snorkelling with Cool Beans was a completely different
story. On the sea, in the sea, she was so full of childlike wonder
that she forgot to hate the tourists. We kayaked out to the Blue
Lagoon, a deep hole just inside the outer edge of the reef, maybe
500 metres off the beach, tied the kayaks together in the middle
of the lagoon and snorkelled around the perimeter. I had never
seen either that volume or that variety of fish in one place
anywhere, including the renowned blue hole off the coast of
Andros Island, Bahamas, and the reef that lies between
Sumbawa and Moyo Island, Indonesia. Cool Beans knew every
nook and cranny of the Blue Lagoon, every ledge under which
fish congregated, which anemone disguised the false clown
anemone fish, which rock concealed the rock lobsters, which
deep holes could be prodded until a one-and-a-half-metre
black-tip reef shark emerged. She showed us greensnout
parrotfish, yellowfin parrotfish, Schlegel's parrotfish, six-
banded parrotfish, puffer fish and painted flutemouth. She
showed us dotted butterfly fish, spot-tailed butterfly fish,
raccoon butterfly fish, painted sweetlips, many-spotted
sweetlips, sombre sweetlips and lots of blue-spotted fantail
stingrays and white-tipped sharks. There was coral every shade
from deep purple to bright orange, from chartreuse to lavender.
The colours of the fish made me picture some eccentric God
gone mad with a box of Crayola markers.

039.

My favourites were the moon wrasse, which had a yellow
tail with purple edges, purple fins and purple lines on its face,
and a green-, purple- and blue-spotted body, and the white-
barred trigger fish, which wore blue lipstick and blue eye
shadow and looked so much like the Ellen DeGeneres character
in *Finding Nemo* that I half expected it to talk.

We paddled back to shore in the heat of the day and headed
to the tent for a nap. There were six tents in all at the retreat,
plus one big tent that served as mess hall. The tents were about
five metres by five metres with a sink, a nature-loo and a solar

shower right out the back door. In the event of a cyclone – and they do come through with some regularity, Cool Beans had told us – the whole resort could be packed down into wooden crates in four hours, and reassembled just as quickly after the storm had passed.

Our tent was the second to last tent from the end, perched between two of the whitest dunes I'd ever seen, about a hundred steps from the ocean. From our front porch (the tents were all on wooden platforms connected by wooden boardwalks, and a two-person macramé hammock hung in front of each tent door), we could look over those dunes into blue-blue Indian Ocean, which changed from teal to turquoise to sapphire and back again over the course of the day.

Gary and I were maybe twenty metres from the tent when I first saw him, stretched out like a big dog in the shady patch of boardwalk the wall tent provided, long and lean and the colour of hot chocolate made with milk, sporting a pair of balls I thought were much too big for him, a kangaroo, upside-down and sound asleep. We came to an abrupt stop practically on top of one another that made just enough noise to wake him, and he rolled over, his big legs hitting the wood with a thunk, and gave us a heavy-lidded glare, like, 'Whhhaaaa? Don't tell me this is your tent.'

We sat down where we were and took him in: his pointy nose, his fine triangular ears, and his soft, brown eyes, which he couldn't seem to keep open no matter how hard his better judgment told him to. Eventually he put his head back down on his front paws with his nose pointed in our direction, but his eyes once again were closed.

Of course, we didn't have the camera. When I was sure he was imprinted on the emulsion strip in my brain, I decided I would try to sneak around to the back of the tent and grab the camera, dreaming of the shot I would get of him from the inside, silhouetted by the tent flap, the white dunes and blue sea behind.

But he wasn't going to have any of it. I no more than touched the rear set of zippers and he was away. Gary got to see his first major leap off the boardwalk. I got to the front door just in time to see him cover maybe thirty metres of dune in three giant hops. I followed him, at a safe distance. We'd heard plenty of stories by then of people being split open *nipple to belly button* by boxing kangaroos. (Yes, boxing. Just like the cartoons, except instead of little boxing gloves, real kangaroos have claws.) He didn't love the fact that I was following him, but he didn't really seem to mind it either. He backed himself in under a little bush, the next best shade after the tent flap, and I sat on the top of the dune and took his portrait. I inched forward and he let me, until I crossed some invisible line and he gave me a little feint charge, up onto his elbows, like, 'Hey, you want a piece of me?' I backed up, took a couple more shots and reclaimed my hammock. Then I took a nap myself.

041.

Later that afternoon Gary and I were splashing around in the strip of water the high tide creates between the reef and the shore. We had left our masks and snorkels behind, but we could still see schools of coral cod and blue-green chromis swimming in the ultra-clear water around us. I caught sight of a shadow in the corner of my eye and stood up in the metre of water to get a better look.

'Gary,' I said, 'there is something really big swimming towards you.' It had the tail of a shark, but the head of a ray; it was at least five metres long and we both hustled to shore and let it slide past.

'Giant shovelnose ray!' Cool Beans called out, on her way down the beach with her arms full of wetsuits. 'Neatoliscious!'

o o o o o o o o o

On the way back to Perth, in the lonely stretch between the Overlander Roadhouse and Billabong, we drove through tornadic clouds and green and yellow curtains of moisture that rivalled anything I've ever seen crossing Wyoming on an August afternoon.

'How do we know this isn't one of those full-fledged cyclones Cool Beans was talking about?' Gary asked.

'We don't,' I said. We'd been the only car on the road for at least three hours. It was a long way in either direction to radio reception. Even if the weather service knew a cyclone was coming, there would be no way to warn anyone out here.

When we got safely to the other side of the storm and the rain had left behind giant puddles in the road, we saw four emus, three of them chicks, rising from under a bush, and shaking out their wet feathers in the rain. The rain had woken up the kangaroos too, and we stopped the car to watch a group of them boing-boing-boing across the desert. The Australians think of kangaroos as tourist attractions, disease carriers, pets or nuisances, but I can't imagine how long I would have to live there before the sight of their particular motion wouldn't fill me with delight.

Once in a great while we passed wide, red, washboarded roads that led inland to places with names like Meekatharra, Sandstone and Cue. Twenty-five years ago the American West had seemed to me this big and unnavigable, a million four-wheel-drive roads leading in every direction and me with nothing but my college girl Corolla. Now I knew that basin and range country so well I could name every campsite between San Francisco and Denver from 39,000 feet above sea level (and I often did, to the dismay of my United Airlines seatmate). How lucky I was to have found yet another place bigger than my imagination. I started dreaming of my return to Western Australia, next time with a Jeep Wrangler, a spare tyre and a couple of five-gallon jugs of gas.

Slowly we re-entered ranch country, the cockatoos came back – we even saw some rare black ones – and then the budgies, and then the fences, and finally a few other cars. We stayed in a lively little town called Geraldton (Gerro, Cool Beans had called it) and got up in the pre-dawn to drive to the Perth airport. I started out at sixty kilometres per hour and gradually worked my way up to 120. We were back in civilisation. I didn't have to dodge one kangaroo.

THE FINEST CAKE IN SRI LANKA

BY CONOR GRENNAN

THE BEACH AT Negombo is hidden from the road by a row of fading hotels, lined up like ageing rock stars lingering at a curtain call. Decades earlier this had been one of the most popular resort towns in Sri Lanka, but those days were gone – tourists had long since moved on, peeling the charm from the place and leaving travel agents scrambling to find a positive spin. Even my guidebook's assertion that visitors to Negombo could expect a lot of 'depressing sales pitches after dark' seemed a bit generous, a carefully phrased euphemism to avoid kicking the town when it was down.

But I had a smile on my face. I was standing in the middle of a deserted street, facing a small stationery store, looking at the handwritten sign taped to the window. The sign was written in English – large, deliberate block letters on yellow construction paper.

The sign read simply: 'Maps for Sale'. And a map was exactly what I needed to get me and my bicycle out of Negombo.

Cycling seemed like the perfect way to see Sri Lanka. I imagined venturing far off the tourist trail, meeting interesting locals, and generally allowing myself to get lost in the hills and jungles of this fascinating island. The danger, of course, was that I would end up *literally* lost. Hopelessly lost. Drinking-my-own-urine-to-survive lost. I was cursed with an appalling sense of direction that could just about guide me out of a paper bag – I knew better than to leave Negombo without a reliable map in hand.

And yet it had been surprisingly difficult to find a road map in this town. So difficult, in fact, that after an hour of searching for one, I could have mistaken this stationery store for a mere mirage – that is, until I opened the door and was hit with a very real, very un-mirage-like blast of body odour whooshing out the door.

I took a last breath of fresh air and entered the tiny shop.

The proprietor, a man the size and proportion of a small planet, sat behind the counter, covered in a glaze of sweat so thick that it appeared to be tidal. He was surrounded by no fewer than six heavyset men, all of whom were squeezed into an absurdly small space behind the counter with him; they could have been escaped convicts, ankles chained together out of view, or perhaps unfortunate passers-by sucked into the grav-itational field of the massive proprietor. More likely, though, they were simply local men escaping the hot morning sun.

We exchanged friendly greetings, and I inquired about road maps.

Without a word, the man slowly stood up, shuffled his colossal figure around until his back was towards me, and carefully untaped the enormous map of Sri Lanka that hung on the wall behind him. He rotated back and spread the map across the counter. 'Two US dollars, please,' he said with a smile. He said something to one of the men, who then shimmied out from behind the counter, walked over to the shop window, and took down the handwritten sign.

While I was in no position to be picky about the unruly size of the map – this was, as far as I could tell, the only one in town – I couldn't help but notice the scarcity of writing on it.

045.

'There are no names on any of these roads,' I pointed out to the shopkeeper.

He bent over the sprawling sheet, then spun it around on the counter so that it faced him and examined it more closely.

'Why you want names?' he said. 'Road is road. No name, not like person.' He spoke with a pedagogical air, like I was fresh off the boat from Jupiter.

'But how do I know which one I'm taking?' I asked.

'Look at map!'

'Yes…but how do I know if I am on the road I want to be on?' I asked, more selective of my words this time.

He held my gaze for a moment, then billowed the map off the counter and pointed at it. 'You can look at map,' he said slowly, unsure if I understood exactly what I was purchasing.

'OK, but if I think I am on *this* road,' I said, pointing to a random road, 'and I actually want to be on *that* road – what question do I ask people? How do I find out where that road is?'

This time he responded instantly, certain that his product was exactly what I needed. 'The map!' he cried triumphantly.

I bought the map – he sounded pretty sure of himself. And who knew, maybe Sri Lankan roads had no names. In fact, the more I thought about it, the more I realised I might not need the map at all – my destination that day was the town of Kurunegala, famous for its archaeological ruins and ancient temples, and an important crossroads between the coast and the hill country. Most roads would lead right to it.

For once in my life, I had a real shot at *not* getting lost.

o o o o o o o o o

Three hours later, spectacularly lost, I stared at my map for the hundredth time. What the hell had this guy sold me? In three hours of riding along strange roads and sinking deeper into the island's jungle interior, not one single Sri Lankan man, woman or child had even come close to deciphering the map. The most promising moment came early on, when I approached a man who appeared to be a village elder. I unfurled the gigantic map for him to examine. He gazed at the map and its dense tangle of dark roads for no less than a minute before looking back up at me and saying simply, 'Your country?'

I was beginning to seriously regret my decision to bike. I was lost, my map was useless, and my hapless pronunciation of my destination – Kurunegala – inevitably brought me looks of unmasked confusion from locals, as if I had approached them with a rock in each hand and begun tapping out questions in Morse code. To make matters worse, I had been so preoccupied with where I was – or rather where I wasn't – that I hadn't noticed the legion of dark clouds rolling in like tanks, swallowing the afternoon sun. I didn't even look up until I felt the first drops fall.

I wasn't overly concerned about biking in a little rain, but it was important to pull over to cover my saddlebags so that my stuff wouldn't get wet. It would have been nice to combine the stop with a lunch break – I was ravenously hungry – but it had been a while since I'd passed anything except banana trees. I stopped by the side of the narrow road to dig out my rain gear.

As I was lashing down the last bungee cord to keep the rain cover securely in place, I froze. Mixed in with the sound of wind-rustled banana leaves and light rain tapping at my bicycle, there was another sound. Voices. I stood up and looked around. There, studying me from a discreet distance, too shy to approach, were two young Sri Lankan men, one tall and thin with a deep ebony complexion, the other much shorter but also thin, with a gorgeously rounded face that looked perpetually delighted. They clammed up the instant I caught their eye, as if they'd been caught talking in class. We stared at each other for a moment, then I waved to them. They scurried towards me excitedly.

They seemed thrilled to see a tourist here, and even more thrilled to practise their English. The taller one, speaking with a deep, rich accent that seemed to belong to a much older man, eagerly asked for my impressions of their country. Not wishing to dampen his bubbling enthusiasm, I thought about the little I knew of Sri Lanka after only one day. The jungles were beautiful, the maps sucked, and, if the cover of my guidebook could be believed, there was at least one elephant. I spent some minutes vaguely praising jungles and elephants, left out any mention of maps, and hoped the questions wouldn't get any more specific.

They clung to every word I said, and seemed satisfied that my enthusiasm for their country matched their own. As they were about to take their leave, the taller man asked me why I had stopped here – there was nothing much for tourists to see in this spot. I held up the rain cover by way of explanation.

It took them a second to register what I was showing them; when they did, however, they laughed gently, like the parents of a child who has tied his shoelaces together. They were clearly of the opinion that I was taking drastic measures by using a rain cover, and insisted that it would not rain.

'But…it's raining *now*…' I said.

'Yes, but it is only two o'clock. The rain only *really* starts at three o'clock during the rainy season,' he informed me.

I straightened up at this.

'The rainy season?'

'We are very happy you come to our country,' he said with sudden emotion. The smaller man nodded vigorously. 'You come even during off-season. Many tourists leave after tsunami – but you stay, you even bring a bicycle. It is…an *honour*…that you visit.' His eyes appeared to be welling up with tears.

'It's the *rainy* season?'

'Make sure you get to your destination very soon. The rain is very strong. But you are a good cyclist, yes?' he said with a generous smile. 'No problem for you, I think.'

It was the *rainy* season? Had I understood that correctly?

I pedalled away from the happily waving men, considering my situation. I tried to look at the positive side. Biking in the rain may not be such a bad thing here, I told myself. At the very least, it would be a nice way to cool down after a hot morning ride. My timing could be rather serendipitous.

'Cooling down' in the afternoon showers of the rainy season in Sri Lanka is a bit like trying to cool down by standing between a fire hose and a burning house. The drops were soon coming down with real weight to them, slapping my head like falling acorns. Within minutes it was raining so dangerously hard that it was difficult to even stay upright. I kept my head down and fought to keep moving. I was caught in the middle of the jungle – nowhere to hide, nowhere to stop, nowhere to even catch my breath. I felt like I was drowning, like I was somehow going to be washed all the way back down the road and out to sea.

Then, miraculously, out of nowhere, on the far side of the road, a small concrete building appeared through the grey sheets of rain.

○ ○ ○ ○ ○ ○ ○ ○ ○

When I think back on that moment, I never imagine it from my own point of view: a lost, drenched, ravenously hungry biker who has just spotted what could be his salvation. Rather, I imagine what the proprietor of this small store saw on that afternoon in mid-April. I imagine him standing at the wide open entryway of his shop, staring vacantly at the sodden jungle, watching the water pooling in the cracks and ruts of the pocked road, the visibility poor through the haze of the downpour, the meditative snare drumming on the metal roof.

Then I imagine the quiet of this daily scene shattered by some preternatural blur heading straight for him, a pale-faced meteorite of a man on a bicycle, missing him by mere inches and emitting a high-pitched shriek that hits a crescendo as he skids to a halt inside the shop itself.

o o o o o o o o o

I sat for a second on my bike, panting heavily but happy to be breathing air rather than rainwater. I looked around – I seemed to have landed in a general store of some kind. I turned to apologise to the owner for almost taking out both him and his merchandise, and for the water cascading off my bike and onto his floor. He stared at me as if I had just climbed down a giant beanstalk.

To break the ice, I asked him if he sold any food. The simple nature of the request seemed to snap him back into coherence; the shock fell away from his face and he became a shopkeeper again. He shook his head, raising his arms to indicate the scant selection of soap and glue and batteries. Then, almost reluctantly, he said 'Except…'

He pointed half-heartedly towards the far corner of the store.

I followed his finger into the corner. In it stood a simple wooden table. And on that table, piled high in neat pyramids, were boxes upon boxes of what appeared to be birthday cakes.

'Are those birthday cakes?'

He nodded slowly.

'You don't have any other food?'

He shook his head.

'Uh, OK…well, then, can I please have one of the chocolate ones? Over there?' I said, pointing to the far end of the table.

He looked at me, then back at the cakes, then back at me again.

'You want whole cake?' he asked hesitantly. 'To eat now? With hands?'

'You got anything else?'

'No,' he said sadly, and took down a box from the pyramid. He paused. 'Well, jam roll!' he said, reaching for another box.

'Just the cake, thanks.'

He brought me the chocolate cake. Then he pulled up another small stool and sat down next to me.

I carefully pulled back the lid of the box, revealing a gaily frosted chocolate cake, complete with small pink roses ringing the edge of the cake like sugary ramparts. I plucked one of them off and popped it in my mouth – it was so delicious I felt my eyes begin to water.

Out of the corner of my eye, I could see the shopkeeper peering at me to see if I was really going to just dig into this cake with my hands. I looked up at him and he quickly looked away, but he was wearing a large grin. I grinned too, and dug in.

It wasn't how I expected to spend my first day in Sri Lanka – lost and drenched and wrist-deep in birthday cake out here in the middle of nowhere. But the man sitting next to me looked completely content, gazing out at the pouring rain. I looked around the shop, at the carefully stocked shelves and the well-worn stools and heavy door propped open to let in the afternoon breeze, and it occurred to me that this was not nowhere – not at all. This was this man's whole life. Everything around me was as familiar to him as it was strange to me.

The rain slowed an hour later. I said goodbye to my new friend, left the empty cake box on the table, and rode back the way I'd come. I had been studying my map; it looked like maybe I'd missed the turnoff to Kurunegala – maybe it was back down the road where I'd met those two guys.

Then again, maybe it wasn't. Maybe, after all, it didn't really matter.

GROUNDED IN IN BINH

BY KARLA ZIMMERMAN

I WAS THUMBING through a Gabriel Garcia Márquez novel when our bus flew off the road and into the lime-green mountain. We heard metal scrape metal, then – for a second – the bus was weightless and drifting. Bushes smashed up against the windows before we ground to a halt, tipped at a forty-five-degree angle against a wall of rock. Someone screamed.

The book's title was *One Hundred Years of Solitude* – an inauspicious omen given that we had just crashed in Vietnam's remote highlands. But this was just the latest omen: we had suspected we were in for trouble soon after boarding in Hanoi.

'I want to introduce you to an important man,' our guide had said when we reached the city's outskirts. 'This is Mr Khanh – K-h-a-n-h.' He pointed to the excitable man behind the steering wheel who was stacking packs of cigarettes on the dashboard. 'He will be our driver to Sapa, twelve hours north through steep mountains – a very dangerous route. So be nice to him.'

Mr Khanh flattened his palm against the horn. The sea of bicycles in front of us parted slightly.

As we moved farther into Vietnam's northern region, the bikes had thinned and been replaced by smoke-belching trucks, but Mr Khanh had been undeterred. A graduate of the 'honk-first, look-later' school of driving, he approached hairpin curves on the single-lane road with gusto. His method – lay on the horn and charge ahead at full speed – had proved effective for the first six hours of our journey, until he rounded a curve straight into a van filled with drunken soldiers.

'Are you OK?' we looked around and asked each other after the crash. There were twenty-four on board – nineteen foreigners and five locals. The bus door was flush against the embankment we'd slammed into after Mr Khanh had swerved from the van. So we all squeezed out the back windows, jumped over the rear tyre, and landed on the road five feet below.

Families trickled from a scattering of houses at the road's side. They stared at us and pointed at our bags, but we weren't centre stage. Yet.

That honour belonged to Mr Khanh and the soldiers, who shouted at each other, fists raised, faces an inch apart, fighting over who was to blame for the wreck. High-pitched cries and cigarette butts volleyed back and forth. An hour later, the soldiers passed a wad of money to Mr Khanh. The dispute had been settled. The soldiers packed up their still-mobile van and clunked away.

Our guide was the next to go. Without a phone, he had no way of communicating our broken-down situation. He flagged down a truck headed back to town, and promised to send a new bus to take us onward.

We were now alone in the middle of nowhere. Waiting.

A man in our group asked the name of the village. The response sounded like 'In Binh.' No phone. No shops. Nothing except terraced rice paddies and eight tidy wood houses.

We smiled at the villagers; they stared back.

Finally, an old woman with black-and-red, betel nut–stained teeth stepped forward and shepherded us away from the roadside, where trucks whizzed by with alarming velocity. She

053.

laughed and laughed about how the males in our group wore earrings and many of the females didn't.

Then the kids loosened up. Twenty of them crowded around us, eager to look at our cameras and guidebooks. They were whip-smart and tried to teach us to say 'hello' and 'thank you' and to count to ten in Vietnamese, an act we reciprocated in English. One little boy rode his water buffalo to the gathering.

When it started to rain the families who owned the two houses closest to the crash site invited us in. Another family farther down the road prepared a noodle dinner for everyone. Their homes were humble – one big room with a bed or two and a table, and no indoor plumbing, though they each had a large working television tuned to Vietnamese variety shows.

Seven hours went by. Darkness fell like an anvil, and knee-high wisps of mist rolled in. We shared fiery home-brewed whisky with our hosts and laughed at discussions we couldn't understand. A gentleman from Saigon translated a local proverb to make us feel better: 'You learn by looking and listening as opposed to talking. That's why you have two ears, two eyes, and only one mouth.'

Since the whisky was making speech difficult even in English, the new bus pulled up at an opportune time. The driver said he'd be taking us two hours north to Bao Yen, the closest place with accommodation for the night.

'A hotel?' we asked.

'Sort of,' he said.

We shook our new friends' hands and thanked them for their hospitality. '*Kom ern*,' we said, using our recently honed language skills for 'thank you'. We boarded the new bus, and the villagers lined up beside it, waving and shouting goodbye. Everyone was jovial except Mr Khanh, who hung back, keeping a protective hand on his sideways bus.

o o o o o o o o o

Truck stops are squalid by nature, but the truck stop at Bao Yen was in a class by itself. The rooms featured three twin-size wooden platforms, where six people were expected to sleep. The mosquito netting seemed to do more to keep the swarms of insects in rather than out. And a raucous poker game serenaded us deep into the night from the courtyard outside.

Still, we must have fallen asleep somehow, because it was suddenly morning when men on motorcycles knocked on the door, their faces hidden beneath thick helmets. They pointed to us, then to the motorcycles, then back to us, chattering with great insistence. What were they saying?

There was only one way to find out.

We climbed on behind, and held on tight. They zipped past women carrying chickens and morning glory vines, skirted potholes the size of meteor craters, and deposited us with a wave at a little restaurant with plastic tables.

Over a breakfast of rice and eggs, we heard a horn honk, and Mr Khanh drove up in our original bus. The bus from last night had to go back to Hanoi, he said, but the original bus was just fine. OK, so it was making some odd noises, but it was fine enough to make it to Sapa. A truck driver had helped him pull it upright and onto the road, and it barely had a scratch. All it needed was a good squirt with a hose to wash off the mud and bushes, a feat that the restaurant manager helped Mr Khanh accomplish.

We boarded, and spent the next four hours winding through fat mountains cultivated with tea, corn and rice. Banana and cinnamon trees lined the road, along with bamboo groves cloaked in cloud. Even Mr Khanh seemed to be enjoying the scenery, evidenced by his reduced speed and honks.

The Black Hmong and Red Dzao hill tribes populate this area that borders China. The former wear indigo clothes that stain their skin blue; the latter add a poppy-red headscarf to the mix. Most able-bodied people work in the fields, so it falls to the old women and little girls to sell opium and souvenirs to the tourists.

We could hear the females coming from far away – they wore jangley silver jewellery, and so many hoop earrings that their ear lobes were elongated – but we could not escape them; they chased us down the street, then surrounded us. We spent the next two days buying useless trinkets like jaw harps and woven bracelets, and then it was time to return to Hanoi.

Mr Khanh pulled up in – yes – the same bus. Only now, the starter wasn't working, and we had to get out and push the bus to kick the engine into gear. As a consequence, stops would be few and far between on the way back, Mr Khanh said.

So we were surprised when, six hours later, he pulled up next to a shuttered house and cut the motor. He must have to pee, we thought.

It took us several minutes to realise we had arrived at In Binh. Little by little, people trickled out of the fields and drifted down the road. The red-toothed old lady was back, as was the boy on the buffalo and all the other kids. We greeted each other like long-lost relatives – waving turned to handshakes turned to hugs all around. We tied bracelets (a practical gift from Sapa, after all) onto each other's wrists, the Vietnamese laughing at how much string they needed to encircle our bones. We exchanged addresses to send photos.

Mr Khanh tooted the horn for us to reboard. 'Goodbye! Good luck!' we called to our friends, then assumed our position behind the bus, and grunted and groaned as we coaxed it into motion. Hopping on, we headed back towards Hanoi's golden dragons and perfumed pagodas, water puppets and grand boulevards. But it was an unexpected bend in the road, and eight tiny houses, that branded our memory the deepest.

CHITIMBA

BY JUDY TIERNEY

PADDY SHUFFLED FROM the three-room wooden shack carrying two warm Carlsberg beers for Christine and me. We'd resisted his offer of a drink and a place to sit since we'd arrived, but we finally relented, collapsing in rickety chairs beneath the leafy umbrella of a mango tree in his front yard and tossing our backpacks on the dusty ground.

I longed for a cool bottle to press against my perspiring forehead, but with no electricity or ice, Paddy had no way to chill them. I pulled my dirty bandana from my shorts pocket and wiped my face.

When the bus had dropped us in front of Paddy's Brothers in Arms Resthouse in Chitimba on Malawi's western shore an hour earlier, our mission was clear – to get a ride out of town as soon as possible. Chitimba was merely a transfer point, Paddy's resthouse the last-resort option for travellers unlucky enough to get stranded on their way to Livingstonia, the hill-top village known for its panoramic views, the country's highest waterfall, and its historic nineteenth-century mission. Paddy's place stood at the foot of the twenty-five-kilometre climb up the dirt road, accessible only to four-wheel-drive vehicles or ambitious hikers. Hitching a ride appealed to our senses far more than the five-

hour trek in Malawi's impenetrable heat and humidity. We'd
also met an American woman earlier in our journey who had
been robbed at gunpoint walking up with her teenaged porter.

'Two or three trucks go up a day,' Paddy had told us when we
arrived. 'One should be coming along to take you just now.'

His words implied a sense of immediacy, as if by living on
the main route he was privy to some unwritten truck schedule,
so we stationed ourselves by the road. We would later learn
that the African expression 'just now' indicates some indistinct
point in the future, which could actually be anytime between
now and several days from now.

A rooster pecked his way through the leaves around our feet,
piercing an unripe piece of fruit on the ground. He appeared to
be the most active inhabitant in town. Across the lawn, at the
edge of the road, eight Livingstonians also sat waiting for a
ride. They waited in silence. Talking required too much effort in
East Africa's intense October mid-afternoon conditions. Two of
the men, wearing loose pants and worn T-shirts with American
slogans – one said 'Baby on Board' with an arrow pointing down
to the stomach, the other 'Beer, It Isn't Just for Breakfast Anymore' – leaned against a tree trunk and passed the time by
staring ahead at the dusty path. The others, surrounded by
cases of soda, baskets of live chickens, and various milk crates
and striped plastic bags filled with items they had purchased
in town, lay on the grass, seemingly apathetic about when the
next vehicle would arrive to take them home to the top of the
mountain.

I heard a motor in the distance and rushed towards the road
to try to negotiate a ride from the driver. The locals sat and
stared, and the oncoming truck sped past the turn-off. My
watch said 2.30pm, and I wondered how many of the two to
three trucks Paddy mentioned had already passed by on this
particular day. I looked over at him and saw him staring at me
from across the yard, looking amused.

'*Poli, poli,*' he said gently when I returned to the shade.

Slowly, slowly. We'd heard the African mantra repeated over and over but Christine and I had not yet been able to embrace it, to put it into practice. It had been only a couple of months since we'd left our corporate jobs in New York. Didn't Paddy understand that we had planned every detail of our ten-day journey through Malawi, and that according to our strict schedule, we were to arrive in Livingstonia by sundown?

o o o o o o o o

A few hours later, as the sun sank behind the mountain, Paddy carried our backpacks into his guest room, a dark, cramped space with one window and a line of foam-mattressed beds. Christine and I slipped into swimsuits, grabbed our towels, shampoo and a bar of soap and crossed the street to the path leading to Lake Malawi. A smattering of straw huts stood behind the tall yellow grass lining the short trail to the beach.

In Lake Malawi's clear water I began to relax for the first time that day. For several minutes, two young mothers and their sons studied us from the beach, then shed their clothes and ran naked into the water. They splashed over to us, laughing and pointing to the bubbly lather dripping down our hair and arms.

'Do you think this is the first time they've seen soap?' Christine whispered. 'Or are they just laughing at how odd we are?'

She handed the bar to one of the women. One lathered up, then passed the soap to the next until all four were covered in suds. Through a series of charade-like gestures, we learned that Joyce and Tabu and their five-year-old sons, Benson and Cone, lived in the small village we had passed on our way to the lake. They followed us to the beach to dry off, and when we left them halfway down the path, the smallest boy was still clutching the bar of soap.

Back at the resthouse, Paddy's wife prepared dinner. Dressed in a bright, flowery sleeveless top, an earth-toned striped skirt, and maroon wool beret, she sat on a wood stump cooking rice in a small skillet over a fire on the ground. The entire contents of the kitchen lay scattered across the bare room – a few old pots and pans, a teakettle, assorted plates, spoons and forks, cups, and two plastic water bottles, recycled and now used for cooking oil. I thought about my kitchen at home, stocked with the latest and greatest Williams-Sonoma gadgets, hand-painted dishes perfectly coordinated with placemats and napkins, and the essential electronics, my microwave, blender and toaster. Yet everything she needed for her daily routine rested within arm's reach on the dirt floor. That evening, we feasted on a mouth-watering meal of rice, beans and fish fresh from Lake Malawi.

When it was time for bed, we asked Paddy if we could bring the foam mattresses onto the porch. With limited ventilation in the guest room, we knew we'd be more comfortable outside with the cool, night breeze, under the stars.

He hung a mosquito net, too small to stretch across both of us, from the porch ceiling. Christine and I huddled together under the net for protection against the ants, stick bugs and other creepy creatures crawling around on Paddy's porch. I anticipated a long, sleepless night, but I slept more soundly than I had since we left home.

o o o o o o o o o

We awoke at 4.30am to a chorus of roosters, dogs, birds and crying babies. It was almost light, and thirty minutes later, when we crawled out from beneath our canopy to watch the brilliant orange sun rise across a powdery blue sky over Lake Malawi, Chitimba was wide awake.

From the porch, we watched Paddy's wife sweep the leaves across the yard to reveal a clean dirt floor. Colourfully dressed ladies with babies saronged to their backs carried buckets of water on their heads from the lake for the day's cooking, cleaning and laundry. We mustered enough ambition to wander to the lake just in time for the local fish market, where fishermen who had been out all night sold skinny, silvery fish from canoes dug out of tree trunks.

We hurried back to Paddy's, sure that an early truck would pass by on its way to Livingstonia. Paddy greeted us and asked if we wanted pancakes for breakfast. In spite of myself, I was beginning to like this place.

The eight Livingstonians waiting for a lift the day before had resumed their horizontal positions on the edge of Paddy's lawn, their belongings spread around them. Paddy told us that they had slept at the homes of friends and relatives who lived nearby. While we wrote in our journals and watched for vehicles, they sat motionless, without conversation, books or other activities to entertain them. I tried to remember the last time I had sat still, doing nothing, for even five minutes. I'd carried the daily pressures of self-imposed commitments and obligations with me to a continent where rushing got you nowhere and nothing ran according to a schedule.

We tired of watching for trucks. Paddy told us later that several vehicles had passed by that day, but none had turned towards Livingstonia. Even if one had, Christine and I would not have been around to catch it.

By mid-morning, we escaped the sweltering heat for a swim in the lake. It was the first of many trips to the beach that day and many encounters with the Chitimba villagers. Two girls, Chris and Savako, wearing taffeta and lace bridesmaid dresses with broken zippers donated by American relief organisations, ran from their huts as we made our way down the trail. They skipped over, grasped our hands, and led us to the water, gazing at us the entire way, with their little brother following at our heels.

Later we met Eton, a mischievous twelve-year-old with a contagious laugh, who loved splash fights and having Christine and I toss him back and forth in the water. And we wandered the beach, exploring abandoned canoes on the sand with a gang of younger boys, their bellies extended from malnutrition and bums exposed through worn-out shorts.

Heading back to Paddy's, we walked with a student who, although he was almost twenty, had not yet completed the eighth grade. 'Many times,' he told us, 'children have to work in the fields instead of going to school, so it takes them longer to finish.' He explained that with too few teachers, the schools have classes of sixty to 100 students. We promised to send books when we returned home so that he could practise reading.

Several of our new friends told us about a big football game that evening. The Chitimba team was going up to play Livingstonia. Around mid-afternoon, hordes of local fans gathered for the long pilgrimage up the hill. I secretly hoped that Christine would not suggest joining them.

Chanting and cheering for Chitimba, the crowd began the procession to Livingstonia. A bright blue, extended-bed Mazda truck overflowing with the town's players followed behind. Christine and I waved at them from the shade of the mango tree, sipping warm Carlsbergs and pondering what Paddy's wife would cook for supper.

We decided we would leave the next morning, not for Livingstonia, but for a different place, and at sundown, we returned to the beach for our final visit. Villagers rested in the sand, bathed or washed clothes at the water's edge. Christine took a picture of the mountains rising over the lake and another of several children playing near a dugout canoe.

Within seconds, a huge crowd gathered, each wanting their picture taken. We took individual photos, group photos and family photos. We snapped serious pictures and funny ones and kept snapping until we ran out of film. We wrote down everyone's address and assured them we would mail copies when we got home.

That night in bed on the porch, Christine and I heard singing in the distance. The voices moved closer in the dark, loud and harmonious, and we sat up listening until lights appeared from the mountain. Chitimba's team had won the football match, and the victory parade, singing celebratory songs, was on its way home.

o o o o o o o o o

The next morning, watching the town come to life, I wondered how Livingstonia's panoramic views could compare to the serenity and beauty of Chitimba at sunrise. Or how the mist from the Chechewe waterfalls could be more refreshing than bathing with the locals in Lake Malawi. Or how exploring the old mission buildings could be more stimulating than discovering simple pleasures through the eyes of Chitimba's villagers.

We told Paddy and his wife goodbye, and he assured us, 'The first bus should be coming along just now.' He was talking about the bus travelling south towards Mzuzu on the M1. 'It comes by here six or eight times a day. Although today is Mother's Day, and sometimes the bus does not run on public holidays.'

We lugged our backpacks across the street and sat on the side of the road where the bus had dropped us off. For a third straight day, the eight Livingstonians waiting to go home emerged from the village and settled down among their piles of belongings.

We sat for two hours, swatting the flies that flocked to our damp skin. The bus never came.

Eventually a pick-up truck drove by, passing the Livingstonia turn-off, but stopping to pick up several locals standing a few yards down the road. Christine and I looked at each other, grabbed our backpacks and ran over to ask for a lift.

'I'm going to a town just south of Mzuzu,' the driver told us. 'Where are you going?'

'I'm not sure where we're headed,' I replied, as we jumped in the back. 'We won't know until we get there.'

THE COPTIC PRIEST

BY LISA ALPINE

WHILE SLAVING AWAY at a waitress job in Switzerland in 1973, I read *Exodus* by Leon Uris. The book ignited in me an overwhelming desire to go to Israel, so I saved my money and flew to Tel Aviv. Did I pay attention to the fact that the country had just been at war? No. Did I consider the impact of the recent terrorist massacre of the Israeli Olympic team in Munich? No. Did I worry when I arrived in Tel Aviv in the middle of the night and slept on the linoleum floor at the airport that the bullet holes strafing the wall above my head had been made within the last two weeks? No. I was nineteen and blissfully ignorant and heading for the Promised Land I'd read about.

As the warm, caramel-coloured Middle Eastern sun rose and bathed Israel in morning light, I hitchhiked to Jerusalem. I stayed at the Methodist hostel in the Old City and spent weeks wandering the alleyways, befriending Palestinian children, old Jewish guards and Hassidic women at the *hamam* (public bathhouse).

I wanted to explore the rest of the country and chose Jericho on the West Bank in the Jordan Valley as my first stop; it is considered by many to be both the oldest city in the world (dating from 7000 BC) and the lowest city on earth (250 metres below sea level). I hitched a ride south with an Israeli in a noisy tin can of a car. He was horrified that I wanted to go to Jericho and adamantly refused to drive me from the highway into town. He said the Palestinians would rape and rob me and I would never make it out of there alive.

I had him drop me off at the junction and walked into the town of Jericho anyway. I bought plump dates and succulent oranges and sat on a bench in the plaza watching dilapidated produce trucks clunk by and short dark women in black dresses zigzag across the plaza, stopping to talk to one another. Jericho was bathed in amber light and warm sun. It felt good on that bench.

I found a guesthouse and rented a room. Then I went for a walk – still no raping or robbing. I walked to the end of a dusty road that led to a tall, mudbrick wall worn down by eons of wind and history. The air caressed my skin; a luscious scent wafted on the whispering silken breeze. The wall surrounded an orange grove and the trees were in full waxy white bloom. The hum of many bees called me. I scaled the wall, dropped down onto the blossom-covered ground and wandered amid the aisles of trees. The drone of the bees pulled me into a hypnotic state. I lay down, closed my eyes.

When I awoke, a dark-skinned man was sitting directly in front of me, staring. He wore the traditional scarf, white and black like Arafat's, on his head and his eyes were bloodshot. He was squatting, arms crossed over his knees. He just stared. I was startled but felt calm. He was calm. He spoke in soft, guttural Arabic, lit up a big newspaper-wrapped spliff and offered it to me. I didn't smoke pot and shook my head. He puffed away and conversed. I had no idea what he was saying but understood he was the orchard guardian. He left me there and I daydreamed as the hills wavered in the heat. It was a timeless, peaceful place.

This became my daily pattern. I wandered the dirt roads leading out of town to the encircling orchard walls of times gone by. I could smell the ancientness, sense the spirits of long-dead residents' robes brushing by me, feel the splendour of great cities bordering the Jordan River. I was a captive of my imagination and I couldn't get enough of that orange-blossom smell.

One day, as I peeked through a gate keyhole in wonder at a particularly fragrant orchard, a man peeked back. The gate opened and there stood the tallest man in Jericho with the biggest ears! He smiled at me and spoke French. Finally, someone I could talk to.

With a grand sweep of his arm, he invited me into his garden. The black robe he wore was frayed and dusty around the edges as it dragged on the ground after him. His orange grove had a unique feature – in the centre was an ornate whitewashed church. I had been befriended by a Coptic priest and this was his residence.

We sat in the shade, drinking mint tea, discussing worldly affairs. He had been born in Egypt, where Coptic Christianity originated, and in the course of many exploits had moved through the Sinai to Israel. His ears waggled as he talked. Suddenly, rocks hit the ground around us, disturbing the harmony of our garden idyll. They were thrown by little boys on the other side of the wall who were walking home from school. They tormented the priest because he wouldn't let them play in the grove. He scurried out the gate and chased them down the road, cursing them, his robes stirring up great billowing clouds of bone-dry dust.

This turned out to be a daily occurrence during our visits when I found myself in his garden listening to stories of his very long life.

On Sunday I dressed up and went to church. I knocked on the wooden gate. The Coptic priest was splendidly attired in a clean robe. Massive ornate silver crosses hung around his neck, and his head was topped with a tall, pointed stiff hat. He ceremoniously led me inside the church. It was dark and small, musty and mysterious; paintings of gilded saints loomed on the walls over the altar.

There was one other person inside, a wizened old lady in black kneeling and praying. Audibly. My friend commenced the service by lighting a gigantic copper incense burner that he swung around and around. As it built up momentum, he circumambulated the miniature room. Billows of intensely pungent copal fumes filled the church. It became so thick, I couldn't see my hand. The clouds of sickly sweet smoke wrapped around like a boa constrictor, choking me. Through the haze I heard him begin to chant fervently, but still he swung the incense burner. Though I was dying from smoke inhalation, I felt obligated to stay and support him as part of his congregation of two – perhaps the only Christians in a sea of Muslims who would tolerate his penchant for ancient, murky rituals.

o o o o o o o o

Two weeks passed, and another church service. I was becoming a fixture in Jericho. The women in town also befriended me on my daily meanderings through the market and plaza. I became an object of lunch invitations and unintentionally initiated a town-wide competition to see who could make the most delectable *ma'aluba* – a greasy lamb-and-rice dish that was not delectable at all since I was a vegetarian. However, I could not refuse their hospitality, so I had lunch many times a day. These abundantly wide women wanted to fatten me up and marry me off to one of their sons who, luckily for me, were all away studying at the university.

As if part of the conspiracy, the Coptic priest was always plying me with drippy, syrupy sweets and tree-plucked oranges.

In spite of this fact, we became good friends. I trusted him and he never took advantage of me. In fact, no-one did.

I felt protected and watched over in Jericho. What more could one ask as a guest in someone's country? I was not a woman to exploit, a pocket to rob, or an American to hate. I was just the blonde traveller from California sitting on a park bench eating dates, savouring the sweet, moist, nutritious fruits that have been nurtured for millennia in the oldest town on this earth.

SECRETS OF THE MAYA

BY LAURA RESAU

THROUGH MOONLIT FOG, I walked from the bus station towards the colonial *centro* of San Cristóbal, Chiapas. I glimpsed rooms glowing yellow behind thin curtains, shops laced with tiny white lights, restaurants strung with red lanterns. My dog-eared *Maya Cosmos* book, nestled in my backpack, portrayed this southern Mexican state as a land drenched in ancient symbols, only a veil of colonialism cloaking age-old rituals. Fluent in Spanish and armed with a degree in anthropology, I was on a break from the university where I taught in the neighbouring state of Oaxaca. For months I'd been devouring books on Maya spirituality in anticipation of this trip. As a little girl, I'd dreamt of entering magical realms, and now, as a twenty-four-year-old, I longed to discover one of the 'portals' that opened to the Otherworld – what my book called the 'Maya road to reality'.

On the first two days of my long weekend, I stuck to the tourist track; this offered interesting sights, but no doorways to the Otherworld. On Sunday, my final day in Chiapas, I decided to head to Tenejapa, a relatively remote Tzeltal Maya village. As my taxi wound up mountain roads, the thick fog turned into a cold drizzle. We passed a hillside lined with towering crosses painted blue and dressed in pine branches, standing as tall as the neighbouring pine trees. Wooden planks were scattered below among smaller crosses, like unhinged, abandoned doors. Despite the gloomy weather, I felt a thrill. I'd read about this place, a Maya graveyard: the planks were portals to the ancestors' dwelling place, where shamans regularly venture.

The taxi dropped me off at the main square in a lush, green valley. On one side was a church, and on the other, a modest, one-storey building that I guessed was the town hall. Verdant hills of corn and coffee rose up behind it. Beyond the square were a few blocks of low, tile-roofed houses. No market stalls or heaps of fruits or vegetables could be seen, only some clusters of men in ponchos fringed with pink pompoms and women in red-and-black shawls. There was a hopeful pocket of activity in front of the town hall, where about thirty people sat on wooden benches facing each other, women on one end, men on the other.

The men wore hats resembling festive lampshades, dozens of colourful ribbons cascading over the rims. Their outfits were elaborate: red embroidered shorts peeked out beneath the hems of black wool tunics; leather straps were slung over their chests, equipped with knives and canteens made of horn; necklaces of silver medallions hung down past their waists. The older men held staffs that gave them an air of royalty. As I walked towards them, ducking my head in the rain, I noticed their faces were serious, rather closed and unreadable.

The women, at the other end of the benches, seemed more lighthearted. Varying degrees of smile wrinkles fanned out from their eyes. They wore two long braids, dark skirts and white blouses embroidered with tiny red stitches. As they whispered among themselves in Tzeltal, their hands flew over their mouths to suppress their giggles.

'*Buenos dias,*' I said, rubbing my hands together. It was cold enough to see my breath. 'Could you tell me where the tourist office is?'

Two men who appeared to understand Spanish grinned, revealing teeth painted gold and silver. There was a flurry of excitement as they translated for the others.

'No. No tourist office here,' the younger man said.

'What about the market?' I tried.

'What market?'

'Today's market day, right?'

'There is no market here.' They laughed with a metallic flash of teeth.

'Oh,' I felt annoyed at the tour guide who had recommended this place. I was sure he'd said Sunday was market day. 'Thanks anyway.' I turned away awkwardly, aware that the men seemed to be laughing at me, not with me. Well, I thought, I could wander around the town and chat with the women and children; they seemed less intimidating than the horde of ribbon-bedecked men wielding staffs and carrying knives.

The rest of the town was nearly deserted, just a few people on the streets, an occasional dog or burro passing by. I tried, unsuccessfully, to strike up a conversation with three women who smiled apologetically and responded in Tzeltal. This trip was rapidly turning into a failure. With my anthropological detective work thwarted, I was, unfortunately, reduced to a typical obnoxious tourist. Against my better judgment I whipped out my camera.

As I took a few shots of the mountains and the church, I noticed a strange structure – two tree trunks with a beam nailed across. With a wave of excitement, I wondered if this was a variation of the Maya World Tree, the source of all life, the pillar supporting the cosmos.

It occurred to me to ask the ribbon-bedecked men about the tree-cross, but truth be told, they scared me. From a distance I observed them, admiring their zany hats and wishing I could snap their picture. My guide yesterday had warned that many Mayas don't like having their picture taken, since a photo makes them vulnerable to witchcraft. But I had only two more photos left on my roll, so didn't it make sense for me to use them before I left? Chilled to the bone and determined to get something out of this trip, I shrugged off my better instincts and devised a plan: I'd pretend to take a shot of the town hall but secretly zoom in on the lampshade headdresses. I casually wandered closer, feigning interest in far-off mountains, and then nonchalantly raised the camera to my eye. In one furtive gesture, I swung the viewfinder from the peaks over to the town hall and zoomed in. There were the men, in clear focus, looking sternly at me beneath the ribbons, wagging their fingers and shaking their heads.

Caught! I felt a deep blush.

What now? I could run to the road, hope a taxi would pass by soon, go back to San Cristóbal, and pretend this never happened. But I wouldn't be able to live with the shame. I took a long breath and headed towards the group. They stared, their faces grave. I stopped in front of them, aware of all eyes on me.

'*Buenos días,*' I said, feeling my cheeks flush again.

'*Buenos días, señorita,*' they replied.

I launched into a long-winded apology about how deeply sorry I was, how terrible I felt, how really, I didn't usually act like this… 'Please forgive me,' I concluded and held my breath. Would they whip out their knives and pry the film from my camera?

The two men translated for the others, discussed my transgression in low voices, and then burst into laughter. Golden teeth glinted and silver coins jingled. An older man raised his staff. '*Mira, señorita*, you may take pictures of the buildings or mountains, but not of us.'

'Thank you very, very much.' I backed up, half-bowing, embarrassed but relieved. Their laughter followed me as I walked across the wet plaza towards the road. This time they seemed a little gentler, as though they were chuckling at a cute, but pathetic, little kid. When I'd nearly reached the road, my eyes rested on the odd tree-cross structure, and I realised I wasn't ready to give up. I'd already humiliated myself beyond repair. It couldn't get any worse. And after all, this could be my last chance to learn the secrets of Maya reality.

The group watched me walk towards them, their eyebrows raised, amused. 'Uh, *con permiso*,' I said apologetically. 'One more thing. That cross by the church? The one with two tree trunks? What does it symbolise?'

They squinted at the church. They murmured to each other in Tzeltal. They conferred with the women. Were they debating whether to divulge some secret? Was the cross what I suspected – a sacred vestige of the ancient Maya, a portal to the Otherworld?

Finally they announced, 'We don't know what you're talking about.'

I pointed to the cross. 'There,' I insisted. 'See?'

'That thing? That's not a cross. That's what we tie banners to during fiestas.'

'So – there's no deeper meaning?'

They shook their heads. 'No, *señorita*.'

'Oh,' I looked at the rows of faces, ranging from apologetic to entertained. 'Well,' I paused. 'OK then.'

As I turned to go, feeling dejected, a young man said, 'Wait. What's your name, *señorita*?'

'Laura,' I said with a flash of hope. 'And yours?'

'Antonio.'

The other man who spoke Spanish well, Alonso, explained that they were the village authorities and the women were their wives. 'You speak *castellano* very well. Better than us!' Alonso laughed. He offered me a seat on the bench, on the men's side, and we chatted about my hometown of Baltimore, what the weather was like there, what crops we grew, what animals we raised – the usual small talk. Several men began playing beautiful, handmade instruments, variations of mandolins and harps. The melodies were meandering and mysterious, far from the salsa and cumbia tunes I was used to hearing. The group of men and women grew more animated by the minute, darting from Spanish to Tzeltal and back again, voices escalating into waves of laughter.

At some point I became aware of a moustached man standing near me with a shot glass and a bottle of clear liquid. He filled the glass, handed it to a seated man, waited for him to gulp it, and repeated the process with the man beside me. I noticed some of the others, especially the women, glancing at the moustached man and at me, and back at the moustached man. The women looked eager, their eyes full of mischief and hands over their mouths, tittering. Now the moustached man stood in front of me, extending the shot glass freshly filled to the brim.

'What is this?' I asked nervously.

'*Posh*.' He grinned.

'What's *posh*?' I thought of the ubiquitous warning to foreigners: don't drink anything that's not boiled or from a sealed bottle.

'We make it from sugar cane.'

I sniffed it. 'I don't usually drink hard liquor.'

'You must drink it,' Alonso told me with a stern smile.

I hesitated.

'You must drink,' the others echoed, their eyes lit up.

I stared at the shot glass in my lap. It looked unusually big.

Deepening his voice, Antonio said, 'You know what happens to people who don't drink *posh* here?'

'What?'

'We throw them in jail.' This sparked a wave of laughter. 'Yes! We are the village authorities. We say you must drink the *posh*.'

I drank the *posh*. It burned and tingled in my chest, and within minutes, my head was floating. I smiled at everyone, giddy.

Then I caught sight of the moustached man again. He was making another round, this time with a pack of Alitas cigarettes. He walked from person to person, handing each a cigarette. I'd never seen indigenous women smoking before, yet here were fifteen of them, taking long drags with gusto. I was not a smoker, but I assumed it was either smoke or go to jail. Trying not to cough, I tentatively took a few puffs.

I bit my lip when the moustached man appeared once again. This time he handed us each a thick glass bottle of Coke, the kind that's been refilled countless times, chipped and scratched and stained. The man opened each Coke ceremoniously. I sipped my Coke politely, grateful for something familiar. Then I noticed the others drinking quickly, filling the air with a cacophony of burping.

The previous day, I'd observed ritual burping inside the church of San Juan Chamula. The church's interior was dark and cavernous, lit by hundreds of tiny candle flames with pine needles scattered over worn floorboards, creating a shadowy forest. Copal incense smoke filled the air; statues of saints lined the walls, adorned with mirrors and flowers; clusters of Maya men and women in traditional dress knelt on the floor, performing spiritual cleansing ceremonies. In one corner, a healer moved a chicken over candle flames, ran it over a sick girl's body to absorb 'evil air', and then snapped the animal's neck. Next she handed the girl a bottle of Pepsi. As she gulped it down and burped, my tour guide murmured, 'She is eliminating the last of the evil air.'

I sipped my Coke with the others, but felt too self-conscious to emit more than a few soft burps. Were we burping out evil air? Was this an elaborate purification ritual? Or were we just, well, drinking and having fun? And I was having fun, warmed by the *posh* and camaraderie, thoroughly relaxed and sinking into the moment. I didn't worry about deeper meaning; it was enough to keep up with the conversation that bounced from coffee consumption to the Zapatista uprising to teenage marriage to Tzeltal verb conjugations to corn cultivation. An unexpected slice of Maya reality.

The moustached man came by again. Now he was passing around a gourd about the size of a fist. Each person poured out a small pile of dried green herb onto their palms, licked it, and passed the gourd on.

'What's that?' I asked Alonso.

'An herb,' he said breezily.

'What's it for?'

He conferred with the others, and a few moments later, came up with, 'It makes you happy.'

Hmmm. I poured some onto my palm and licked. The smell was unfamiliar, definitely not marijuana or any other herb I'd encountered. It tasted like dried grass, and I couldn't distinguish its effects from the alcohol and nicotine and caffeine already coursing through my veins.

After the mysterious herb, the moustached man still wasn't done. Now he circulated with a huge bottle of Superior beer and a single, yellow-flowered glass, the kind I might find in my grandmother's kitchen. He stood like a waiter as each person chugged a beer, and then he moved on to the next. I was never much of a beer-chugger. I took a succession of quick sips, which made the women crack jokes in Tzeltal while the men urged me to drink faster. *'Rápido! Rápido!'*

I finished the beer, laughing along with the others, feeling a proud part of this Maya version of a frat party. I smiled warmly at everyone, the drunken kind of smile that gushed, *Aw, I love you guys!* 'This is a nice fiesta,' I said to Antonio. 'Really communal.'

Antonio grew serious. 'This is not a fiesta. This is a ceremony. This is special, what we're doing now.' He didn't elaborate on its significance, and this time I didn't ask questions, felt no need to analyse it. I just nodded and burped.

When the moustached man came around with more *posh*, I reluctantly declined. I had to get back to San Cristóbal since my bus would depart that evening.

'Stay!' Antonio cried. 'Later there will be a meal and dancing. Spend the night in our home.' The women realised I was leaving and raised their voices in protest. 'Stay!' they repeated in accented Spanish. I shook hands with every single person, saying goodbye in my newly learned Tzeltal. Finally, with a dazed grin, I strolled across the plaza to a taxi that was magically waiting for me.

I never found out what vestiges of ancient Maya rituals, if any, were hidden behind the veil of beer burps and happy herb on my Sunday afternoon in Tenejapa. And in the end, that was fine with me. I had found my own Maya road to reality.

LOST IN BEIJING
BY MICHELLE RICHMOND

UPON MY ARRIVAL in Beijing in the sweltering summer of 1998, I was in possession of three basic facts: Mr Yiu was the president of a large trading company, my job was to help him improve his English, and I had flown to Asia on a one-way ticket with no definite date of return. Three weeks earlier, I had answered a classified ad in the *New York Times*. The interview took place in a posh apartment in Midtown, where Mr Yiu asked a series of polite questions before offering me his soft, moist hand and saying, 'You begin tomorrow.'

During my first four days in Beijing, Mr Yiu did not appear, and I began to wonder if he existed at all, or if I had merely dreamt him. Every morning, I woke early and walked to Ritan Park to watch the elderly people at their exercises. Then I wandered the *hutongs* behind the train station, where the smell of breakfast noodles and hard, unsweetened pastries filled the air; to this day the word 'China' conjures for me the image of a slender preteen girl kneeling in the courtyard of an ancient stone dwelling, brushing her teeth over a metal bowl. Later, I would venture into the chaotic maze of streets near the centuries-old observatory on Jianguommen Way. There, in the shadow of the elegant astronomical instruments, the newer residences, uniformly square and white, gleaming like cheap bathroom tiles, seemed like something out of a futuristic horror film.

During our fifth and final rendezvous in New York City a week before – lunch at an expensive Italian restaurant where I taught Mr Yiu the words 'eggplant' and 'basket of bread' – he had informed me that, once we arrived in China, our study sessions would take place in the afternoons. Thus, following my morning adventures those first four days, I made it a point to be back in the apartment by noon.

Despite the relative modernity of the building in which the company apartment was housed, there was no telephone in the unit, no Internet. The enormous television picked up only Chinese channels, and I quickly exhausted all my reading material. The refrigerator and pantry were glaringly empty. In this utter absence of stimulation, I would sit in one of several expensive, uncomfortable armchairs, gazing out the sliding glass doors that opened onto a narrow sixteenth-floor balcony, and wait. 12pm. 1pm. 2pm. 3pm. No word from Mr Yiu. Finally, an intensely grey dusk would settle over the city, which even in its brightest hours was darkened by soot and smog. Around 7pm there would be a knock at the door, and a young man, no older than nineteen or twenty, would stand nervously at the threshold, proffering a carton of soy milk or bottle of water, perhaps a cellophane package of dried fish, and once, three crisp bills whose markings I could not decipher.

'Hello,' he would say, thrusting the strange gifts into my hand. 'Tomorrow.' Then he would nod and disappear.

Late in the afternoon of my fifth day in China, I was sitting on the living room floor in a tank top and jeans, trying to figure out how to work the karaoke machine, when the door to the apartment swung open without warning. It was Mr Yiu, dressed in a rumpled black suit; like all of his clothing, the suit looked very expensive but was slightly too large. Mr Yiu glanced at me and quickly looked away, blushing.

'We go to dinner with someone,' he said softly. 'Maybe you better change.' He pointed to his neck, as if to indicate that more fabric was needed in that general region. 'I wait downstairs.'

After he left I rifled through the bedroom closet, where my meagre shirts and pants shared space with the more expensive clothing of some size-two female whose identity was entirely unknown to me – his previous tutor? An estranged wife? I changed into a conservative black dress, pumps and pantyhose, aware of the absurdity of this outfit in the muggy heat.

When I arrived downstairs, I could see Mr Yiu through the lobby's glass wall. He stood on the curb beside a black Mercedes, beckoning me impatiently. Outside, I was hit by a wall of heat. The frowning driver wore a gold necklace and shiny black button-down shirt. His skin was disturbingly shiny. 'Mr Feng,' Mr Yiu said, by way of introduction. I climbed into the back seat, Mr Yiu into the front. I hadn't even gotten the door shut before we screeched away. For the next hour, Mr Feng drove at a maniacal speed, taking us further and further away from the centre of town. I watched the odometer click off the miles while the two men talked excitedly in the front, neither of them saying a word to me. During our brief time together in New York, I had come to feel almost comfortable with Mr Yiu. Now, he seemed like an entirely different person.

I became suspicious, uneasy. Who was this Mr Feng, and where was he taking me? I tried to memorise landmarks in case I needed to make a daring escape, but it was impossible. The randomly placed street signs were no help, as I couldn't distinguish one Chinese character from another, and even those signs that were translated into Pinyin all looked maddeningly similar – Fuxingmen Wai, Fuchengmen, Beisanhuan Dong, Beishuan Dong. The first couple of miles took us past some of Beijing's most affluent properties – high white luxury hotels, the massive Friendship Store, the gleaming Pizza Hut and

Dunkin' Donuts. Gradually, however, the scenery changed: row after row of dingy high-rises, curious eyes studying me from the roadside. For the first time in my life I felt the discomfort of being a minority. With my red hair and pale skin, I was an oddity, a point of interest, a freak. I tried to roll down my window, but it was apparently controlled from the front seat. The lock on the door was also secure. Claustrophobia set in.

Finally Mr Yiu addressed me. 'We go Mr Feng's apartment,' he said, without turning around to meet my eyes. 'Maybe you have dinner with him.'

Me? Dinner with Mr Feng? What about English lessons? What about vocabulary? At that moment, it occurred to me that perhaps the classified ad for an English tutor had been a scam, and I was the unwitting victim of an international prostitution ring. 'Dinner' could be a euphemism for any number of involuntary acts of perversion and subservience. I imagined Mr Feng's shiny hands on my body, his mouth on my neck. I tried to come up with ways to overcome him. Once in a made-for-television thriller I had seen a woman drive the heel of her stilettos into a rapist's eye. I glanced at my serious black pumps, but the heel was too wide and blunt to do any damage.

From the map I had studied upon my arrival, I knew that Beijing was laid out in a series of ring roads. By this point, I was certain that we had travelled past the fifth and final ring, into some sort of no-man's-land. While I silently plotted my un- likely escape, Mr Yiu picked up his cell phone and engaged in a brief, animated conversation in which I recognised the improb- able English phrase, 'one hundred dollars'. So this is my asking price, I thought. My first instinct was to be offended, although perhaps I should have been flattered: at the time, $100 consti- tuted an entire month's salary for the average worker in Beijing.

'Where are we going?' I demanded, trying unsuccessfully to control the quiver in my voice. When Mr Yiu did not respond, I repeated my question more loudly, adding, 'How much further?'

'Not far,' he replied coolly.

A couple of minutes later, Mr Feng swerved off the main road and whisked us through a maze of narrow backstreets crowded with bicycles, pedestrians and vendors. The high-rises disappeared, giving way to scattered apartment blocks. The sidewalk was the centre of life. Here, all the things that most Westerners do behind closed doors were exposed to the plain light of day. The tools of every trade, the playing pieces of every game, the ingredients of every meal, and the contents of every life were spread on rickety tables or arranged on little pieces of cloth on the ground.

An elderly woman was giving haircuts on the sidewalk. Her salon consisted of a rusted metal chair, a yellow comb, a bowl of water, a pair of scissors, a hand-held mirror, and a tin can. Her current customer was shirtless and grey-headed, and his hair had been shorn to military proportions. The haircut she was giving him – the haircut that seemed to be most popular here – was a shorter version of the fifties buzz cut once worn by Elvis. Nearby, a boy in red shorts squatted on the ground, selling ears of corn from a plastic bucket wedged between his legs. Every few yards, another group of men crouched around a card game. Children stood in shop windows, slurping noodles with chopsticks. Toddlers in split-crotch pants stopped in their tracks, squatted, and peed on the sidewalk.

The air buzzed with entrepreneurial eagerness; it seemed that everyone had something to sell or trade. A young woman in an incongruously dirty dress withdrew freshly pressed white linens from a steaming basket. A man with no legs sold incense sticks from the back of a rickshaw. A wheelbarrow loaded with watermelons stood right next to a fancy ice-cream freezer, which was decorated with pictures of popsicles and drumstick cones.

Before long, the car came to a halt in the shadow of a white-tiled building, and my heart skipped a beat. Mr Feng and Mr

Yiu got out and began walking. Mr Yiu looked back at me, almost as an afterthought, and jerked his head, a silent command for me to follow. It occurred to me that I had reached a moment of decision: I could go with them, or I could flee. But where would I go? The only Chinese words I knew were 'hello' and 'thank you'. Reluctantly, I climbed out of the car and followed, struck once again by the oppressive quality of the heat; it reminded me of the Alabama summers of my childhood, the air so thick and moist it was difficult to breathe. Little droplets of mud spattered my ankles, and a thin ribbon of sweat trickled down my spine. We passed off the street into what looked like an abandoned apartment complex. The ground was littered with concrete blocks. A few dozen feet of freshly laid sidewalk began and ended arbitrarily, apparently leading nowhere.

Soon we turned a corner, and Mr Feng punched a series of numbers into an electronic keypad beside the front door of a five-storey building. There was a terrible buzzing, the door opened, and I followed the two men inside, into a windowless stairwell that echoed with our footsteps. I felt my way along the wall in the dark, touching cold, smooth concrete. The air smelled of garlic and something chemical, like burning glue. I walked four or five steps behind the men. On the fourth floor they stopped, paused, and muttered a few words to one another. Mr Feng knocked on a door. No-one answered. I lingered in the stairwell, terrified. Mr Yiu motioned me forward. From inside the apartment came the sound of male voices. I wondered how long it would take my family to come looking for me, and how they would ever find me. Unlike Hansel and Gretel, I had left no trail of crumbs.

Then the door opened, and a burst of cool air hit my face. An attractive young Chinese man in wire-rim glasses and a New York Giants T-shirt stood before us. He had the smart, casual air of a university student. Moments later I heard one of the loveliest sounds I have ever heard – a female voice, and an older woman came to stand behind the young man. Something about her posture, the tender familiarity with which she touched the student, made me realise that she was his mother. A relief verging on gratitude washed over me. What is it about maternal figures that puts us at ease in an alien place? We instinctively trust them, willingly resign ourselves to their care. The most threatening situations are instantly rendered harmless by the presence of a certain kind of woman.

As it turned out, Cheng Shee was no quiet homemaker, but a professor of Arabic at Beijing University. She had studied in Cairo in 1976, among the first wave of students allowed to attend university abroad following Mao Zedong's death. She offered me a chair and a banana-flavoured popsicle, then went to the kitchen and returned with a bowl of lychee fruit. In broken English she asked how I liked China. Her husband, a bespectacled man in a blue button-down shirt and grey trousers, asked me a series of polite questions, which were translated alternately by his son and by Mr Yiu.

Later that night as I lay in bed, watching a red China moon rise over the city, I pieced together the facts: when I thought Mr Yiu said, 'Maybe you have dinner with Mr Feng,' he had actually said, 'Maybe you have dinner with Mr Cheng' – the kind man in the blue shirt and trousers. And by *you*, he meant *we*. In the tonally complex but grammatically simple landscape of Mandarin Chinese, pronouns, gender and number do not exist. Mr Yiu's benign intentions had been lost in translation, as had the city's geography – our journey had covered less distance than I thought. Mr Cheng's apartment was located within the boundaries of the third ring road, not outside the fifth. Furthermore, the building was not in ruins, as it first appeared; to the contrary, it was still under construction.

I drifted off to sleep, only to wake a few hours later in a dark, unfamiliar place. As I always do while travelling – whether in

China or Charleston, Buenos Aires or Baton Rouge – I went through my mental filing system, trying to get my bearings. Though I recognised nothing in that first moment of waking, I wasn't exactly afraid, for I trusted in the time-tested alchemy: simply by remembering, by naming this spot on the earth, I could be somewhere, rather than nowhere. In a matter of moments it came to me: Asia, yes. Beijing. The apartment on Dongchang'an Street, sixteenth floor, the middle of July.

Again and again in the days that followed, sleeping or waking, I would experience this same feeling of being lost in some unidentifiable dream. Finally, sometime in August, I woke one morning, glanced around, and felt the comforting certainty that comes only with time. I did not need to orient myself to the white bedside table, the large picture window overlooking the city, the hint of soot in the air-conditioned room. No, I could pinpoint my location with comforting exactitude. And that could mean only one thing: I was, at least for that moment, home.

CROSSING OVER

BY ROSE GEORGE

THE *CANMAR PRIDE*, though a cargo ship, has begun taking passengers, seeking to augment its income by attracting those travellers allergic to cruise crowds. Usually there are enough of these to fill its half-dozen passenger berths, but as no-one else is lunatic enough to pay money to sail through hazardous winter waters, I am to be the lone woman amongst 2200 containers and a twenty-two-strong Indian crew on this ten-day Atlantic crossing. My family worries for my safety and my boredom threshold, but there is a VCR, an exercise bike and books. The crew is courteous and the captain – a genial Parsee from Mumbai – happy to welcome me on his bridge, where two sofas have been installed for passengers. As we pull away from our berth on the Medway River, out towards the English Channel, I'm standing next to him, surrounded by machines spitting out weather reports and warnings of 'ice-infested waters', and wondering where else I would be granted such a privilege.

Other safety worries are groundless: the ship is brand new and the length of two football pitches, with a bow stronger than an icebreaker, and a BW engine (in shipping terms, a Rolls Royce) that can storm through force-ten gales. If I am to sail

John departs at night, climbing far, far down into his little tugboat – little, but worth £3 million and with 40,000 horse-power, whereas the *Canmar Pride*'s bow thruster has only twenty-three – and I sleep easily in my luxurious bed, lulled by the humming of engines seven decks below. As the only passenger, I dine with the officers in their mess room, and they eat early. A 7.30am phone call informs me in Hindi-accented English that it is time, so I pull on clothes and sneakers and run up five flights to the small mess-room, furnished with a couple of tables and small portholes. 'Sweet corn,' says Stanley the steward, by way of a greeting, and puts a bowl of it on the table, by way of breakfast, along with various curries. This is something of a culinary shock early in the morning, but luckily, Stanley is from Goa, and Goans make good curry and the best stewards. One of the officers, perhaps to soothe my obvious unfamiliarity with spicy breakfasts, tells me a joke: 'A man says to his Goan friend, "My son's just been promoted to captain!" "Oh, that's nice," says his friend. "But when is he going to become chief steward?"' Stanley is unfazed by my vegetarianism, just as the supposedly vegetarian Hindu officers, I learn, are unfazed by meat. 'Yes,' says an officer, helping himself to chicken, 'we believe the cow is sacred. But it's also tasty.'

The ship has sidestepped to Antwerp to gather cargo. I need film, and go into town, but it's snowing hard and I get back to my bridge quickly, more interested in cranes and containers than picturesque medieval squares. A friend had told me that cargo ships were less intriguing now that everything was hidden in metal boxes, and there were no more tarantulas. But there is still mystery, when even the captain doesn't know what's in the boxes (it's a security measure, says the shipping company). I stand by him on the bridge, in front of the bank of windows that run its width, and picture mounds of peaches and perfume – though it's probably Hyundais and hydrogen chloride – while the captain tells tales. Once in West Africa he watched armed pirates steal containers ('I wasn't going to argue with an Uzi'). In East Africa, the deck list is removed from the stairwell, so thieves can't find what they want. In Canada, another gang once hijacked an unremarkable container that held millions of dollars in gold coins. I recall what someone had whispered to me before sailing, that stowaways are still often found in the containers, though the metal boxes get colder than freezing.

Late in the evening, the *Pride* sails into the Channel. The last landmark is Bishop's Rock, which floats past next morning, and the sea is now officially an ocean. It's too dangerous for me to walk on deck without an escort, so the captain takes me for a stroll around the ship, moving carefully between the containers and the rail. 'Ships are always losing people,' says the captain. 'It's the wind.'

This is an oversized world of industrial beauty. The containers look like New York skyscrapers, the rope is giant's rope, the chains are supersize. Everywhere, there is the orange-red of Canmar's corporate image, and mysterious doors and hatches that I never see open. The crew move within the labyrinth of cold metal swaddled in industrial boiler-suits, brown skin and white teeth gleaming in the depths of heavy hoods. Their work looks thankless, but they still manage a grin for the strange woman who thinks freezing cold and ocean seas mean entertainment, not hard slog.

The captain has never seen *Titanic* – though there is, oddly, a copy of the video in the crew lounge – but he escorts me to the bow, where there's a platform on the forecastle to hold the floodlight that ships need to transit the Suez Canal. I step up and prepare to recreate the film's most famous scene, though I am wearing a hard hat and thermals, not eveningwear, and when I spread my arms wide, the wind knocks me off my feet. When I do lean over to watch the ship slicing through the deep, it's with both hands firmly on the rail.

Later, I see a fishing vessel going along next to us and she's pitching up and down as she hits the waves. The *Pride* hardly notices. But there are two 'complex storms' ahead, and the master is not yet sure we'll avoid them. At dinner, I notice a ridge around the table edge has been raised, in anticipation of rough weather, to keep the plates from falling off. Old seamen, says the chief engineer, are always removing things from the tops of their fridges at home, in case they fall off in a storm. And their wives are always putting them back on.

The weather picks up and they laugh at me when I say I'm feeling sick. This is nothing. When it's really rough you can come to the mess room and find the fridge halfway across the room, and the chairs on top of the table. The captain tells me to sleep in a locked position, diagonally, so the pitching and rolling doesn't affect me. The highest waves he has endured were fifty feet. With those, he says, the bow goes straight up in the air and – whack! – hits the water. 'When you're stuck between two swells, that's bad,' he says, like a teacher to a child. 'You can't navigate through it and your ship is rolling forty-five degrees each way.' I decide I no longer want some bad weather for excitement, but it appears to be too late.

The next day we hit the Atlantic Ridge, and leave Europe for America. We're now in the fast lane of European immigration, following millions of hopefuls to the new world. There are other ghosts, too, as we are fleeing the weather, and our more southerly route is the exact one taken by the *Titanic*, forty-five-to-forty-six-degrees latitude, says the captain, who knows the facts better than the film fiction. 'If she'd gone straight onto the iceberg,' he says, 'she would have survived. The mistake was to turn her to port.'

On the bridge, an officer says a ship is heading in our direction. 'Well, get on the radio, then!' says the master to the chief. 'It's probably the Croatian.' He says 'the' not 'a' because there are few foolhardy enough to brave these seas in winter, and the master knows them all. The chief gets on the radio, then reports back. 'Filipino, going from Honduras to Spain.'

'Filipino!' yells the master. 'Monkey!'

Indian crews compete with Filipino ones, in the competitive world of shipping and shippers, and the captain has decisive opinions about them. 'Filipinos are the worst. They drink and drink and then they fight and get their knives out. But they work hard. Indian officers are in demand, because they work, they don't really drink and they're cheap.' If the captain left Canmar, he says, he would have no shortage of work; the young men who are his second and third officers are spending their lives in isolation to pay for brides and houses, and because they know their careers will last.

But those are thoughts too practical for these waters. We're now in the western seas that lay beyond the pillars of Hercules, where the ancients' sacred resting places were. This is where the Greeks had their Isle of the Blest, and the Welsh their Avalon. It's the site of Atlantis, and Atlantic sailors still swear they see the mythical island of Hy Brasil although, like the rest of the sacred isles, its existence was ruled out in the mid-nineteenth century.

Still, though the Atlantic is now officially relatively island-free, it's not a blank. In the shallow brown drawers of the radio room, behind the strangely antiquated-looking machines that steer the ship, which are actually the latest and best of their kind, there are charts that reveal the emptiness is filled with names. Around, near and far, are the Faraday Fracture Zone, Maxwell Fracture Zone, Olympus Knoll 1562, Kings Trough, Azores Biscay Rise, Kurchatov Fracture Zone, Charlie Gibbs Fracture Zone (named for a weather station called Charlie and a man called Gibbs), Porcupine Abyssal Plain and West Thulean Rise. In the radio room, someone has switched on the BBC World Service, and a presenter is talking about politics. He says, 'We're in uncharted waters here.' I think of what's outside and thank the explorers who set off into nothingness and dared to anchor it with names.

There are means to connect with the outside world on the bridge – computers, an Internet connection, satellite phones and faxes. The captain is often to be found at the computer, perfecting solitaire. But I don't want communication, having sunk by now into a languorous life, and into a daytime routine of sleeping and reading and sleeping some more. I have brought, ambitiously, *St. Augustine's Confessions*, but prefer to read trashy novels from the passengers' lounge, or my *Oxford Companion to Ships and the Sea*, if my brain tends towards the catatonic. I don't mind the doziness, but sometimes it's a relief to leave the sealed portholes of my cabin for the bridge, where the side windows open, and I stick my head out to blow away the torpor, to sniff the freshness and saltiness of outside, and to watch the waters change from aquamarine, in balmier times and places, to stubborn slate-grey, in those places furthest from anywhere.

The day's meanderings end with a sundowner in the captain's cabin – a whisky for me, always, but 'only a beer' for him, he says, patting his stomach. Then dinner with the officers, who talk of house prices in Bombay, and why they went to sea ('I don't know,' says the second officer, who is from a non-seafaring family in landlocked Lucknow, as if it's just one of those things). Then, always, up to the bridge, to sit on the sofa or a stool at the windows, my nose pressed to the glass, though there is nothing to see but black and stars, listening to voices crackling on the radio. The second officer, who usually has the late-night watch, thinks I am odd to come up here every night. But it's my favourite time, when I feel smallest of all in this immense sky and sea, when even the watch officer forgets I'm there, and the mechanical chirping and clicking of the bridge's machines mix with the blank pitilessness of the nature outside, and I feel I am taking a holiday from being human, from the daily grind of being conscious. It could be crushing, but it's a comfort.

At eight o'clock, as usual, the second officer makes his announcement. 'Clocks will be retarded by one hour this evening.' There is no crude jet lag, no brutal loss or gain of hours by a bewildered body. I am being propelled gently into a different time, on an icebreaking Indian restaurant, and I need nothing else but this amount of nowhere.

This serenity of mine is not matched by the sea. One morning I wake at 4am to find my possessions being hurled across the cabin, having failed to obey point number four in the MV *Canmar Pride* Safety and Quality Management Action: 'to secure all loose personal effects to avoid personal injury or damage to any equipment.' I get up to rescue my camera and computer, and that's the first of many forays, putting things in drawers, shutting doors, sliding shoes back across the room to the other bed. The wardrobes are particularly enraged. I doze feeling my outer body move and my intestines follow a second later as the *Pride* shoves her bow through nine-metre swells.

Later, in the mess room, my toast escapes from me across the table, the chairs do a jig and the galley door slams shut. I go back below but the master calls me back up to see a rainbow, and anyway, the bridge is the highest place I can be, and the higher I am, the less sick I feel and the less I collide with low-flying objects. The ship is battling, the horizon is grey water, the spray is white and the sun is shining. The furious waters show their mood, now, by the blackness of their blue, dotted with white wave tops and – for a brief while – the captain's promised rainbow, hitting the middle of the steel containers, blurred by the spray slamming against the windows on all sides. I don't bother looking for the rainbow's end; everything is too huge and too distant, and my stomach can't take the rising – up, down, up, down, mercilessly – of the horizon. I stop watching and take refuge in my sofa. The captain, usually keen to ensure his passenger isn't bored, offering tours of the bridge machinery, or a perusal of the storm reports constantly spitting out of the storm report machine, is less talkative than usual, concentrating on the swell. He's annoyed because we've lost a day already, as we're going at thirteen knots instead of twenty-two. That's 100 miles less a day. Our sea is the result of low pressure off Ireland, he says, affecting us all the way down here. 'And I've taken a more southerly route,' says the master. 'If we'd done the normal route…' and he makes a gesture of frustration.

I wonder what day it is, but don't bother asking. Normal indicators of time and place are irrelevant. 'Where are we?' I ask the master. He says, 'At sea.' 'Where are we?' I ask the third officer. He says, 'In water.' Possibly, I've transgressed some code, like I do when I joke about bad weather in the presence of anyone, or engines in the presence of the chief engineer. When I say 'Any collisions?' the master groans, 'No, never,' and touches the wooden chart drawer in front of him.

When the waters are calmer, the captain lets me steer. Autopilot is turned off, and I'm holding $200 million of ship in my hands. I'm scared stiff.

'Of what?' says the captain.

'Colliding.'

'With what?'

He's right. It's hard to collide with nothing. Even the whales have gone south for the winter.

Afterwards, the captain tests Surindar the cadet on his ice code, using ice charts from the Canadian Ice Center. Surindar will have to learn fast, because the captain has decided to take a shortcut to take fifty miles off the journey, though the chief officer thinks it will risk the ship.

'Risk?' roars the captain. 'You're insulting my ship! This is the strongest ship going to Canada. It's stronger than their icebreakers.'

I suspect he also wants to show off. A few days earlier, when I'd asked to see the moon, there was a similar roar – 'The lady wants the sun and now she wants the moon!' – but he tried to accommodate the lady, nonetheless, setting the third officer to work with pencils and charts to figure out when the moon might be visible. '18.30, a few days from now,' said the third officer, with a quizzical look. Don't I know that the moon rarely emerges from clouds in winter? So if the captain can't give me the moon, and not much sun, he's determined to give me ice.

The waters heed him. One morning I'm awakened by a summons from the bridge to discover we're in the mouth of the Saint Lawrence River. Disappointingly, there is nothing but fog. 'Ten minutes,' says the captain, sagely, and ten minutes later the heavens open, the sun bursts through and the third officer and I run up to the monkey deck to stare at a stunning polar landscape. The ice stretches from bank to bank. It's a gorgeous, deafeningly quiet white-out, with only the muffled swish of the bow cutting a blue streak through the frozen river. I say to the third officer, so excited he's in shirtsleeves, 'We've got sunshine, good visibility, ice. What more do we want?'

'Seals.'

Inside, though I scour the river with binoculars, the water seems as empty as the houses that line its banks. Only Quebec City shows any sign of activity, sitting prettily on its cliff top. The captain tells me about the French defeat in 1759, when the British climbed the cliffs overnight, met the French army at the Plains of Abraham and routed them in less than fifteen minutes. He's laughing, and a minute later, he whispers the same story to the chief officer, out of earshot of the Quebecois river pilots.

Farther on, at Cape Charles, we pass the home of Charles, the elderly man who usually blasts each ship's national anthem from enormous loudspeakers set up on the roof of his house as the ship sails by. The crew love this, especially since the man, after realising this Bermuda-flagged ship wasn't crewed by Brits, has been playing the Indian national anthem instead. 'I feel so good when I hear that!' says the captain, who has now emigrated to Canada. But today Charles is silent. Like the whales and the seals, he won't perform in winter.

The empty river is spooky, but that could just be my mood. Three days ago I was begging the ship to stop moving. Now I dread land. I even ask the captain to let me stay overnight on the ship in Montreal, a request that the crew find as odd as my decision to sail in the first place – some have been on for seven months and can't wait to get off.

Eventually, I too have to leave, and a shipping agent gives me a lift into the city, stopping at the customs office at Sugar Quay, where Canada's sugar is deposited. From here, I can still see the *Canmar Pride* sitting passively, a steel Gulliver crawling with Lilliputian cranes. She's still mesmerising, and still magnificent, but she's no longer mine.

IN THE WAKE OF ALBATROSSES

BY KERRY LORIMER

ON A GUSTY bluff on a speck of an island in the farthest frigid wastes of the Southern Ocean, a pair of wandering albatrosses performs a balletic and beguiling mating ritual. Encircling each other with their three-metre wingspan, they dance a flat-footed *pas de deux*, uttering a loose-throated gargle that rises to a shrill, whinnying honk, ending in a wet *pop* and a sharp rattling of beaks. Periodically they pause and delicately preen each other's snowy breast. The elaborate tenderness of their greeting is understandable: in the two years since they last saw one another, each has flown many thousands of solitary kilometres, possibly circumnavigating the globe, and never resting on land.

Their performance is played out on a tussocky, blustery stage, back-dropped by black mountains mantled with glaciers that reach down to a wind-whipped turquoise sea. Bruise-coloured clouds and a chill wind chase squall shadows across the broad sweep of the bay. The birds' only audience – to which they are oblivious – is two humans who have sailed 1200 nautical miles east from South America to see them in their nesting ground on Albatross Island, a tiny fracture off the Sub-Antarctic island of South Georgia.

As we sit, transfixed and shivering in the near-freezing temperatures, they shuffle ensemble towards us until we have to scramble out of their way. Their heads are as big as a child's, their bodies the size of well-upholstered Labradors.

A sound like a small buzz bomb cuts through the low howl of the wind and we involuntarily duck beneath another wanderer coming in low overhead. The landing gear goes down, huge webbed feet dangle disconnectedly and the whole bird develops speed wobbles as it brakes and loses lift. There's a moment's apparent panic before it lands with an audible *whump*, completing a three-point landing with an undignified beak plant.

These birds are designed to fly, not to land.

Their brethren have been our near-constant companions for the past couple of weeks at sea, but seeing them up close – their size and exquisite beauty – I can feel tears stinging my eyes.

o o o o o o o o o

Our adventure had begun as most such expeditions do: with a surfeit of alcohol. At a wedding banquet in South Africa, as Zulu warriors danced around a bonfire, I'd waxed lyrical about the wonders of South Georgia – the icy Eden where animals know no fear of man – to Bernardo, owner of the aptly-named *Beagle IV*, an eighteen-metre sailing ketch, who'd long dreamed of sailing there. After downing his 117th 'springbok' cocktail, he turned and slurred, 'Let's do it.' I squinted back at him through my own springbok haze and said, 'D'ya wanna?'

And so we found ourselves – along with John and Rachel (whose wedding it was) and two of Bernardo's friends, David and Julio – plotting our course: we would set sail down the Beagle Channel and turn left at the southern tip of South America, then head deep into the wilds of the Southern Ocean, south of the Roaring Forties, into the Furious Fifties and skimming gut-clenchingly close to the Screaming Sixties.

More than a few seasoned yachties suggested we were off our chumps: sailing a smallish, unreinforced fibreglass yacht to one of the planet's most isolated outposts in a heavy ice year. Although I'd already clocked up a respectable number of sea miles, in preparation for (or trepidation about) this expedition, I'd undertaken a safety-at-sea course. This had involved jumping into a swimming pool, fully clothed in heavy foul-weather gear, in pitch darkness, with fifteen strangers. Fire hoses had been turned on us to simulate sea conditions and we'd had to clamber into a tippy inflatable life raft without drowning anyone in the process. This experience had convinced me that I never, ever, wanted to have to abandon ship. On our upcoming trip, however, it wouldn't make much difference: if we hit an iceberg and had to take to the life raft, our chances of being found would be close to zip – and we'd probably freeze to death anyway.

We set sail and quickly settled into a routine of sleep, eat, stand watch, sleep, eat. The lethargic funk and mushy brain feeling of the first few days at sea – and my unvoiced fear of our foolhardiness – finally lifted on our third day out. Dragging myself from my bunk after three hours' damp, cold sleep and swathing myself in enough thermals and foul-weather gear to out-frump an elephant seal, I poked my head out of the companionway to see a wandering albatross soaring in a rare blue sky. For two chilly hours – until my fingers felt like they were welded to the wheel and my toes had become frosty pebbles – I steered the boat alone, down the face of cresting rollers across an endless blue disc, while ten wanderers and a host of smaller albatrosses wheeled about me.

They soared past close enough for us to look one another in the eye, descended to parallel the water as they overtook the boat, arced up until they almost stalled, then wheeled about and took long dives low along the surface, their vast wings stretching just a little further as they reached azimuth, wing tips flickering above the wave tops. I tracked the continuous helix-shaped flight path of one bird: in fifteen minutes it didn't flap once.

A couple of days later we spotted our first iceberg – a large blue smudge on the horizon – and matched it to the green blob on the radar. That night, we had one person on the wheel and one down below, scanning the radar screen for telltale green splotches. But the next morning we got a nasty scare: a 'growler', a chunk of ice big enough to sink us, drifted by – without registering the slightest blip on the radar. We resolved to heave-to at nightfall in the future.

That was fine by me. Nights gave respite from the minus twenty-five degrees Celsius wind chill and the corn-size sleet that blew horizontally on the forty-knot wind, peppering my ski goggles and drifting down the neck of my jacket to settle and chill at about belly level. It felt almost novel to stand upright rather than at forty-five degrees, not lurching and tripping about below decks like we were in the superwash cycle of a washing machine. It was a relief not to have to hang onto something to avoid being ejected from my bunk while I slept – and to be able to pee without worrying about either overbalancing or backwash.

o o o o o o o o o

In another couple of days we were weaving between icebergs – glowing, flat-topped chunks strafed with electric blue fissures – and we had to put another reef in the main to slow us down, lessening the odds of a *Titanic* moment. Then the sea erupted: from utter aloneness, we were suddenly surrounded by life in dazzling profusion. King penguins and fur seals leaped and twirled about us and the sky was full of birds. The peaks of South Georgia spiked the skyline, the ponderous curtain of grey clouds rolled theatrically back and we were in sparkling sunshine, beam reaching at ten knots towards a flooded mountain range.

It looked like a stage set: black mountains, so sheer and jagged they appeared as two-dimensional outlines drawn by a shaky hand against the sky, soared from the ocean to snag their snow-streaked summits in piles of pancake-shaped lenticular clouds. The sea turned a vivid, glacially opaque turquoise and every passing wave carried a surfing seal or penguin. Frothy whitecaps cantered across the surface to smash against icebergs that had calved from the glaciers of Antarctica itself.

On every sheer, shattered cliff top, emerald green tussock grass was dandruffed with nesting albatrosses – the tiny specks the only thing giving a sense of scale to the huge, wild landscape. After so many monochromatic days of grey sea and grey skies, the technicolour intensity and variety of colour sizzled the retinas. We closed with the coast as bullets of katabatic wind, gravity-driven from the mountain peaks, whipped the water to smoke, spiralling in williwaws across the water and hitting us with fifty-knot blasts that laid us on our side.

Giddy as kids at a funfair, we tucked into a sheltered bay and dropped anchor for the first time in eight days. The constant noise and movement of sailing abruptly stopped and we looked at each other, momentarily stunned into silence. The plaintive cries and howls of a nearby seal colony whirled on the wind. We peeled off our foul-weather gear; with our matted hair and wind-bitten faces, we looked like we should be howling ourselves.

After a hot meal from a plate that didn't leap about, we pulled out the charts and pored over the possibilities, matching them against the weather fax, which was looking ominous. Low-pressure systems wheel unfettered around the Southern Ocean like horses in a chariot race, circling Antarctica, their attendant cold fronts streaming behind like reins. At that moment, there was a low to the south of us that looked like a thumb print – very nasty – so our plans were hedged by the need to always be close enough to duck for cover in a sheltered bay if necessary.

o o o o o o o o

We continued sailing down the northern side of South Georgia; the coastline here is frayed into numerous bays and islets, but few give adequate shelter. Though 170 kilometres long and forty at its widest point, the island is more than fifty per cent covered by 140 glaciers, and most of the rest is near vertical. Still, it's the only speck of land for a thousand or so miles in any direction, so if you're a penguin, seal or bird and you need to get out of the water to breed, this is the place. Between November and March each year, the waters boil with beasties and the beaches are packed tighter than Bondi on a sunny Sunday. Two-and-a-half million pairs of macaroni penguins manage to shoehorn themselves onto every rocky surface, while 400,000 king penguins and their offspring pack the beaches so that, from a distance, the squirming mass stretching to the glacier-framed horizon looks like 3D animated wallpaper. It even creates its own heat haze.

Thanks to its extreme isolation and lack of any permanent human population, South Georgia's wildlife has next to no fear of man. Each time we landed on a beach, baby fur seals would follow us about like puppies, and if we sat at the edge of the penguin rookery, we'd soon have king penguin chicks – looking like mink-coated babushkas – pecking determinedly at our shoelaces. The adult kings, surfing waves onto the sand, would pick themselves up and stand momentarily bemused, their brilliant blue-black and silver-white plumage with the bright orange ear muffs glistening in the sun, before waddling away to join the wallpaper throng.

On a chill and misty afternoon, we searched for the narrow entrance to Cobblers Cove and found it guarded by a large berg with a row of chinstrap penguins on top. We surfed between savage-looking rocks and dropped anchor in a tiny inlet just big enough for the boat to swing around. The fur seals' querulous laments echoed off the surrounding cliffs; above us light-mantled sooty albatross couples performed their immaculately synchronised aerial courtship.

We dinghied ashore, keeping a paddle handy as a 'bodger' to fend off any advances from the bolshy fur seal teenagers that were loafing, jostling, and mock-fighting in their hundreds along the shore. The shore line wriggled with tiny

youngsters that were frolicking in a natural wading pool formed by long streamers of orange kelp. Further up, elephant seals lay like overstuffed cigars, stacked in scrofulous heaps, occasionally giving out hot, pink yawns and only raising their heads and tails to belch and fart in our general direction as we passed by.

We scrambled up through muddy tussock and startled a herd of reindeer, which galloped away up the steep, velvet green hillside. After so many sedentary days at sea, we were breathless by the time we reached the top and gazed down on *Beagle*, looking like a toy in its very own bathtub. Yet at this height we found a gentoo penguin rookery: the crazy critters somehow made the climb every day from sea level to here. Such was the premium on prime property.

o o o o o o o o o

Our time in South Georgia is nearly up when Rachel and I find ourselves alone with the wanderers – and I find myself quietly sobbing in the face of such inestimable purity and beauty. The island has been overwhelming on every level, but it has saved the best until last.

Our final harbour is Elsehul. The air is thick with birds – albatrosses, giant petrels and thousands of Wilson's storm petrels, tiny, fragile creatures the size of sparrows whose domain is the roughest ocean on earth. We jump in the dinghy and head towards a patch of grey: a colony of 50,000 macaroni penguins. The next hill-top along is speckled with albatross nests: it's a veritable suburbia.

It's too steep for us to land, but not for the penguins. We drift for an hour, watching the little birds porpoise through the water at full tilt, launch themselves to smack face-first into the steep rock face, then scrabble wildly to get up to their nests. If they make it, they stand slick and shiny and shake their yellow eyebrow feathers loose; but just as often they slide backwards into the water, flippers flailing, and knock their buddies off with them. A young fur seal tries the same trick and comes off looking rather sick. It's all very Buster Keaton.

There's not a breath of wind, the water is a surreal, still, teal blue, so clear we can watch the fur seals metres below us, somersaulting their lithe and sinuous bodies through the strands of kelp. They're intelligent and curious and before long, as we putter around the bay, we have a teenage gang of twenty or thirty seals playing tag in our wake, rolling and tumbling over each other – I'm sure they're laughing as much as we are.

With no wind or waves, the only sounds are the cries of seal pups for their mothers and the buzz and whoosh of swooping albatrosses. A cloud of tiny Antarctic prions takes to the air; the patter of their feet on the surface of the water as they lift off sounds like a waterfall, and they dance around us on flickering wings.

Sadly and suddenly, it starts to sleet and we leave our private paradise and head back to *Beagle*: it's time to leave. The boys lean over the charts and there's much head-shaking: the ice conditions have apparently worsened, with many more bergs in the area and the prevailing winds will be right on the nose, making the sail slow, wet and bumpy as we force our way against the swell. That's to be expected – the only question is one of intensity: how bad is bad going to be?

o o o o o o o o

The ensuing six days are something of a blur. When we're not on watch, we're in our bunks; it's just too cold and miserable to do anything else. Everything is wet and slick with salt; the saloon floor is like a skating rink and getting about is like playing Twister. It takes two hands and all your strength not to be thrown across the boat, the motion is so rough and muddled. It's too rough to cook anything elaborate so Rachel and I rustle up some 'hoosh' in the best Shackleton tradition: grab the six most accessible tins of food – whatever they might be – and throw them in a pot.

I yearn to be warm, dry and vertical, not wet, cold and in the middle of the ocean. We seem to be getting nowhere and I start to feel like a hamster: there's a big, blue ball rolling beneath us and we're sailing like mad, but we're not really going anywhere.

Then we cross north of the Antarctic convergence and instantly the air and sea are warmer. The wind takes a friendlier direction and the world looks sunnier as we surf the last hundred miles to the Falkland Islands.

Soon we're tied to a dock, with a smiling Falkland Islander waiting to clear us through customs. It's the first 'civilisation' we've seen in a month and it's all a bit of a shock.

Even though this is but a waypoint on the journey – and the worst is possibly still to come in the notorious stretch between the Falklands and South America – we feel like we've made it. We slap and hug each other, recognising a bond between us that's formed for life – and a huge sense of relief. Rachel and I head for town, returning with the essential ingredients for some celebratory springboks, and we party till dawn.

The next day there's a feeling of quiet dread (not to mention hangover) as we cast off the lines and head out of Port Stanley, accompanied by a pod of bow wave–surfing hourglass dolphins. But this time our fears are unfounded and we have ludicrously mild conditions.

We can't decide if the weather gods are feeling benevolent or just toying with us. There's another thumb print low to the south, ready to thump us, but we're sailing through a massive high pressure system – much of the time there's barely enough wind to sail. Still, we're making good time, so good, in fact, that we're two days ahead of schedule.

Tracing our rhumb line on the chart, fingers start drifting south, and soon there are mumblings about Cape Horn. It's often called the yachtsman's Mt Everest, and is the graveyard to some 800 vessels, but eventually the words are spoken: 'Maybe we should try to round the Horn?'

There's a unanimous reply: 'D'ya wanna?'

THE END OF THE ROAD
BY BILL FINK

WE LOST THE side-view mirrors somewhere outside Nakhon
Ratchasima. They shattered when Ben steered our jeep too close
to the thick Thai jungle choking the roadside. The gas gauge and
speedometer went at Bua Yai, the transmission failed near Khon
Kaen, and we snapped the driveshaft twelve long miles from
Udon Thani. Only the broken driveshaft really slowed us down,
adding a day's delay in our quest to see the Real Thailand.

On winter break from a study abroad programme in Japan,
Ben and I had decided we would skip the typical backpacker
trip to the tropical Thai party islands of Koh Samui and Phuket.
And we certainly weren't going to go on one of those packaged
air-con bus tours of the country, sharing our seats with grey-
haired old ladies from Peoria and honeymooning Japanese
couples in matching sweatsuits.

No, our plan was to discover the true Thailand by driving
straight to the middle of nowhere. We felt the further we left
the beaten path, the better chance we'd have to meet the locals,
experience the culture, and become one with the people. We
rented a jeep to help us navigate the harsh backroads terrain.
But we had to give up on the idea of blending with the locals,
because the only jeep we were able to rent had bright yellow

flames painted on the side, big chrome bumpers and a decal that said 'Pattaya Party Cruiser' on the hood. Plus, we were two long-haired, bearded white guys who couldn't speak a word of Thai, and had a bit of trouble remembering which side of the road we were supposed to drive on.

But we were as friendly as we were filthy, and we figured a little sincerity would go a long way towards bonding with the locals. At the start of our trip we had decent luck befriending Thai people, especially as we revitalised village economies with all the money we were spending on jeep repairs. But as we headed to the hills of the northeast, people became a little less open and a little more cautious about engaging with us. The area at the intersection of Thailand, Myanmar and Laos, infamously known as the Golden Triangle, had been a vortex of the opium trade, cross-border battles, tribal insurgencies, and general mayhem for generations. In the months before our arrival, a military coup in Myanmar had resulted in the slaughter of protesters, closing of borders, and rebel fighters using the Thai countryside as a hiding ground. The Laos–Thailand border was also closed, due to a simmering border dispute between the two countries that had been sparking small military skirmishes.

This information was very revealing when we learned it a month later, after our return to Japan. But as we drove into the Triangle, we were blissfully unaware of why Thai troops manned roadblocks at every mountain pass, and why they looked at us like we were raging lunatics. We figured it was business as usual as they searched all our gear for guns, drugs, or some other clue as to why we were driving through the middle of nowhere. The troops were friendly enough, but as the day progressed we noticed bottles of Singha Beer and Mekhong Whisky strewn around the barricades, and the soldiers getting a little more pushy with their searches, waving their M-16s around a bit too recklessly.

To avoid the roadblocks, we followed smaller dirt roads into the hills. Low on gas (or at least we thought so, not having a working gauge) and lost in the mountains, we crisscrossed rocky paths looking for any sort of town for a fill-up. As we crested a hill, I spotted a village tucked into the forest. It consisted of about a dozen tidy but faded wood houses surrounding several larger two-storey structures that looked like stores. Children played in the hard-packed dirt of the central square, kicking around a *tákrâw* wicker ball, while elders sat in the shade on the porch of the main store, hiding from the late afternoon heat.

The villagers' heads rose and turned in unison as our jeep rumbled downhill towards town. By the time we had pulled into the square, every last man, woman and child had fled. They dove into doorways, ducked behind buildings, or flat out ran for the hills.

Ben and I sat in the idling jeep, smiles frozen on our faces, hands not even finished with our hello waves.

'What'd we do?' I asked Ben.

'Oh, we're idiots. They don't wave here, they do that *wâi* thing, you know, hands together in prayer, close to the chest, fingers near chin, like this.' Ben demonstrated, and sat in the driver's seat like a bearded Buddha with his *wâi* ready to welcome the villagers back to their own town.

'Or maybe we should turn off the stereo; they might not like Hendrix,' I added, clicking off the cassette deck along with the ignition.

We sat silently for ten minutes, but still no townspeople appeared. Ben's *wâi* drooped as the sun beat down on our open-topped jeep. Here we were, parked smack dab in the centre of a town in the middle of Thailand, and we couldn't have been further from connecting with the spirit of the country. We were just two goofs in a jeep who might as well have been in a Wal-Mart parking lot.

A door creaked open in the wooden building across the street from us. A pot-bellied middle-aged Thai man emerged. He straightened his wire-rim glasses, buttoned his collared shirt, frowning as he patted down the creases, adding a couple of taps to his stomach. He turned his face towards us, smiled and shouted, 'Friend!'

We smiled, gave him a *wâi*, and hopped down from the jeep, ready to bond.

'Hello,' said Ben. '*Sawat di krap*,' he added.

'Friend!' shouted the Thai man, still smiling. He extended his hand.

I reached to shake the hand, which he did with vigour. But he didn't let go. He put his other hand on my back, and not so subtly directed me back to the jeep.

'Friend! Peace!' he added, still shouting, as he gripped my hand with renewed intensity.

'He must be the mayor,' Ben guessed. 'Let's ask him where we can find some gas for the jeep.'

We tried to get some information out of our greeter, but couldn't get beyond 'friend' and 'peace', which certainly are two very good words, but weren't going to move the jeep very far. In the background, we noticed a few kids creeping out of the shadows to see what was happening at the Showdown in the Square.

Giving up on English, we pointed to Thai words in our phrasebook, but still couldn't get an answer from Mr Peace. We pointed to our jeep, the cap of the gas tank, and the road out of town. At this, our friend brightened.

'Nan! Nan!' He shouted out the name of the next large town to the east. We figured he probably wasn't offering us Indian flatbread.

'OK, thanks, yes, we know it's up the road a piece, but we need some gas, petrol, *nahm man baehn sin.*' I tried some Thai out of the phrasebook.

115.

He shouted 'Nan!' again, pointed to the east, then escorted us back into the jeep, gesturing to the road ahead.

'I believe we're being run out of town,' Ben said, as he was cordially shoved into the driver's seat. The mayor recoiled slightly as our stereo started along with the motor, but he never lost his smile at the prospect of the two hippies leaving town.

We drove east, meandering on unmarked roads for half an hour before seeing another army roadblock. It was the standard long tree branch, painted red, held across the road by a tattered rope. Sandbags lined a wooden guardhouse; slouching soldiers stood with guns loosely hanging from straps at their shoulders.

'Here we go again,' said Ben. 'Grab another pack of chewing gum for a gift, and see if they'll tell us where a gas station is.'

'Whoa, you think these guys are Special Forces? They're wearing blue uniforms instead of the usual green.' I scanned the soldiers as we slowed to a stop. They gave us the same astonished look that we had been seeing all day. And as usual, they began shouting at us. We smiled, shrugged our shoulders, and pointed at our ragged map to demonstrate we were lost.

'*Arrêtez! Pourquoi vous-venez ici?*' One soldier began yelling at us in French, moving in front of the gate, hand resting on his gun, which had the characteristic forward-angled banana-shaped ammunition clip of an AK-47.

'Wait a minute, what's this guy speaking French for?' I asked. 'Since when do Thai people speak French? And um, he's not carrying the same weapon…or wearing the same uniform…'

'Oh crap, welcome to Laos,' Ben muttered under his breath. In our search for the centre of things, we had driven clear off the edge of the map.

'*Aimez-vous gum?*' Ben smiled and offered a pack of Doublemint to the increasingly agitated Lao soldier. The soldier shouted in a mix of French, Lao and just plain Pissed Off, all the while pointing behind us. We were all too happy to turn around, retreating to the main road where we soon came upon a medium-sized Thai army base, complete with armoured cars and helicopter. Sent away from that camp, we stopped at a roadside stall where we bought two gallons of gas in plastic jugs. When queried for directions, the gas man just said 'Nan' and pointed north.

The light was fading as we bumped along the rutted dirt road, hoping it was the one that would finally lead us to Nan. We drove by miles of sugar cane fields before we reached a surprisingly modern village, with electric lights lining the streets, concrete houses with corrugated tin roofs, perfectly aligned gates in front and…

'Where the hell are all the people?' asked Ben, scanning the streets. 'There's not even a dog. Everyplace we've been has had dogs running around.'

'Weird,' I said. 'It's like *The Martian Chronicles*. You know, the Bradbury story where the Martians created a perfect little town in imitation of what they thought a home town should look like. The Martians gave the foreign visitors a false sense of security before they killed them all in their sleep.'

'Dude, that's not helpful at all.'

'Or wait,' I added, the quiet darkness fuelling my fear, 'this is like one of those Vietnam War resettlement towns – where US soldiers burnt down villages supporting guerrillas, and moved the people to a controlled area. This could be the resettled village of some opium-growing rebels who have run back to the hills to continue their fight. That'd be a more realistic explanation, right?'

As an answer, Ben quickly accelerated the jeep out of the brightly lit ghost town.

The narrowing dirt road led us through an expanse of planted fields. In the darkness we couldn't tell if the fields were planted with short sugar cane or tall opium crops.

'Outstanding,' Ben said. 'If we run into someone out here in the dark we're screwed. The drug traffickers are going to shoot us because they'll think we're government agents, the government agents are going to shoot us because they'll think we're drug runners. We better find that town fast.'

'Wait, I think I see light ahead.' I pointed to a glow coming from an area on the other side of a mountain a few miles to the north. 'That has to be Nan.'

'About time.' Ben gunned the motor, then braked the jeep to a skidding halt. I looked at him in confusion, but he just pointed ahead of us. A thirty-foot-long wooden bridge crossed a crevice with a river rushing through twenty-five feet below.

'You think this bridge is meant for cars?' I asked. 'It doesn't look like it can hold much more than a mule.' Long flat planks lay irregularly across raw logs stacked crosswise on the bridge supports. Crudely sawed boards created two tracks on either side of the bridge that *might* be meant for the wheels of a car. Or they might be meant for inbound and outbound mule traffic.

'We gotta get to Nan,' Ben said, and edged the jeep onto the first set of planks. One snapped. I stepped one foot out on the running board of the jeep.

'Where you going?' Ben asked.

'If this thing collapses beneath us, I don't want to go down with the jeep.'

Ben laughed, 'Come on, have some faith,' but he slid to the edge of his seat, steering with his left hand with his right foot ready to launch him away from the soon-to-be-imploding bridge.

We crept across a couple of feet at a time, wincing each time the bridge snapped, creaked, and moaned beneath us. It sounded like we were driving across a large, sick water buffalo. With ten feet to go, Ben gunned the jeep, and we flew across to the other side, leaving a chorus of breaking wood behind us. The bridge still stood, but we weren't sure for how much longer.

'Thank God, we made it!' Ben sped the jeep down the still-narrowing dirt road. The brush scraped the sides of the jeep, scratching what was left of our beautiful flaming decals. But the lights ahead became brighter as we approached the hill. Ben cheered as we reached the summit, practically singing, 'Hello Nan, goodbye Killing Fields, we can finally relax!'

We crested the ridge and sat speechless, the only sound the jeep's motor idling in the silent night air. From our vantage point, we could see the road descending into a wide valley fronted by a large forest. We had finally found the source of the light: the forest was on fire.

We had begun our journey with a quest to find cultural enlightenment by going to the middle of nowhere. Instead we found the end of the road: that exact spot where you can't go forward, can't go backward, and really don't want to stay where you are.

POSTCARD FROM THE EDGE

BY PICO IYER

THE WIND WAS whistling over the black volcanic rocks at the edge of the small lawn that ran down from our motel-like rooms. All the buildings of the island were clustered in small groups of such bungalows between which Polynesian women with hair down to their waists sashayed in the late afternoon sunlight. For most of the day nothing seemed to stir. Behind us were the monitory statues that stand across the island, luring people to the loneliest inhabited place on earth. But more powerful by far were just the signs of ordinary life on an island that seemed to have seceded from the world and staked its claim in a far-off corner of the imagination.

On Sunday, a man in a robe with *rongo-rongo* symbols written all over it presided over an unlikely mass, while altar girls walked among the fifty or so in attendance, collecting coins. The rest of the time, the island displayed all the features of a place where every other shop said 'Closed' and the ones that were 'Open' looked little different. When it was dark, three white crosses shone on the top of a lonely hill.

Easter Island is one of the most Nowhere – which means Nowhen, and even Nowhy – places you could visit even in your dreams. And on the eve of the new millennium – I had brought

my mother to see in a new century in this place that defiantly
held to the old – the sense of isolation was more resonant than
ever. Long, long roads on which I would walk for half an hour
or more, no sound but the wind whipping in my ear. A few visitors (mostly very elderly) sitting around the tiny pool in the
ranch-style house that was our 'hotel' for the new century. No
furnishings even in my room – no chairs or clothes hangers, no
minibar – and just to phone my mother in the next room involved placing a call through an operator who was never there.

We had come here in order to step out of a century we knew
too well, and to ground ourselves in what belonged to the
collective past, as it seemed: something totemic, ancestral, all
that we associate with Easter Island's iconic stone figures
(moai), which move across the island after dark, the locals
believe. We had never thought to recall that man cannot live by
sight alone.

To put it simply, my mother had to eat. And a Nowhere place
where almost no-one comes is ample mostly in the supply of
nothing. A single menu in our little dining room (which looked
out on the emptiness, a silence you could feel and taste
whenever you gazed out of the window) covered breakfast,
dinner and lunch. It began with that South Seas specialty Spam
and travelled (so it seemed) to Spam again.

On every table in the echoing room sat a jar of Nescafe,
which came to seem as forbidding to us as the stone statues
dotted enigmatically across the grassy hills. Next to it, a bowl
of Sweet 'n' Lo. Part of the fraught joy of going to any Nowhere
place is that you soon realise that the sights are less important
than what you can't see (or, in this case, what you can, but never
expected to see). The traveller seeks to slip into the cracks
between meanings and fixities and there he finds – on Easter
Island at least – nothing, in great abundance.

Occasionally, rumours of a restaurant would reach us from
the more fearless visitors who had come to the place in the

121.

spirit of looking in on one's grandparents at Christmas. The fish there was…well, edible, came the not entirely persuasive recommendation. My mother, however, born in India and of good Hindu stock, does not eat meat or fish or poultry. We'd come to Nowhere to get away from it all and now we were beginning to crave it all again.

My days went very strangely on Easter Island, as if I had attained a dream-space in which I walked through parallel passageways in my head. To get to town meant wandering along those empty roads, quite car-less, or waiting for a bus scheduled to arrive six months from now. To call a colleague in New York meant finding a public phone booth, as in the old *Dr Who* television series (or the haunting travel-movie *Local Hero*), and listening to a man in the fury of midtown Manhattan talking of deadlines while phones jangled in the background. The one Internet parlour I found was a three-seat travel agency run by a small elderly Swiss man with tufts of hair behind his ears, who'd pinned a tiny snapshot of a beautiful island girl and child on the wall, silent explanation of how his three weeks here had become seven years.

My mother, soon, was looking like an elegant excerpt of herself. Canned peas for lunch gave way to canned corn for dinner. Canned corn for lunch gave way to canned peas for dinner. When I reminded her that resources were so scarce on the island that in the nineteenth century people had been reduced to eating one another and the population had dwindled to barely more than one hundred, she looked not fortified at all.

A Nowhere place offers one more ironies and curiosities than any of the places that are cluttered with associations and activities. As the mind is brought to a point in a bare Japanese room decorated only with a flower, so in a place like Easter Island, it fastens upon every detail. A Nowhere place can become like a monastery, in which the silence rings outside you and the absence of external distraction opens up expanses within. The days stretched out like the water on which I looked, leaving one nothing to do but wander (in one's head, across the grass). I handed over a credit card to pay for a $6 purchase in the museum and, when the transaction was over (forty-five minutes later), the woman at the cash register came round to hug me, thrilled at having completed the first such exchange in her not-young life. I sat on my chair on the lawn overlooking the black volcanic rocks, the blue stretching out towards sheer emptiness, and imagined what it might be like to come here as a priest, hoping to convert the locals, and find oneself turned around instead, won over to a different way.

The three crosses shone in the night. Samuel Butler's curious utopia in *Erewohn* (I thought) was just a 'Nowhere' rearranged.

My mother, however, was now looking something like the supermodel Kate Moss, and urging me to take on the aspect of Moss' swain, Johnny Depp, when he rampaged through the Mark Hotel in New York. We were growing increasingly rich in peculiarities and discoveries – a luxury in Easter Island was a piece of wood – but in more discernible ways we were shrinking fast.

At last my explorations disclosed a hopeful possibility: a blue-painted building with Tibetan flags outside it and stirring quotations from Pablo Neruda scrawled across its windows. Two hippies from Chile had decided they would go Nowhere, slowly, and now had come up with a menu that offered won ton curiosities and 'non-instant coffee'. We joined the long line of anti-Nescafe revolutionaries and saw just how noninstant coffee can be.

Time began to slip away, and space, and reality itself, as my mother poked into a plate of plain white rice while a man in a tribal topknot at the next table told some television crews from Chile that Easter Island was losing its hold on eternity.

It became easy, in the silent, largely unpeopled days that followed, to wonder whether Everyman was really meant to come to Nowhere (it seemed a better place for no-one – and no food – and the Everymans around me began to long for Everywhere: the very McDonald's fries and Starbucks cacophonies of possibility that we had come all this way to flee). The generic global city that we had put behind us now shone in the memory as a place where my mother had managed to find tacos, spaghetti, even decaf coffee, everywhere I'd taken her (Angkor, Luxor, Kyoto). 'Going nowhere' began to seem a way of embracing absence and becoming nothing.

The millennium arrived, at last, and a spray of fireworks went up into the heavens as the 3000 islanders gathered on a grassy mount overlooking the sea. The television cameras from Chile wove Hanga Roa (as the village is called) into the global pageant, turning a new page in the collective calendar and embarking on a new century. The next day, when I awoke, there was still no place of higher education on the island, and the hill where I went to look out over the ocean was as empty as the horizons that I overlooked.

We got onto an Air New Zealand plane – almost able to fit into the same seat now – and flew to Papeete, the famously overweight, spoiled Tahitian port of shopping malls and restless kids and all that Denny's has to offer. Austin Powers was at the local cinema; a man was playing 'My Way' in a Chinese restaurant; roaming bands of teenagers dreamed and spoke of Everywhere. The virtue of going Nowhere, I began to feel, is that it made Everywhere – and everything – seem irresistible.

INTO THE DARKNESS
BY CHRIS COLIN

126.

I WAS PEERING out the grimy couchette window at the moonless German forest when I thought of a hole. The hole belonged to a story told by my great-grandmother, an honest woman who died recently at nearly a hundred. She'd written down much about her childhood on Western ranchland, and this particular story had stayed with me since my own. It was not a sweet great-grandmother story but a terrifying nightmare of an account:

A hole had been discovered out there on the stark, red earth of Colorado; a crowd gathered when a local man agreed to be lowered. This was murky territory, where hopeful new towns built schools and markets, but also where Indians had slaughtered and been slaughtered. At first they lowered him slowly, I imagine, then a little faster as they realised just how deep a thing they were dealing with. Down he went. It's the darkness that I imagined as a boy, levels unknown to me but somehow known, too, deep in my heart. Further and further he went until finally there was too much quiet for anyone to feel good about. The others looked at each other and reeled him in. The man who finally surfaced was not the one who'd descended. Ghosts? Dead bodies? His own unravelling? Here

the account was deliciously unsatisfying: what happened in
that hole would remain a mystery because the man never spoke
another word for the rest of his life. He'd lost himself.

A grown man myself now, I still dread and long for such a
fate in embarrassingly equal proportions. One feels similarly
divided on the Golden Gate Bridge, on the deck of a ship: Oh
please don't let me sail over the edge…But I wonder what it's
like to sail over the edge? I'd bet an Indian penny Columbus
half-believed the earth was flat and that an awful plunge lay
ahead. Who isn't drawn to uncertain places? For every
lighthouse we build, its inverse hovers in the periphery – a
pinprick of darkness beckoning us from the dull safety of a
clear, sunny day.

But I wasn't beckoned, not really. Instead I built a life of
lightness. Via busyness and easy California fun, my wife and I
strayed far from that hole; the Colorado story became a funny
old anecdote. So six months ago Amy and I looked at each other
and decided to let out the line.

We were flip at first. We staggered around Amsterdam's
Schiphol airport, exotically bright, tickets in our fists. We had
seven months ahead, multiple cities, a gradual descent into the
small Balkan city of our disrupted new lives and so, we
thought, a descent into darkness itself. We'd quit jobs, rented
out the house, even purchased coats – technological things,
feats of fabric mastery – to better facilitate the descent. We
laughed in different accents, moved the savings into checking.
'Are we being too cavalier?' I'd asked a good friend the drizzly
afternoon we moved our belongings into long-term storage. We
were leaving him and others and all family behind. But my
question rang hollow and my friend and I both knew it. I was
already gone.

We miscalculated the exchange rate that first day, lived
briefly as kings: a beer at lunch, the finer species of postcard.
We walked and rented bikes and listened to conversations in

the rain. When the wind came up the Prinsengracht I felt
pleasingly fortified in my new coat, as the castle guards must
have when the mongrels were coming and the hot oil had been
readied. The homes were wonderfully squished and the cars,
too, more like a drawing of a car; cosily they puttered past on
the little brick roads. Life in Amsterdam seemed as cheerful
and clear as a Richard Scarry picture book – this man's
climbing a ladder for the phone company, that one's delivering
bread!

And so we moved along. Cheerful and clear are fine but not
for getting lost. We wanted uncertainty, risk, confusion of the
self. To the vast Central Station in the heart of town we dragged
our suitcases and boarded the twelve-hour night train to
Prague via Frankfurt.

This is where I found myself in the dirty couchette, staring
out at moonless woods and the occasional creepy village
nestled therein. Werewolves live there. Lonely patches of dirty
blue snow live there. The trees thicken impossibly, darken
impossibly. We told each other ghost stories. They were the
cheesy kind, leaning too heavily on bad spooky voices, but we
shuddered dutifully. On a slow curve I fixed my eye on a
lonesome cottage far into the trees and shadows. Were the train
to stop and an official-looking person to order us off – there in
the pitch-black, no choice but to rap on a yellowed window –
the heart would crack apart from fright and solitude. This is
nowhere, I thought.

But I was kidding myself. Depressingly the fantasy fell away
and I conceded this wasn't nowhere – it was Germany. Sure, the
terrain was peculiar and the trees a different variety, but the
strange souls who inhabit these fairy-tale spots, well, they still
get the zipper stuck on their coats, still shake their heads at the
to-do list on the fridge. In this I, myself, was still recognisable,
was not lost. The train shuddered through more woods but I
put my head down. At 3.30, when the border police rapped

urgently on the door of our couchette, danger vaguely
suggested itself again. Grimly they searched my backpack –
perhaps they'd find that half-smoked joint from Amsterdam? –
but it was a superficial search. They smiled and stamped our
passports and moved on to the next door with a stern nod.

Four days in Prague, four in Vienna. At the giant Disney
castles and the Ringstrasse of Habsburg extravagances, we
futzed with the camera; meanwhile I squinted around for the
eerie sublime, for passage to the unknown and terrifying. I
found souvenir crystal shops. I also found deeper things – at
the architecturally miraculous Hundertwasserhaus I recalled
that the sublime lurks in joy as well as in mysterious holes –
but mainly I put my eggs in the dark Balkan basket looming
ahead.

Down we went. Some dirty patches of snow, pale sky like a
dishrag and at last our train crossed the Slovenian border.
Studies in loneliness dotted the countryside: a windswept bus
stop on a deserted highway, an old woman shuffling along a
gravel path, a single sooty European bulldozer moving bleakly
over some carcinogen mound. Meanwhile streams and rivers
meandered in unholy sour-apple green.

We squealed into Ljubljana. Our friend met us and we drove
to his concrete, Socialist-era apartment; we'd stay there until
we could rent one of our own. '*Dober dan,*' we said to Slovenes
we saw. It was a promisingly dark greeting.

o o o o o o o o o

'It is a quiet building,' the agent told us in broken English, five
days after our arrival. 'Many ladies.'

With that we accepted the key to our Slovenian apartment,
an unexpectedly modern and luxurious building: how did this
country find out about recessed lighting, we thought, and
what's with all the settings on the oven?

I quickly realised I'd been wrong about everything. I knew better but still I'd expected a bombed-out capital, a crater. Instead Ljubljana was tidy and lovely, untouched by the madness that engulfed neighbouring countries just fifteen years ago. Along the narrow river dividing the small city, locals sipped coffee and discussed philosophy. Or at least I imagined they were discussing philosophy. They'd grin and reach in the air for ideas, buy second rounds of grog. All around, sparkly lights pulled warm yellows and oranges from the old buildings. Sure, Ljubljana's castle floated ominously on the hill over town. But it was a pleasant kind of ominous, and I heard the café at the top had good coffee. In the Balkans, Bram Stoker wrote in *Dracula*, 'every known superstition in the world is gathered.' But he hadn't been to Slovenia.

And so we began a life. If I was disappointed at all the swellness – it was swellness I'd wanted a break from, back in cushy California – I chided myself for my foolishness. Anyway, there were linens to buy, spatulas to buy… Our first night in the apartment we spread a makeshift tablecloth and cooked lentils.

I didn't see it coming. Nobody sees things coming when they're chewing lentils. But it hit me harder than any haunted German forest, any imagined Balkan pandemonium. I put my spoon down.

Where am I?

The weight of our gallivanting came to me. In an impulsive moment we'd cut friends, family, television, Internet, magazine subscriptions and every other diversion from our lives; all that remained were the bones. For all my interest in finding a heart of darkness on the road, I've never been good at confronting my own. In practice I prefer to glimpse the inner realm in short, sideways glances, if at all. The embarrassing truth descended on me, there at the table: I'm a flitter, a reader of the backs of cereal boxes, a phoner of pals. It didn't matter that this was happening in Slovenia, we could just as easily have picked St Louis – I was briefly, invisibly, lost.

I considered writing a postcard, beating a path back to familiar ground. But I had not come here to retreat, I told myself. I stared, and I think Amy did, too. The evening stretched before us like a desert; there is panic as well as opportunity in the unbroken, unbusy expanse of time. All that remained for us were the bones, yes, and the sight of them opened a dark, bottomless pit in the middle of that desert.

This is the essence of travel, or at least travel taken to completion: it's not the change of scenery, or the new way of preparing lamb – it's *you*. You are lost to yourself, you don't know who will emerge from the pit.

After some time I cleared our bowls. A partner knows uncertainty when she sees it, but Amy said nothing. We washed the dishes and dried them, noting minor differences in Slovenian soap. The lentil bag received a knot and returned to the cupboard. We gave the kitchen a final inspection and went to the living room, where we parked ourselves on the stark white couch. We'd bought a crossword puzzle book at the airport, and it beckoned us from the floor. But we didn't open it, not this night. Instead the time somehow passed, and later we were in bed, a place both reliable and foreign when on the road, and I assume we fell asleep because we awoke the next day and it was bright.

180°

160°

140°

120°

180°W

100°

80°

60°

40°

THE WORST COUNTRY
IN THE WORLD

BY SIMON WINCHESTER

IT WAS AS I was lying in a hospital bed in Oxford in one of those high-tech emergency isolation wards – all the nurses in spacesuits, all visitors banned, air pumps keeping my room at artificially low pressure so that none of my germs would flow out and infect passing strangers – that I first began to wish that I truly had been nowhere. The doctors were feeding me quinine, intravenously, and the odd thing about quinine is that in large doses it makes your ears ring with a high-pitched whine, just like the sound of an approaching mosquito – which is, I guess, where the trouble started in the first place…

Technically it had all begun three months before, in a pub called the Blue Lion on Gray's Inn Road in London. There we all were: David Blundy, Jon Swain, Cal McCrystal, Stephen Fay, others I can't remember, and maybe not even these four. All I really recall is that I was the very junior man among them – a crew of some of the best-known foreign correspondents of their generation. In our time we had all been just about everywhere, covering wars and insurrections and famines and goodness knows what from Aden to Zanzibar. We all kept carry-on bags packed beside the bed, ready for the call from the foreign editor to get moving, oftentimes not knowing exactly where to until the taxi arrived at Heathrow. We were very rarely all in London at the same time; but on this wet February day it happened that we were: the world must briefly have paused to catch its breath. So there we gathered, having a beer together, and reminiscing, sort of, about where we had been, about girls (no doubt), about expenses (as in: their role in the making of fiction) and about what we had lately done in the practice of the petty crime we knew as Committing Journalism.

And then slowly the conversation became a little more structured and turned to something rather interesting: which place each of us thought might be justly given the title of the Worst Country in the World.

I think it began when someone remarked how perfectly bloody it was being stuck for weeks in Iraq – then, as now, a fairly grim kind of country. Someone else then chimed in to say that if you thought Baghdad was bad, just wait till you see Kolkata. Or maybe it was Luanda. Or Sudbury, Ontario. I forget. And then it turned to countries to avoid, countries that were Really Nasty – and under the influence of more rounds of beer, the ways in which they were so horrid began to evolve until we were talking animatedly about real, sensible criteria.

Before long we were agreeing that to enter the lists, to have some standing as contender for Worst Country in the World, the places we chose had to have a) no scenery, b) awful food, c) dreadful people, d) a terrible regime, e) a wrecked economy, f) uncontrolled hordes of hostile and pestilential local fauna, and, g) in all other senses no redeeming features whatsoever. One by one we listed countries and ticked off the criteria – and in all cases found that there was indeed a redeeming feature that excluded each from the running.

So – Iraq. Dreadful food, foul regime, an unredeemably grisly climate mostly involving flying sand, and horrible locals (yes, yes, I can hear the Stereotype Police reaching for their citation pads, but what I mean is the people we journalists encountered were not very pleasant – I'm sure most Iraqis of the time were the kind of folks you meet in *Little House on the Prairie*). But then, to counter all of this, there was Babylon. And Ur. And the relics of Nebuchadnezzar. And the country was *Mesopotamia*, for heaven's sake. So no, on sober consideration it proved neither possible nor desirable to list Iraq among the Nasties. Let's try again – let's try Cambodia.

And that – at the time the Democratic Republic of Kampuchea, with that most unamusing desperado Mr Pot running the show – was duly considered next. Foul, we all agreed – except for Angkor Wat and, of course (since one of our number was married to one), the Cambodian people, who were universally loved (save those from the Khmer Rouge). So Cambodia was out. As were, in turn, East Germany, Honduras, Albania, North Korea, Libya. We had all been to these places, and of each we had fondish memories – perhaps of that blonde barmaid in Rostock or the sunsets in Tegucigalpa or the funfair of sheer idiocies to be found on the streets of Tirana – that managed to cancel out the notion that any of these places could really be adjudged supremely dreadful.

We could find nowhere that fit the bill – until we began seriously to consider tropical Africa. And more specifically, West Africa. And here were indeed plenty of unsavoury places. Mali, for instance, was the one country on the planet that still officially practised slavery. The Central African Republic's then leader was a crazily self-styled emperor who sat on a throne made of gold eagles wings. In Liberia they were busily shooting people tied to telephone poles on the beach. And up in the north of Nigeria local priests still ordered the stoning-to-death of adulterers, especially if they were women. But once again, in each of these places there were saving graces – whether Ashanti gold, or the Atlantic sunsets, or the astonishing beauty of the local birds – that provided to all of us who had been there good reasons for rather liking each of these otherwise hellish spots, however perverse such a liking must have seemed.

But then – it was late afternoon by now, and our pub had officially closed, but the bartender seemed as fascinated as we were by the direction of the conversation – we finally narrowed our search down to one country to which none of us had been but which had the strangest and darkest of reputations.

It was a former Spanish colony tucked into the fetid armpit of the continent between Gabon and Cameroon, and named Equatorial Guinea. Ah yes, we all agreed: of this eccentric and unknown place we had heard much – and what we had heard made it sound wonderfully, magnificently and memorably abominable.

For a start, it had two dominant tribes – one called the Fang, the other the Bubi, and so far as we could make out the Fang hated the Bubi and the Bubi hated the Fang. (You couldn't make this stuff up, chimed in someone.) Then it had a post-independence leader who had specialised in 'terror and economic chaos', and who was said, among other things, to be a cannibal. When not eating schoolchildren he liked to ban things, on a whim: he had proscribed the wearing of spectacles and the ownership (except by his friends) of all wheeled vehicles; he tried to ban money; he closed down all religious institutions – all the convents that the Spaniards had left behind, for instance; and he closed down the American embassy by accusing its staff of practising voodoo.

So terrified was this leader of another coup d'état like the one that had first brought him to power that he refused to have any Guineans around to guard him. He hired giant Algerian mercenaries instead, but since they spoke French and he spoke only pidgin-Spanish and a tongue called Biokan, there was perpetual uncertainty about the orders these troops were given. The only other foreigners who lived in the country were Albanians, Chinese and North Koreans, and reportedly one

German former concentration-camp guard who had tried to run a bed-and-breakfast inn, but for some reason had no customers.

All told, Equatorial Guinea sounded just the ticket. Not a saving grace in sight. No-one had a kind word to say about the place. It appeared to be, in short, a total, unreconstructed, utter and complete dump. Yes, we said, this was our undoubted winner. We cleared the table, asked for the bill, rose unsteadily to our respective feet and, blinking, made for the door, the street and the fast-fading winter daylight. Conversation over.

But then a hand was placed on my shoulder. 'Not so fast,' said a familiar voice. 'I'd like you to go there.'

It was the editor of the *Sunday Times* magazine. He had been sitting quietly at a nearby table, listening to it all. And he decided, quite properly, that it would be a magical story. The Worst Country in the World. A First-Hand Eye-Witness Report. 'Stay right where you are,' he said. 'I'm telephoning your photographer.' He went over to the pub's payphone.

I knew who he would be calling: Don McCullin, a man whose nitrate chronicles of the dreadful had made him one of the most sought-after photographers of the day. He would be sure to want to come along. He had made his name in dysfunctional and photogenic places like Biafra, Bengal, Lebanon, Northern Ireland – wherever people were suffering in picturesque squalor, Don liked to be. And sure enough, the editor returned from the call box, smiling. 'Don will come,' he announced. 'He'll meet you in Paris tomorrow morning.'

And that's how it all got under way. Don and I met in Paris, we managed to acquire our visas from an Equatorial Guinean embassy, which seemed more than a little surprised by our claim to be tourists – but was happy to take the $100 fee for issuing two sixty-day entry permits for clubbing and sunbathing – and we flew to Madrid for the once-weekly flight to the Guinean capital city, which all schoolboy swots know, of course, to be the great conurbation of Malabo, on the tropical island then known as Fernando Po. We arrived there three days later, our aircraft sliding off the runway into a field of liquid mud. We walked into town – no taxis, of course – through a furious storm of hot rain, and we eventually bedded down in a warehouse, sleeping for the next four weeks on bags of rotting beans.

Equatorial Guinea, we discovered, was as close to being nowhere as any place could be. Nothing good ever happened there – and indeed, there really was no *there* there. Malabo was a shanty town, without palaces or offices or hotels (hence our need to sleep in the warehouse). There was a scattering of markets, and a restaurant that served us an unremitting diet of bananas and stewed rats – except for one golden day when we were given a plate of a darker and marginally more succulent meat that, after we had eaten it, was said to have been cat. The streets were lonely places, populated only by slack-jawed youths and suspicious-looking thugs and a scattering of very large Algerian soldiers, and with the occasional lugubrious East German spy to add a bit of social sparkle to the scene. And at night all was quiet, except for the intermittent rattle of gunfire and the hooting of vultures out in the abandoned cacao plantations.

It was the nights that were the most unnerving. The warehouse was barely locked, and most nights strangers would break in and loot some of the bags piled up on the rafters. The roof was broken, and we had a glimpse of a night sky that seemed perpetually alive with vampire bats. But most scary of all was the whining of the mosquitoes: every night they were there, hovering right by our ears, keeping us awake, driving us half mad, and no doubt biting us and offloading some pestilence borne up from the swamps and fetid lagoons with which Malabo was so liberally supplied. After a week or so we became inured to their Zero-fighter whines; but our arms and

137.

necks were covered with evidence of their bites, and the heat didn't help the itching one bit.

The adventures we had during our six weeks in the Republic were legion, and bizarre, and journalistically splendid. But they belong in another essay, not here – in perhaps a future Lonely Planet anthology with a title like *Dispatches from Planet Incredible*. The country was like a continuous series of episodes of *The Far Side*, where nothing was as it appeared, where no-one was to be trusted, where everything was wrecked. Tom Waits would have been quite at home: 'I'm tired of all these soldiers here, / No-one speaks English and everything's broken…'

But eventually we got home. They dug our plane out of the liquid mud, and we flew back up north to Madrid and to London. Don developed his pictures, which were as macabre and brilliant as we had hoped, and I wrote my piece, and it was duly published and there was the kind of praise which made everyone pleased, and those who were in the pub that afternoon all those weeks before looked ruefully at me years later when next we all turned up, and wondered what we should talk about, and whether it might make the papers too.

And newspaper life wore on. I went off to America to write a profile of Nancy Reagan, then to Ireland to profile an IRA man, then flew away east to spend a week in Afghanistan. Six weeks of such work went by before the foreign editor relented and sent me back to my family in Oxford for a weekend, even though I knew I would be wondering idly most of the time where I might be going the week after.

It was Saturday night, just as I was settling down to dinner, that what turned out to be a virulent bacillus named *Plasmodium falciparum* first began to make its presence in my bloodstream rather dramatically known to me.

I suddenly felt terribly cold, I began shivering, and every muscle in my body became swiftly locked in a rictus of pain.

My head began to pound and once I was in bed a thermometer showed the mercury rising past 103, 104, 105 and into what Jon Krakauer, if he were writing this story, would tell us was the Death Zone. Whatever it was, it was very uncomfortable, and family members called doctors and ambulances and before long – before midnight on that same night, in fact – I was in the isolation ward and tubes were attached and neat quinine by the pint was being pumped into me and my head was whining, whining and I fancied I could see the vampire bats whirling and hear the vultures hooting as they circled and waited over the ruined cacao plantations...

But of course, it all got better. The pain eased, the mercury inched down, the head cleared and they took out their tubes and the whining stopped. And then a rather worried-looking doctor in a mask and a white coat approached me, with a form.

Duty, he explained, compelled him to inquire, formally, how I thought I had managed to catch a disease so rare in Britain that its appearance had to be reported to the government. It was falciparum malaria, and it was dangerous, often fatal. 'You were lucky,' he grinned. 'So – what do you do? And where have you been?'

I racked my still-addled brain. 'Oh, you know,' I said, 'Washington, Belfast, Afghanistan. The usual places for a foreign reporter. *Nowhere in particular. No, haven't really been anywhere.*'

He looked disbelieving, a little cross. 'Come now,' he said. 'That can't be quite true. Because there's been another case reported. Not just yours. It's a case in London – exactly the same time as yours, in fact: Saturday night. A chap called' – and he consulted his notes – 'a Mr McCullin. Yes. Mr Don McCullin.

'And he tells us he's been in a place called, let me see – Equatorial Guinea. Not a place I've ever heard of, I must admit. But tell me – does it ring a bell? Pretty nasty place, he said. Worst place in the world. Do you want to tell me about it?'

ON THE TRAIL

BY KARL TARO GREENFELD

WHEN I WAS working in China, it seemed that everyone I needed to see was not where he was supposed to be. He was away, at the county seat, or at the provincial capital, or visiting relatives in a distant region. Or I couldn't find out where he was, exactly, but he certainly was not here, in this office or bureau or work unit I had travelled a thousand miles to reach. 'Here' was always past the edge of a town where stores sold nothing but tractors, motorcycles and spare parts for trucks – gleaming new manifolds, greasy axles and engine blocks, laid out in the swept dirt before a darkened showroom, beneath a red banner advertising Donfeng and First Automotive Works. Then I passed factories that seemed abandoned. And then sub-divided collective farms cultivating crops I didn't recognise. And then a winding dirt road until, finally, I arrived.

And despite all my previous disappointments, the regularity with which I had failed to meet with any of those officials or politicians or civil servants I had set out to interview, my hopes would rise as I drove through the gate, past the indifferently manned guard house, to the parking lot in front of the ministry or bureau or people's hall. I remained optimistic as I climbed the three concrete steps to the unlit, dusty lobby and then

waited a few moments at the reception desk. I stayed
enthusiastic while the middle-aged man with the huge mug of
tea, muddy with what looked like chewed tobacco, mulled my
request and then shook his head because he didn't know if the
official or civil servant or administrator or deputy director or
under assistant or section leader or work-group subchief was
in today. He would tell me where the office was – inevitably it
would be on the fifth floor, and there was never an elevator. And
I climbed, fulsome with aspiration, and I reached the door,
stained wood with perhaps a few simple documents tacked to it
outlining recent regulations and new ordinances and changes
in the schedule and the announcement of a clean-up-the-city
campaign and an end-littering drive, and then I knocked on the
door. And I waited.

141.

And he was not there.

And nobody knew when he would come back.

And no, under no circumstances, would they give me his
mobile number.

Writing my book about the deadly new virus that would
later be called SARS – tracking down through government
officials the first patients afflicted by this mysterious disease –
meant a hundred of those trips, long voyages of hope that
ended by crashing into closed office doors.

And then we would retire, my assistant and I, to a local
restaurant, where we would order the local hotpot delicacy,
some freshwater fish cooked with chillies, some rabbit stewed
with scallions, some chicken knuckles mixed with hot peppers,
and try to figure out how many *li* away was the county seat, the
provincial headquarters, the big city offices. (A *li* is, technically,
the distance a fully burdened imperial porter could travel in 24
hours; I don't know that anyone actually uses *li* as a measure of
distance anymore, but I've always liked the sound of it and it
works very well to express my exasperation at the great
Chinese distances I always had to travel.) The food was always

pleasantly surprising. The distances daunting. Six more hours in the back of a smoky hired car with the driver's cassette of that German song that goes 'Da da da' on auto reverse. Could he change it?

Yes, he said, but then I will fall asleep.

And so we let him play 'Da da da' all six hours, until we were at the county seat or provincial capital and then I would find out that the official, the deputy director, the workers collective boss, he was gone. And then another night in a local, even smokier hotel where I couldn't pick up a cell phone network and the Internet connection was a slow-speed dial-up that wouldn't let me read any sites that weren't in Chinese.

o o o o o o o o

Is there a word for hopes that persist though we know they are certain to be dashed? It is with such totally unjustified optimism that we drive today to the village, at the end of a two-lane macadam road, past the shops selling spare truck parts and the women who have laid out a crop of some sort of red beans by the side of the road to dry in the few hours of late autumn sun. We climb the concrete steps and query the informationless receptionist, and then ascend two more flights to the office of the deputy director of the local branch of a government agency dedicated, at least nominally, to fighting infectious disease.

We knock once and then walk into a narrow, sunny office with two tall windows facing south. On his desk is the tea mug, thick with its composting vegetative matter, an ashtray, a pack of Panda cigarettes and a plastic lamp with a calculator and paper calendar built into its base. And he is here! The sight of him, smoking his cigarettes, sipping his tea, poring over a medical-supply magazine, is as reassuring to me as finding a cheque in the mail from a magazine that has published a story of mine – unlikely yet still, despite everything, expected.

He is a squat man, with a short neck and a boxy, fleshy head so that if you had to render him very quickly you might start with a rectangle as his abdomen and then a smaller rectangle as the head, topped with a few quick pen strokes representing shocks of black hair combed at a forty-five degree angle down and to his right. He appears well fed and has a sleepy air that could also, in a pinch, serve as a buffer to keep unwanted visitors from overstaying.

We bow. I explain myself and my project in terms that will in no way be perceived as politically controversial. This is dry, academic stuff, he should understand, of interest only to scientists, doctors, public health officials – very unlikely, in other words, to ever catch the attention of government officials in Beijing. Yet I need to appeal to him, to his vanity, to any lingering pretensions to serving the commonweal that have survived his decades in the Chinese civil service. His cooperating with me should be understood as a totally risk-free salve for whatever might still be troubling his conscience.

He listens in his somnambulant manner, once even closing his eyes for a few seconds, and then he rouses himself and offers me a cigarette. I have a fondness for Panda cigarettes – Deng Xiaoping's brand. They were traditionally available only to high Chinese officials and a tin of them openly displayed on a bureaucrat's desk used to be an unsubtle display of connectedness – *guanxi*. The cigarettes can today be purchased in some duty-free shops and from the myriad tobacconists and cognac vendors lining the corridors connecting Hong Kong and Shenzhen in the south.

Those Pandas sold in the south, however, have a stale quality absent from the cigarettes I smoke in the presence of those officials I have met. Also, those Pandas sold on the market come in flat aqua tins while the officials always have big, round, red cans. The cigarettes from these cans, somehow, taste like illicit privilege; you know anyone smoking these cigarettes is someone or knows someone.

And now, sitting in this distant office, I know someone.

He opens his flip phone and reads out a mobile phone number.

'Is this the patient?'

'No,' he shakes his head, 'this is the neighbour of the patient. Or the patient's parents, anyway. They live in a godforsaken place, a trash heap practically. It has a name like Wasteville – no, that's not it. Waste Land? Garbage Town? Trash Village?'

It sounds like that. The man I am looking for, he has no phone. Nor do his parents. It isn't even a village, where they live. Just a collection of shacks, lean-tos. These people are not even native to this place which doesn't have a proper name, only a few words denoting that it was built around things other people don't want.

'This is the person you need to talk to,' the official explains. 'I have the number of the man who owns the land where all these people make their shelters. They are dirty people. Filthy.'

'Is he there? The patient?'

The official nods in a way that means maybe, maybe not.

And I know that means another ten hours sitting in a car, driving through the Chinese night, looking for a place and a person who I hope will be there, but who I am sure will not.

o o o o o o o o

I changed assistants a month or so ago. My first was a rough woman named Hu who dressed like a boy and seemed indifferent to whether we succeeded in any of our intended visits. She walked with a rolling gait, like a cowboy, and she never carried a pen or notebook into any of our non-appointments. This shouldn't have bothered me. These were, after all, nonappointments. No-one was ever there so there were no interviews so why should she have bothered to bring a pen or paper. But I felt it jinxed us, somehow, to not even maintain the pretence that our official, our deputy director, our little mandarin, might actually be here.

My luck was rotten, I concluded, so I needed to change it. And I hired this lovely little Sichuanese woman, Zhu, with pointy shoes, a narrow waist, wavy hair and big, round, brown eyes. And she was still excited enough about the idea of journalism, of working on a story, a book even, that she always carried a little dossier inside of which was a pen, a fake leather notebook and even a few extra pens.

And here she sits, leaning forward in her chair, her little notebook open before her, those big eyes beaming at this Panda-smoking official. His phone is flipped open, and Zhu asks in her sweet little voice, does he have any other phone numbers that might be helpful, other doctors, government officials, hospital directors, epidemiologists? He takes a drag on his cigarette, looks us both over, lingering for a while on Zhu's exposed calves, and then begins to read off the phone numbers he has saved in his mobile, his web of contacts and secret phone numbers.

We scribble furiously, at least two dozen phone numbers, names and titles, many of them names we have read in newspapers and World Health Organization reports. I don't know that Zhu understands what we are being given; part of her charm is that she takes for granted her access and ability to win confidence. I also try to take it in stride but I am overjoyed and can't help but feel that finally, all those journeys of 10,000 *li* have not been wasted.

We start with the very first number he has given us, the phone of the man who knows the man I want to see – the first patient, possibly the index case, the embodiment of emergence, at which the incident that I am writing about begins.

Another long drive, this one with a taxi driver who does, at one point, fall asleep for a few seconds before alert Zhu nudges him awake from her seat beside him in the front. Every hundred kilometres or so, there are huge pyramid-shaped gas stations at the side of the road, little pennants drooping from nylon cords attached to the broad eaves. Sometimes, as in the West, convenience stores are attached, with their antifreeze and cans of motor oil and packs of cigarettes and cans of Pringles. (Pringles are everywhere in China. I don't know how or why, but there they are, on sale in myriad flavours next to baskets of live grub beetles and strands of dried roots and bound coils of copper wiring.) Finally, we pull into a parking lot, rent rooms at a hotel, and I crawl into a wood-framed mattress that smells of nicotine, in a cold room with a concrete floor that has an open drain in one corner. All night, I imagine that I am hearing insects crawl from the drain into my room. In the morning, when I wake up, there is a centipede halfway out of the drain, its antennae whirling in the frigid air. Before it can finish its reconnaissance, I bring the heel of my loafer down, making a wet crunching sound much like smashing a grape.

At breakfast, the driver sits at a separate table and slurps down a bowl of rice porridge between cigarettes as I drink green tea and eat Pringles from a can.

We drive another four hours and arrive, finally, at the bottom of a foothill covered with pale trees that look, from a distance, like stunted spruce trees. At first glance, this little mountain looks pleasingly sylvan, the high ground beside a slow-moving channel of greenish water. There are numerous trails of smoke rising from what I imagine are cooking fires, the hearths of the encampments of the hardy woodsmen living in this alpine hamlet. We call the number given by the official, and the information we receive is the usual vague information cloaked in what we take to be the standard suspicious misdirection. The man may be here, members of his family certainly are, somewhere. We may find them. We may not.

Now we have to find the man who knows the man. But he, alas, is now away. At a meeting. In another town. Many *li* away.

o o o o o o o o o

We do learn where we might find the first patient or at least his family. They are up the hill. Zhu and I start climbing a muddy, switchback trail, and very quickly I realise how mistaken I was about the bucolic nature of this little mountain. First of all, these trees aren't stunted but have been systematically denuded of any material that might serve as fuel. What I had taken to be a ground cover of foliage is actually a form of refuse I have never encountered, the discarded, broken-up plastic shells of old computers, televisions, fax machines, high-tech waste of familiar brand names, slightly burned, muddied and trod into the ground. I have never seen this sort of trash extruded and dumped in this manner, as if birds had defecated vast amounts of plastic guano.

At the first encampment, we see that what I had assumed to be cooking fires are actually smelting pots in which bright, liquefied metals shimmer like undulating tin foil. It is beautiful. It smells lethal. We ask a withered fellow sitting on a cement block and wearing sandals made from an old tyre for the man we have come to see. He does not know him. But he knows his clan. They are further up the hill, at another encampment. And we climb some more, the plastic casing cracking underfoot. Finally, near the top, where another pot simmers a liquid that is more dull and pewterish in colour than that which cooks down the hill, we find another scavenger who has bundled himself in a drab, olive parka as he sits on a bench made from what looks like the casing of an old, orange iMac computer. He does not greet us. Not knowing where to stand, and feeling out of place

147.

in my fancy loafers, blazer and pea coat, I pause for a moment by the fire and warm my hands until I inhale some of the fumes emanating from the cauldron. The poison makes me take a quick step back.

Zhu asks the man if he knows the patient for whom we are searching.

'Yes.'

'Is he here?'

'No.'

'Will he be back?'

'I don't know.'

'Does he have a mobile phone?'

'No.'

'Oh.'

Zhu tells him who I am, what I am doing, and I suggest that we will pay something for the man's time, if and when he ever returns.

We descend the foul mountain.

o o o o o o o o o

Over a dinner of some sort of ground poultry cooked in a stew with cabbage, I wonder whether I will ever gather what I need to write this book from a country so impenetrable and vast, where no-one is ever where they ought to be, where appointments are rarely kept and phone calls never returned, where, when I am bivouacked in lonely towns like this, there is not a soul I know besides my assistant for a thousand miles. But I have already invested months seeking and interviewing those who could be located. My ego is linked to the completion of this book in a manner that makes me embarrassed to consider abandoning it. Books, I tell myself, are more the accumulated product of overcoming these moments of doubt and insecurity than they are the star bursts of inspiration.

Also, I have already spent a good portion of the publisher's advance.

The restaurant has rough plank walls festooned with fading beer posters. There is a woman seated behind a gouged wooden desk, which has soda and beer bottles lined up along one side and an abacus in the centre. Just as we are finishing our chicken and cabbage, three men in drab grey and olive clothing enter the restaurant. They recognise Zhu and before they can sit down at another table, she very quickly rushes to them and, it seems to me, forcefully guides them to our wobbly table. Ah, these are the men from the mountain! I recall them seated before their steel pots, melting down their salvaged precious metals. In the fluorescent light, their creased faces are sharply contrasting, narrow bands of white and shadow. I hurry to the girl at her desk and gather three bottles of beer and three more glasses. Once the men have each downed a drink, I pour another round, and then another.

They are taciturn, bashful around Zhu and a foreigner, but also, as they drink, they become less reluctant to express their curiosity about why I am here, what I am doing. They remember the virus, of course, for they themselves have a close relative who has been stricken. But they are vague about where he is, this first patient, this fellow who had the virus before it even had a name. When he fell sick, one of the men explains, everyone just assumed he had caught one of the innumerable coughing diseases that burn through China in the winter.

As Zhu pours them more beer, and encourages them to order whatever they wish, they forget for stretches that I am even there. I slide my chair back to make myself less obtrusive, and look down at my pants, study my hands, fold them, wiggle my fingers. I never make eye contact with the men who are chatting eagerly with Zhu, peppering her with questions about Sichuan, about her village, about the sorts of dishes they prepare there, and then about Beijing, where she lives, and whether she misses her family and what her parents think of her living in the city. They assume she lives in a dormitory, with other women who have jobs like she has, and they say that if they were women then perhaps they would seek that sort of job, an office job, instead of tearing apart old computers, monitors, fax machines and printers and stripping their CPUs, circuit boards and disc drives of traces of aluminium, copper and gold. They are able to extract about five *jiǎo* worth of metal from each CPU or circuit board, that's about a half-penny for each man. The work is dirty, and, the men worry, unhealthy. They have been told by a doctor who travelled up to see them that they are at risk of being poisoned by the fumes that rise as they burn off the precious copper and gold. It is mercury, they have been told, and it will kill them slowly. This doctor had offered to sell them medicine but the men found it too expensive.

'And whose land is this?'

'It belongs to a mining company a few hills over.'

That was where they used to work, they explain. Two of them are even entitled to minute pensions. They supplement those irregular payments with the work up the hill.

'Does it have a name, this place?'

'Jianxi Area Mine #6.'

'No, the little mountain where you work.'

'No.'

From the woman behind the desk I collect four more bottles of beer. Since we are now the last party in the restaurant, I also slip her four hundred-*kuài* notes, as a tip for letting us stay late. This turns out to be another stroke of luck, as she orders the kitchen to produce a dish far better than any we have eaten so far: a hotpot of some sort with at least two medium-sized fish stewing in chillies and peppercorns. I don't know where in this landlocked province they caught these fish, but their arrival signifies that this dinner has turned into a banquet of sorts. I dish out the seafood into the chipped porcelain bowls, giving the men almost all the meat. They slurp it up happily.

'If I worked in an office,' one of the men comments, 'I would always eat seafood.'

As I gaze at the men gathered around this scratched wooden table, each of their faces withered and creased and shiny from the grease and red from the beer, I feel for the first time a pang of guilt at seeking to manipulate them by sating their hunger and thirst. Why should I take advantage of their appetites? And in a larger sense, who am I to assume that I should be able to extract from this vast country, the hardship of which is embodied in the faces of these three men who ply starvation wages from high-tech waste, anything that I could then take back to America and sell to those enjoying easy lives?

'Forget it,' I tell Zhu, 'don't worry about it.'

She looks at me strangely. She points to a fellow with a crew cut removing a fishbone from his mouth with a pair of chopsticks. 'But this is him.'

151.

o o o o o o o o o

That dinner in that remote province is where my luck changes. Zhu and I begin a series of interviews and meetings where instead of closed doors and absent officials and doctors and hospital chiefs always in distant cities, they are at their desk and are happy to meet with me. We are handed documents and hospital admission forms and official communiqués and, twice, top secret, internal memos. And when I return home from these trips, I begin to write down what we are discovering, to make sense of the information we have gathered. As hard as it was before, it is inversely easy now. A friend of mine, an accountant, loans me a little office in the central district of Hong Kong where I unpack my files and open my computer and begin in earnest. I can write this book, I now feel. What I am typing might actually amount to something. Oh, it is awkward and forced and full of sentences, paragraphs, entire sections that have no place in any published work, and it is unwieldy and unsound in the way that a bridge constructed from just one bank might appear. But it is slowly, accretively, emerging, on my hard drive, 10,000, 20,000, 30,000, 40,000 words. I am nearly halfway to a finished manuscript.

In the afternoon, when I am finished writing for the day, I take a walk up Pedders Street to the Foreign Correspondents Club, where I can check my email, or I cut over to Lang Kwai Fong where I can buy a coffee at Starbucks or browse in the Front Page bookstore. I love that sense of a day's work done and stored in my computer, diligently backed up on an iPod, and of just dawdling for a few minutes, watching the pedestrians, admiring the women, scanning the crowd for anyone I might know. It is a totally earned waste of time. I'm not expected anywhere for a few minutes, and I have nothing to do.

It is on an afternoon like this that Zhu calls me and tells me the most improbable news yet. A very high official, a mandarin among mandarins, has agreed to meet with me. He wants me to come to Beijing, tomorrow, to see him.

I go, of course, packing my computer and roller bag and taking the plane from Chep Lap Kok to Beijing and then a car to the St Regis, where I sleep fitfully. In the morning, I meet with Zhu and together we go to the ministry. I am greeted by several officials, the most senior of whom is a woman with a stack of curly hair and wire-frame glasses, who gives me her card. We are led into a meeting room where there is a mural of the winding Great Wall on the southern wall and a bank of windows facing east. The seats are upholstered with white doilies laid over the chair backs so that as I sit down, I feel the bumpiness of the stiff fabric against my shoulders. Cups of tea are positioned on small, dark wood tables arranged between each chair.

The four officials sit down on chairs beneath the east-facing windows. I sit with Zhu beside me on a bank of chairs opposite the mural. Finally, the minister himself enters, makes a very slight bow in the direction of his colleagues and then comes over to where I am standing and shakes my hand, bows again and takes the seat beside me. He wears a dark blue suit, white shirt and shiny silver tie. His jowls dangle slightly over his collar, so that when he sits I can't see his neck. One of his underlings strolls over and hands him a folder which he leaves unopened on his lap.

The interview itself does not provide me with much new material – he repeats the government position that it did everything it could, that no-one could have known this was a new disease, that the cover-up was the work of misinformed local officials who have been punished, and that the circumstances that allowed for this outbreak have been altered. Yet the meeting is symbolically significant for me. I have secured access to one of the highest officials in the land. And he is here, right where he is supposed to be.

o o o o o o o o o

I decide to return to Hong Kong via Shenzhen, to make another visit to one of the neighbourhoods that had been among the earliest points of infection. I have come to know this area well. The collection of eight-storey tenements is a grid of dank, wet, unpaved alleys just two metres wide. There are numerous barber poles skirling red, white and blue. (The barber pole, in China, very often denotes a house of ill repute.) The hookers in skin-tight lycra pants and tube-tops grab my arm as I walk past. Because I am a foreigner, they proffer *'Amore, amore'* – Italian here, for some reason, being the language of love. There are several tiny piecework factories of three sewing machines each; the workers sleep under their machines at night. There

are four fellows who can repair your shoes, and one fellow who
converts old tyres into sandals. There are a half-dozen key
duplicators. And no less than a dozen doctors in one-room
offices – fifty-square-foot shop fronts featuring, usually, a
bench covered with newspapers, a cabinet full of pills, maybe a
diploma on the wall and a stool on which the MD sits, smoking
cigarettes. They all specialise in treating venereal diseases,
besides a frightening few who practise cut-rate plastic surgery.
But it would be easier to bypass the doctors and head straight
for any of the half-dozen pharmacies that do a thriving
business in aphrodisiacs and antibiotics. There are the pay-by-
the-call phone centres, the pay-by-the-hour hotels and the
pay-by-the-tablet ecstasy dealers. You can buy one of anything
here: a cigarette, a nail, a phone call, an injection, a piece of
paper, an envelope, a stamp, a match, a tablet, a stick of gum, a
bullet, a brick, a bath, a shave, a battery, even a feel.

There are shops punched through the walls where for a kuài,
you can pick out a DVD or VCD from a box and watch it on a
monitor and listen to the audio through headphones. You take a
seat in a darkened room alongside others who are killing time. I
flip through the box at a VCD parlour and choose the latest
Matrix instalment. When I pay my kuài and am seated in my
moulded plastic chair, I find myself instead watching
Zoolander – in Korean. I try to explain to the proprietor, a kid
with spiky black hair and knock-off Oakleys, that Stiller and
Ferrell in Korean are no substitute for Reeves, Moss, Fishburn
and Agent Smith, but to no avail. In the end, I have to pay
another kuài for another flip through the box. I end up
watching the first ten minutes of *Outbreak*.

I walk a few *li* through crowded streets to the border
crossing at Lo Wu, past the corridors of tobacco- and brandy-
sellers with their tins of Panda cigarettes, where I catch the last
MTR train back to Hong Kong. I listen to a few songs on my
iPod and watch as the businessmen around me replace the

Chinese SIM cards in their mobile phones with Hong Kong versions.

When we come screeching to a halt in the bowels of the station, I slip off my iPod headphones and shove the music player into my briefcase, next to my computer, sling the black briefcase over my roller bag and disembark, heading up the escalator.

There is a long, cavernous hallway down the western side of the station that is open to On Wan Street and the numerous bus lanes between that and the wider avenue beyond. In the dull fluorescent light, the commuters' tan trench coats and leather jackets are shineless and muted, seemingly as fatigued as their wearers scurrying from the late trains to the taxi stand at the front of the station.

I am also tired but with a sense of wellbeing. My many trips to nowhere Chinese towns and often futile attempts to locate officials and administrators are now paying off in the book that is growing on my laptop, right here beside me. That it will all – the reporting, the writing, the fretting – somehow add up is as optimistic an outlook as I can ever have as a writer. I stop at a corner where the corridor intersects with another from Hong Chong Road to replenish my subway and railway pass at a vending machine. I set down my rollerbag beside me, leaving my briefcase perched on top, and then fumble in my pocket for my wallet. I slide the card into the ticket machine along with a red hundred-dollar note. A few other commuters walk behind me, one coming close enough so that his coat seems to brush mine.

I turn around, shoving my wallet back into my pocket.

My briefcase is gone.

My computer, my iPod – my book has been stolen.

I howl. I have never made such a sound before.

I look both ways. There are at least a dozen people walking away from me, going in any of three possible directions. I grab my rollerbag and run down one hallway towards the bus lanes, but stairways descend from this covered walkway every twenty metres. Whoever stole my briefcase could have made off in any of a dozen directions. For some reason, I keep returning to the site of the theft, as if in so doing I can turn back time.

I felt him for a second, I think. I can almost see the person, his black coat just glancing off mine, or was that my own bag that I felt being pulled away? Why hadn't I turned sooner?

The thief can have no idea of the value of its contents. He would be delighted at the US$700 in travellers cheques stashed in a zippered pocket, at the $2500 or so Hong Kong dollars in an envelope, at the Gucci sunglasses, the Palm Pilot, the iPod and, of course, the computer. He wouldn't even be aware of my book, my transcribed notes, the thousands of hours of work that digitised information represents. These are as valueless to him as the notebooks in which I have sketched images of Guanzhou and Shenzhen, as the collection of business cards I have amassed. A magnet will be swept over the computer's hard drive to erase it, the notebooks will be tossed into a waste bin.

o o o o o o o o o

The police station is brightly lit, with cartoon posters advising what to do if you are cheated or in a traffic accident. There is a Cantonese couple seated in plastic chairs before a white counter, speaking rapidly in Cantonese to a uniformed officer who nods once in a while and keeps attempting to draw their attention to a form he has laid out on the counter in front of him. Behind him is a plain white wall and beyond that, I imagine, is the rest of the station. I had assumed that the two officers who had responded to my complaint would have radioed ahead to let the station know that I was coming before they put me into a van to the station. But now I realise that I am just another robbery victim and will have to wait my turn to file my complaint.

Finally, the Cantonese couple rise to leave and I take a seat. I explain to the officer why I am here, what I am doing, and he asks if I would like to file a report.

'Yes.'

He asks to see some identification. I hand him my Hong Kong ID card, which he takes with him back into the station while I wait.

I am led to a small room where I am told to sit down and the officer says, 'Robbery?'

I nod. 'Yes.'

'Did you see?'

I shake my head. I shrug. 'Sort of.'

He doesn't understand me.

'Not really,' I say. 'Is there anything you can do?'

He doesn't seem to understand this either. He looks over my ID card and begins writing my name and other information on an official report.

'What taken?'

'A computer – my book,' I tell him, almost crying again, 'my book.'

'One book,' he says, carefully writing it down. 'How much?'

I shake my head. 'My book was on the computer. I'm writing a book, and this book was on the computer.'

'Com-put-er.' He carefully enunciates as he writes. 'How much cost?'

Later, I will be told by others who have dealt with the Hong Kong police that you have the option of writing the report yourself, which would have saved an hour of watching Sergeant Yiu struggle to write, '1 pom pirate adres book w/ kebored'. But after a while, I realise that these hours of dealing with the police, of laboriously transcribing what has been stolen, of explaining, over and over, that I am writing a book and that my book was on that computer, this is part of the grieving process. I recite the litany, sounding out the words to help Sergeant Yiu phonetically spell out Macintosh, travellers cheque and Tumi. I watch as he laboriously transcribes the contents of my brief-case, never once writing down the most important thing stolen.

When he is finally finished with the report, he leaves the room and returns with a photocopy of the report and a card, which has his name, the report number, case officer and the station's telephone number and Sergeant Yiu's mobile phone number. I take the card and look at it for a moment. It is what I have been given in place of thousands of miles of travel and thousands of hours of research. I slide it into my wallet.

'Do you ever catch them?' I ask. 'Do you ever recover the stolen stuff?'

He shrugs. 'Sometimes. But I have to be honest, not so much.'

o o o o o o o o o

I don't know why, but I didn't expect that when the police were finished taking my report they would simply show me to the door. I'm not sure what I expected, but I wasn't ready for that to be it, for my book to be gone and the actual police response to the theft to have amounted to this. But Sergeant Yiu led me to the door and out into the waiting room with the cartoon pos-ters and then I walked out into the street, a narrow, sloping road glistening from a steady rain that had started while I had been in the station. It was four in the morning and there were no taxis in sight and I was disoriented, not even sure which direction I should walk in to find a cab.

It didn't matter really, which way I went, because I was totally lost.

o o o o o o o o o

I have that card Sergeant Yiu handed to me now, more than two years later. I still carry it with me in my wallet. The Report

Number is 03027895. There is his name, his DPC number, whatever that is, and then a line reading DVIT 2/HH DIV, which I believe refers to the Hung Hum Division, though I could be wrong. There are the phone numbers and, at the bottom, for some reason, a fax number. There is no date on the card but I will always remember that: 18 November 2003.

On 19 December 2003, I began to rewrite my book.

HIS PICTURE NOWHERE

BY JOSHUA CLARK

THERE'S A HOUSE across St Louis Bay in Mississippi and no-one knows where it came from. It wasn't there when twilight fell away on 28 August 2005, the first feathery outer rain bands tickling the mansions that lined the opposite side of the bay in Waveland. When light returned, about noon the following day, breaking through the last spasms of rain and gust, those mansions had vanished, not shifted or splintered or hurled from their foundations or torn apart like those further inland, but vanished, leaving nothing to photograph, not a tricycle or trinket somewhere up in a tree for the reporter who looked hard enough, not anything. Nothing but a one-storey white house, far from being a mansion, barely large enough to be seen, whole, sitting on the shore across the bay all by itself surrounded by virgin forest. It was the final place Katrina made landfall.

The first was Buras, Louisiana, a shrimping community that stretches its tiny self thin along the Mississippi River upon land that once was the Mississippi River, land that now shoots crazily alone out into the Gulf of Mexico with the river eighty miles south of St Louis Bay on the Mississippi Gulf coast. When noon came and light returned, both places were suddenly

empty of anything but day and heat and a silence you expected
at any moment to be filled with the bird's call that unfailingly
swoons into the quietest pockets of the world. But it would not
come. There wasn't, of course, even an insect. And I wondered
what thing would be the first to claim this silence.

Until Alcedia took it. It was almost three weeks later, but she
took it. Down in Buras. Screaming for her granddaddy's picture.
Alcedia through the halls of Buras High School, Alcedia in the
high school cafeteria, Alcedia over the mud caked into pieces
with their edges curling up like maple leaves upon the lunch
tables, screaming for her granddaddy's picture, Alcedia down
the hallway, the ceiling hanging, wires, cords like tentacles
wrapped around books and balls overhead, Alcedia through the
open lockers, an Algebra II textbook heavy as stone, solid with
sediment and water and Alcedia, Alcedia through Wild Cat
gymnasium home of the 1990 AA basketball State Champions,
Alcedia filling the entire gym right up to the windows high
above the bleachers, screaming for her granddaddy's picture
louder than the water that poured through those windows
three weeks ago, Alcedia through Principal Wilkes' office,
across the principal's computer monitor wedged between the
top of the door and the ceiling, across his note crusted to his
overturned desk reminding him to tell his wife to pick up more
Honey Nut Cheerio's and Rogaine, Alcedia still calling for her
granddaddy's picture as I finish my Snickers, pull Principal
Wilkes' waste basket out of the wall, set it upright in mud rank
and wet without the sun, and toss the wrapper in, then shout,
'Yo, Ride!'

'Shut up, dude.' He sounds far away, upstairs in a classroom
or something. 'You just ruined that shot.'

Ride's convinced sound can ruin a photograph. Like me, he
never left New Orleans, another place between the horizons,
northern and southern, Waveland and Buras, of a new American
nowhere. But at least the media had found New Orleans, had

fixed it back in the country's consciousness. Buras will not have that opportunity. So, when we heard the water had receded enough, Ride and I rented the last working pick-up truck we could find in New Orleans and drove down here to see for ourselves, he with his camera, me with my tape recorder, hugging the Mississippi River an hour and a half south, through the last puddles, over ashen earth now dried and hardened and split to pieces like a brittle leaf that's been stepped on, until the first sign of life – Alcedia's hot pink minivan parked along the levee.

Throughout Katrina and its aftermath, the Mississippi River levees held. It was other levees that failed. But in addition to pushing a tidal surge onto the Gulf coast that vanished Waveland, the storm pushed water up into the river, so much water that here, at Buras near its end, it overtopped the levees, and the longest river in the world levelled out into Alcedia's home. Her sister Mary was by her side, holding a child that looked too young to fool with words. Others – sisters and sons and cousins – were scattered around their own shattered homes to either side. It was not the homes, the debris, or the tears that made the whole thing unnerving as we got out of our truck and approached them. Ride and I had become used to this, our new landscape. It was the hush that still got us, just standing there, hearing every movement, every creak of bone, every swallow, breathing in pulses of silence while we gazed vacantly at what was once someone's everything, my tape recorder recording the nothing. Until Alcedia took the silence.

Alcedia: Now you know. You watch it on the TV, and you see devastation in other countries, and you go back to your life. Now you know.

Mary: The older folks is gonna grieve, I'm gonna tell you that, they gonna grieve.

Alcedia: They gonna catch heart attacks.

Mary: You seen my kitchen floor?

Me: I think I saw one back there. Over there, that tile floor?

Mary: That's a wall.

Me: Oh. OK. Hey, what's your name?

Alcedia: Tell him your name, tell the man your name, Corrin.

Me: Corwin, is that right?

Alcedia: Corrin. He's almost two.

Me: Corrin, do you want to come back and live here? This is a tape recorder.

Alcedia: Corrin, you want to come home? Tell the man with the recorder.

Me: You want to go home?

Corrin: Yep.

Me: Yeah?

Corrin: Yep.

Me: You want to –

Corrin: I fix it.

Alcedia: You want to fix home?

Corrin: Yep. Fix house.

Me: Yeah? You gonna fix it? You want to see? See, it's a little tape that goes around that records. Say something and it will record it. You want to hear yourself? OK, talk. Say something about your home.

Corrin: Hello.

–tape breaks–

[Corrin laughing]

Alcedia: It's like death.

Mary: This is it for me, and, I praise the one that can see it happen, coming back, but me, I just can't, I can't see it happening.

Alcedia: Where my home is? Where?

Mary pulled another porcelain rooster out of the ground, wiped it off as best she could with her hands, and added it to her collection of roosters upon the top of the cement stairs that once led to her porch, the only thing still standing in its original place. Her dog was curled up on the slab of her foundation exactly where its favourite couch used to be. If not for the blue sky everything but us would be beige and ash. I walked alone with Alcedia away from the road, away from the first set of foundations, trying to find her home, and all I could think about was whether I should eat the Snickers or open the Cheetos when I got back to the car. I wasn't even that hungry. Alcedia bent down, pulled a Spiderman video game out of the ground.

Alcedia: Nobody knew about this place, we a little dot. Now we nowhere. This whole neighbourhood is just our family, eighteen grandchildren here, nine boys, nine girls. I'm a be a great-great-grandmother in a month. I wanna see them raised up, there's a lot of things we have to tell them. We're lost, you know, we're displaced. We're displaced with housing, we're displaced in ourselves. We don't know how to function right now. You know, we just waking up in the morning, and opening our eyes and starting wherever we gotta start. I guess what it was, we became so complacent, you know, that we weren't focusing on the outside. We had our own world here. We weren't focused on other people, we were just focused on our little town, you know. I worked at the high school right there; I was the secretary there. That was my place over there.

Me: Your house was right there?

Alcedia: Yes.

Me: Where's it now?

Alcedia: That's what you helping me look for. Come on.

Me: Whose foundation is this one?

Alcedia: This is where my granddaddy's house was. Don't know where that is either.

Me: These names, written in the foundation, are these you guys?

Alcedia: Yeah. Well, this is my daughter. This is June, that's my niece. This is Mary, this is me. And this is Wanda my niece. Natasha, Jaquelyn, Jobu, Shawna, Will-Will, my granddaddy Bud – he built this whole community, he's the one, and he just passed last year – and there's Mac and Big Fuzz and Lil' Fuzz right here, and –

Me: Is his grave OK? Your grandfather's? Did you check on him?

Alcedia: Yes. It's fine. Everything's intact.

Ride found the family graveyard just past their satsuma grove, the sun-bleached above-ground tombs, every one overturned, skulls, bones strewn on the ground. A lot of them had been buried together. The grandfather Bud's hip placement looked like the ball on a trailer, he told me.

'Ride? Where are you, man?' I say as I walk up to the second floor of the high school, my footprints the first into the mud up here, Alcedia flooding into every one of them, fast on my heels, still calling for her granddaddy's picture, as I walk into the library, paper everywhere, every book still in its place, stepping around the broken glass peeking out of the floor, light slanting over it through shattered windows, sun paling into autumn, the clock on the wall stopped. 6.37. *Leatherneck* magazine, a whole booth, still upright, full of Marine pamphlets, Army, National Guard.

An hour ago, about 300 feet from the road, a couple hundred feet from the nearest foundation, I had pulled a ribbon out of the ground, brushed off the brass-coloured medal, wondered what war it had come from, tried to hand it to Alcedia but she paid me no attention. She was staring at what I thought was an enormous black tarp on the ground ahead of us until I realised it was a roof. It was just lying there on the ground, its highest point about up to my shoulders, flimsy and twisted like a quilt on a bed left unmade and rumpled over the other bed sheets and pillows and maybe even a person who'd just hit snooze. Alcedia ducked down close to the ground, looked below the roof to see what was under it.

Alcedia: That's his house. That's his house under there. Oh, my granddaddy's house. Oh my God, my picture is in there. My granddaddy's picture. Oh, look at my granddaddy's house. Oh my, oh God. My granddaddy's picture. Where my granddaddy's picture?

Me: Are you looking for a photo?

Alcedia: My granddaddy's picture. Oh, my granddaddy's picture. God.

Me: Ma'am, it's probably under there, and probably what you're going to have to do is get someone with a chainsaw to come back here and cut this wood off and remove it, carefully, and you'll find the picture under there.

Alcedia: My granddaddy's picture!

Me: Please, you need to climb out of there. You'll only hurt yourself.

Alcedia: It was my picture. I kept it in his house after he passed last year. Oh God. Where his picture? My granddaddy's picture. His picture nowhere.

She kept climbing up onto the roof, peering down through the framework exposed like bone. Always, the first thing they go for is family photos. The ones that still exist are invariably ringed with rainbow stains – green then yellow then red then purple then blue – that swirl one upon another more violently than gasoline in dark water. I wondered if I could run back to the car and eat that Snickers, get back before I missed anything good.

Where his picture. My granddaddy's picture. It follows me up to the third floor of the high school, nipping at my heels, even when the mud stops on the second stair. Again, my footprints are the first, this time dirt on clean, carpeted stairs. I come into the band room. All by itself up here. A little third-floor room, a cupola, untouched since the last day of school. The only place in Buras untouched, every window unbroken. I open them. No breeze but at least it bleeds the heat out of the place. And I can hear her louder than ever, where his picture, my granddaddy's picture, flecking off the trophies like the September afternoon. There are trophies everywhere. There's even a whole locker room up here for the band. They take this band shit seriously, I guess. I can see into the river, coffee-coloured, convulsing with conflicting currents, sluggishly fighting its fall as ever into the Gulf. And, on another side, their land. Alcedia is not, of course, there now.

She left with her family half an hour ago after I'd cut myself up pulling her out of the roof, kicking and screaming about her granddaddy's picture. The rest of her family followed her back north in her pink minivan, afraid that if they let her go last in the caravan she would turn around and go back for the picture.

My granddaddy's picture. I put down my tape recorder, hit a bass drum with my hand. Alcedia stops. There is the hush again. Not even an insect. Blood on the drum. My palm still bleeding from a nail in the roof. I find a pair of drumsticks and start pounding on everything I can find – snare drums, bongos, cymbals, xylophones, bells, a tuba. Ride comes up to tell me I'm ruining his photos, then takes pictures of me, then joins me. We throw ourselves in and out of rhythms, ecstatic and wild-eyed sweating beating on anything we can find including each other until we give up and chuck the drumsticks out the window and I collapse on the ground. The tape recorder's still on.

'Goddammit, man,' says Ride finally, looking out the window above me. 'Check it out.'

I sit up. The hot pink minivan's back. And there's Alcedia halfway to her granddaddy's roof again.

'I'm not pulling her out this time,' I tell him, falling back to the floor. 'Your ass can do it.'

'Maybe she won't go back in.'

'Yeah. Where is she now?' I ask.

'Walking toward the roof.'

'Maybe she won't go back in.'

'Yeah,' he says.

'I'm hungry.'

'Yup. There she goes.'

'Dammit.'

'How the hell a great-great-grandmother can do that shit, I got no idea,' he says.

'How old you figure she is?

''Bout fifty.'

'That's impossible,' I say, then sit up. 'She couldn't have that many kids if she was fifty. Goddammit! She's crawling down in it again.'

'Let's just let her be.'

'Yeah, that's great. I suppose when she busts her neck or gets one of those big ass nails stuck in her butt we can just go downstairs and call her an ambulance, right?'

She's lying on top of the roof, only about five feet above the ground, with her head and shoulders down through a hole in it. Then she slides her entire upper body into the hole until all we can see is her legs sticking up in the air, kicking back and forth as she lowers herself further into the roof's framework like she's swimming down to the bottom of the sea real slow, until she's down in it up to her knees. We make our way back down through the school, out the shattered entrance, across the street, back through all the foundations of Alcedia's family's homes, until we're at the roof. Only one of Alcedia's black Reeboks is sticking up out of it now, wiggling around.

'Where his picture,' she's saying to herself over and over. 'My granddaddy's picture.'

'Alcedia?'

'What? What?! Who that is?'

'It's us. Ride and Josh.'

Her foot stops wiggling. 'Did y'all hear that racket up in the high school?' she says.

'What? The drums?' I ask. 'Alcedia, please, please, come out of there.'

'That's ghosts,' she says. 'You used hear it every night here. They banging up there in the high school. But these is new ones, sounds like, because they're in the daytime. None of my family stayed, but I know someone stayed and died, some children, because that's them making all that racket up there. I like that. They happy ghosts. Only someone ought to go up there and teach them how to play all them instruments because they awful. God awful.'

169.

'Alcedia, are you OK in there?'

'Oh Lord, I got it. I found my granddaddy's picture. I found the picture.'

'Can you please climb up out of there now?'

'No.'

'Please, Alcedia, you got to. You're going to hurt yourself. We'll come back, Ride and I will, with a chainsaw and we'll get through the roof and open it all up for you, OK?'

There's nothing for a while. Just pulsing silence. And I think about that last bag of Cheetos still in the car.

'Alcedia?'

'What? Who that?! What you want?'

'I want you to please for God's sake stop talking about your granddaddy's picture and get out of there right now.'

'I already told you, I'm stuck.'

'Jesus.'

'This ain' Jesus' fault. Don't you go curse Jesus. Oh, my granddaddy's picture. I got my granddaddy's picture. Oh God.'

Ride crawls up, sticks his head down into the framework of the roof. 'Alcedia, you'll have to let go of the picture,' he says, 'then give me your hand.'

'Oh Lord, oh God no.'

'Alcedia, let go and then we'll find something to pull it up with,' says Ride.

Her Reebok disappears as she falls all the way in. Thump. Then she pokes her head up out of the roof. 'My granddaddy's picture.' She hands a large framed picture to Ride. 'You please, please be careful with that now.'

Ride takes it. It's almost half as long as him. An electric plug dangles from it. The glass shoots sun all over his face. 'This is the picture?' he asks.

'Help me out,' she says.

'This isn't your grandfather,' says Ride as he hands the picture down to me. He's right, it's not her grandfather. He pulls her out, then walks down the roof with her. She snatches the picture back from me, hugs it to her chest. Her forearms are cut up but not bleeding.

'Oh my granddaddy's picture.' She releases it, holds it out for us to see. It's Manhattan's skyline at night, the Twin Towers highlighted with a gaudy pink glow. The sky portion is a mirror. It seems impossibly clean, doesn't share a bit of the dirt we have all over us.

'I felt so sorry for those people,' she says, 'what happened in the Twin Towers. It's in good condition still. And it lights up. See all the tiny dots around the buildings, they lights. You have to plug it in. That's his picture. He went to New York and brought this back for me. I treasure this, because I felt so sorry for them.'

'Sorry for them?' I ask, me and Buras High School framed in the mirrored sky above Manhattan. 'What about you? Your family?'

'We have our lives, our family. But you know your life is, oh God…They didn't know it was the last. We had a chance to get out. New York is more devastating to us. New York had lives. They lives is gone.'

'You think there's someone in New York with a picture of Buras?' I ask.

'Yes, I think so. And I think they relate what we going through.'

The path of her belongings, which wound its way away from the river to where we were now, had stopped somewhere behind us. There's nothing more but sediment.

'What did your house look like?' I ask.

'It was white, one storey, real long. Gone. But I got New York. That's what I saved. New York.'

White. One storey. Real long. Gone. And I think of that house on St Louis Bay. Found. All alone surrounded by virgin woods, looking out over the bay into a distant, empty shore once lined with mansions, too far away to touch. And I touch things untouched by destruction, my own New Orleans apartment, for example, where I type these words. But more than anything, I want something created from all this. A house that never existed before, white, one storey, real long, in the middle of nowhere, and no-one knows where it came from. No, not a house. A home. With a single picture on its walls, of what was there before, its sky a mirror, how we see ourselves. And Alcedia is heard in its hallways, always. Oh Lord, I got it. My granddaddy's picture. I found –

ALMOST NOWHERE: LIDICE

BY DAVI WALDERS

AS WE TRAMPED the soft grass from marker to marker, the young mayor of Lidice answered our continuous stream of questions: Why did the Nazis burn the town to the ground? How many were killed? Did anyone survive? What happened after the Nazis left? It was the first site on a trip sponsored by the US Memorial Holocaust Museum to death camps and World War II monuments, and we wanted to know everything. Towards the end of the tour of the new Lidice, the mayor asked if we would like to talk with a survivor of the Nazi destruction of the village. We immediately said yes. So our small group trekked into the sparkling new town hall reception room and waited.

We were a group of fifteen: museum supporters; religious leaders, both Christian and Jewish; a writer; accompanying scholars. I was the writer. I had been working on a collection about women who had resisted throughout Europe during World War II, and when I heard about the trip to the Czech Republic and Poland – ten death camps in ten days, seeing first-hand where so many had struggled to survive or had perished, lectures at each site – I knew I had to sign up. I dreaded it, but I had to see these horrific places. When I tried to get my husband to accompany me, all he said was, 'You must be nuts!' But I resolved to go, no matter how gruelling, and was actually relieved at the prospect of having a hotel room to myself; there, I hoped, I could deal with my terror and horror and write myself sane at the end of each overwhelming day.

The museum had designed our trip to explore the full devastation of the Nazi years, including sites such as Lidice, which were only minimally connected to the near-destruction of European Jewry. From our starting point in Prague, it took only half an hour by bus through the green, rolling hills of the Czech Republic to reach the tiny, now-rebuilt village. So we began there, wandering its sparkling white buildings, looking at markers, listening to the young mayor, taking notes. But it was the end of the afternoon that I will always remember.

Under a puff of silver hair, Mrs Anna Nesporova walked slowly down the aisle of the large, sunny town hall reception room and took a seat in front facing us. The mayor said he would be happy to translate for her. He told us Mrs Nesporova wanted us to ask her questions. It would be easier that way, she had explained. She was short, plump, white-haired – a sweet-looking woman. She wore a pink dress, a pin, a brown sweater. She smiled a bit and seemed relieved that several of us raised our hands.

How she survived the annihilation of this town and all its inhabitants near Prague is a long story, she said in Czech. A young bride, she was away giving birth in a Prague hospital in June, 1942, when the Nazis randomly selected this idyllic Catholic mining village in the countryside of Bohemia for retaliation after Hitler's Reichsprotector, Reinhard Heydrich, was assassinated by the Czech underground. No-one in the village was in any way connected to the assassination. It was just the Nazi way of retribution, of maintaining control through random terror.

She was not in Lidice when they came and rounded up everyone in the village. The men were shot in batches of ten behind the town's largest barn. First 192 men were shot; then, seventy-one women. All the women in Lidice were made to watch the men die before being shot themselves or shipped to slave labour in Ravensbruck. The Nazis filmed each step of the destruction of this village as a training film – the shootings, the burning of bodies and homes, all evidence of a town burned into oblivion, ploughed under. A training film. To help others learn to leave no traces behind.

Did any of the village children survive, someone asked. A few, she said, those that looked Aryan enough were sent to Germany and adopted. Two of these children were found after the war and, after long negotiations, brought back to the village. Those that were a bit darker, a bit suspect, were sent to Chelmno or Auschwitz. They did not come back.

And her? What of her and her baby girl? The Nazis came to the hospital. They took her baby. She begged and pleaded to keep the child. For that, they sent Mrs Nesporova to Ravensbruck. For four years she endured slave labour, near starvation, beatings. Then the war ended and she slowly made her way back to the village that no longer existed. She returned to silence and absence. There was no record of her child or the town. Lidice had been completely razed and expunged from Nazi records. During her long months of slave labour, she had known nothing of her town, her husband, her child. She had been driven to survive by the dream of someday reuniting with her family.

Slowly, with the help of world organisations, the town had been rebuilt and she had resettled here. It was her home and always would be, she said. Did she find her child? No, she said, she still knew nothing about the baby who was taken from her breast. And her husband? Her then-husband had been murdered with the rest of the men of Lidice.

Yes, she said, she – like other survivors – had somehow managed to resume life when the war and cruelty were over.

Yes, she had married again and had other children. But that one child, her first, she said with quiet dignity, she still carried in her heart. She looked out the window at the rolling fields and blue sky above Lidice, then turned back to us to say she had been searching for her for sixty years.

Anna Nesporova walked with us through the green memorial grounds, pointing to a large marble statue with many names, so many of them children, one of them, hers. On the way back to the bus, she held my hand, patted my arm. She said she was glad we had come. She had one more thing to tell us, her translator said: 'You must always try to be happy,' she said, smiling.

As we climbed back on the bus, we could not take our eyes off petite Mrs Nesporova, who kept waving. And as the bus backed down the hill and turned towards Prague, we tried to absorb the new Lidice, whose every home, street, and shop had been rebuilt so that the world would not forget. And the old Lidice, the village that had almost ceased to exist, whose courageous survivor had passed on an unforgettable lesson.

A PICTURE OF A VILLAGE
BY ANGIE CHUANG

IN THE GRIM days after 11 September 2001, when a United
States attack on Afghanistan seemed imminent, pundits and
late-night talk show hosts often would tell the same joke. If
President Bush wanted, as he had said in an outburst of
wartime rhetoric, to bomb Afghanistan back to the Stone Ages,
he didn't have to do much. The barren, war-scarred nation was
already there. In our evening news broadcasts, we came to
know the dirt-brown Afghan countryside as a land of endless
conflict and misery. Occasionally, a missile would go astray,
and we'd see wailing villagers in front of their obliterated
mudbrick homes. This place of land mines, veiled women and
Kalashnikov-toting men became a constant companion on our
television sets during that time. Before Iraq subsumed it, we
hoped whatever our bombs and soldiers were doing in that
foreboding land held the antidote to the nightmare to which we
awoke on 11 September.

In those days, I avoided the shrill tones of television news as
much as a person in the news business could. Instead, I found
real insights into this nation we were bombing at the home of
an Afghan immigrant family who lived near me in Portland,
Oregon. I'll call them the Shirzai family, in order to protect the

anonymity of their relatives who remain in the volatile climate of today's Afghanistan. The Portland family members, eleven in all, had fled Afghanistan during the Soviet war of the late seventies. Their two-storey house, nestled amid fir-lined hills, was filled with pictures of their homeland. On those walls, a tangle of tribal horsemen grappled for a headless calf, a headscarf-clad woman smiled at an unnamed photographer, and a pre–Soviet War tourist poster of backpackers on a mountain trail screamed irony. But a small, unassuming snapshot in the hallway kept drawing me back.

The silver, department-store frame gave me a window into an alternate universe: a village of sun-bleached adobe buildings the same colour as the naked, dun earth against a wide azure sky unadulterated by trees or telephone poles. This place, not marked on any map of Afghanistan I had seen, was the Shirzais' home town. They had all been born in the remote village of 400 families with no running water or electricity. For the Shirzais, the photo depicted a location in their psyches, at once distant and ever-present. In their Portland home, surrounded by conveniences none of their relatives who lived in those mudbrick homes could have ever dreamed up – a refrigerator, television, heat, running water, flush toilets – the village and the country they left behind weighed heavily on them.

From the first time I saw it, I wanted to climb into the frame of the picture and walk in that lunar landscape myself. This place was nowhere, really. Had the terrorist attacks never happened, I would have lived a lifetime without ever knowing the village existed. But my work as a newspaper reporter had brought me to the Shirzais exactly a week after planes flew into the World Trade Center towers. And within a month, I was a regular at their home and in their lives, seeking understanding as much as they were seeking a witness to their distant grief for the country they had fled. At that moment, this village in southeastern Afghanistan had become the one place in our suddenly changed world that felt real. And it was real because a Portland family had put its picture on their wall so they would not forget. Sitting in the Shirzais' family room on those evenings in the fall of 2001, I knew it: I had to go.

One October evening, Maiwand Shirzai, who had fled Afghanistan after his brother was killed by the Soviets in 1979, caught me staring at that photo. A stolid, square-jawed man, he was sceptical of journalists and had taken time to start warming up to me. Even then, he wasn't prone to grand gestures.

'You should go with us,' he said. He smiled wryly, as if he wasn't sure whether I'd think he was crazy.

'I should,' I replied.

And so it began.

o o o o o o o o

About two-and-a-half years passed before I stepped off an Azerbaijan Airlines jet onto the tarmac of Kabul Airport. I was travelling with my friend Stephanie Yao, a photojournalist. Maiwand's twenty-five-year-old niece Jamila, whom we had also befriended in Portland, had gone to Kabul ahead of us. We were planning to meet her there. During months of planning for the trip, the Shirzais had been clear about the conditions under which they were allowing us to travel and stay with their family members in Afghanistan. They had agreed to do so because Stephanie and I, both Chinese Americans, would not appear obviously American. We would be safer; hence, their family would be safer. In traditional women's clothes, they remarked, we might even be mistaken for Afghans from the north, some of whom have Asiatic features.

Anything but Americans, I had joked at the time. As it turned out, we left for Kabul as the first stomach-turning photos of US troops abusing Iraqi prisoners at Abu Ghraib prison hit the news. Suddenly I really wanted to be anything but an American.

Arriving at Kabul Airport, Stephanie and I stood near the end of the passport control line. Seeing that we were the only women in line, a man in an olive-drab uniform approached us and beckoned us to cut to the front. I slid our passports under the window. Another uniformed man sat behind the bulletproof glass. He had a trimmed beard and a tight-lipped smile on his face. He looked down at the passports, and then looked up at us, wearing *shalwar kameez* and headscarves, and did a double take.

'You're *American*?'

I nodded apologetically.

He guffawed to himself, shaking his head in disbelief that he had gotten suckered into letting Americans cut to the front of the line. I tried to look contrite. He shoved the passports back, more bemused than angry. I tucked my stamped passport away, grateful that I wouldn't have to show it again until I was leaving the country.

o o o o o o o o

From behind the scarf I had pulled over my face, I saw only the distinctly curved, black metal handle of the AK-47. The wiry hand wrapped around it could have belonged to anyone – Afghan army, coalition forces, warlord, Taliban insurgent, some random robber looking for money-laden foreigners. These kinds of checkpoints, under vague authority, lined the lonely Kabul-to-Kandahar highway. Eventually, this highway would take us to an unmarked set of treacherous dirt roads, which would in turn lead us to our destination for this day-trip: the Shirzai family's village. In the back seat of a Russian sedan that had seen better days, I was a faceless woman at the mercy of whoever had commandeered this piece of nowhere. Decorum and safety dictated that I keep my eyes averted, headscarf shielding my face from the male gaze.

Our driver slowed, and rolled down his window as the man with the gun approached. I willed myself not to stare.

'Please,' the driver said apologetically in Dari, nodding towards me, Stephanie and Jamila in the back seat. We were all covering our faces, with only our downturned eyes visible. 'There are women in the car.'

The checkpoint guard must have waved him on, though I did not see it. We were off again.

Every now and then, the highway's desolation was interrupted by a mine detection centre; these were windowless buildings marked with 'MDC' in red-and-white block letters and a number. Around them, white-painted rocks signalled safe areas and red-painted rocks alerted of mines. At times, construction detours took us off the highway, mere feet away from the red rocks. I sucked in my breath every time we passed one. Nevertheless, amid all these reminders of stagnation and human cruelty, the landscape had a startling beauty to it. Rising from sheer blankness, the mountains ringing Kabul towered in the distance, at once voluptuous and austere. We had left at 4am, the ethereal music of the morning call to prayer echoing as we drove out of the city. The rising sun filtered through clouds in the expansive, uninterrupted sky.

Several checkpoints and countless MDCs later, we arrived in the small city of Ghazni and switched to a twenty-year-old Toyota Surf 4x4 that would take us over the bone-jarring dirt roads leading to a region called Shilgar, where the village was. As we bounced along on the truck's taxed suspension, clusters of homes began to appear amid the monochromatic bleakness. The adobe structures seemed to have sprung up from the earth itself, as those granite mountains around Kabul had millennia ago. The jewel tones of the women's and children's clothes – emerald green, royal blue, electric purple – and the bright yellow and red plastic water jugs they carried to communal wells offered a startling contrast to the blank canvas around them. We then turned off the main road, past the shells of homes that had been bombed by the Soviets. The remains of their jagged mud walls reached skyward like misshapen fingers. Past those ruins, the Shirzais' village emerged, a collection of mudbrick buildings that didn't look different from others that had preceded it. But knowing this was the very place in the photo I had stared at in Portland two-and-a-half years ago made all the difference to me.

I was here. The circle had come full round. Never again would this village be just a picture on the wall to me.

o o o o o o o o o

We pulled into the double doors of the Shirzai family's expansive walled compound. This new thick-walled adobe home with modern windows and a sizable courtyard was the yield of money sent from family members in America. But that money couldn't buy a power grid, pipes or sewers. Like everyone else in rural Afghanistan, the family of seven that had stayed in the village lived without electricity, running water or modern toilets, as villagers had for centuries. From the moment we stepped out of the truck, we were received into a warm world of rooms lined with red carpets and cushions.

Jamila's aunt Fahima, who was twenty-eight, emerged with pots of black tea, piles of puffy flatbread, fruit jam and a thick, sweet cream. She embraced each of the three of us like old friends, offering the traditional greeting between women: three cheek-kisses in rapid succession, left-right-left. Fahima wore the traditional shawl-like headscarf that rural Afghan women wore. The folds of voluminous white cotton framed her weathered face, handsome with deep-set eyes and a long, straight nose.

Then the man of the house, Jamila's uncle Jumagul, greeted us. Like most Afghan men, he kept a polite distance from us women; we nodded vigorously to acknowledge each other. In his late thirties, he wore a long black beard and glasses. He had been legally blind since birth. The shy man hesitated to talk to us at first, but flashed astonishingly white teeth when he smiled, which was often. With his brown eyes half-obscured by thick Coke-bottle lenses, he bore an endearing resemblance to a Cheshire cat. Fahima and Jumagul had four disarming, curious children – three boys and a girl, aged two to nine, all of whom had their father's jaunty, lean frame and their mother's pretty, healthy eyes. After the long, bumpy and sometimes scary journey, I revelled in the stillness of Jumagul and Fahima's home. Bread and tea never tasted so good.

Jumagul's initial reticence quickly thawed. 'We drink a lot of tea here,' was the first thing he said. 'I hope you can keep up.'

Concerned that our presence as outsiders might stir things up in the village, we kept a low profile. Even if we were not immediately pegged as Americans, this rural society was so insular and so scarred from decades of conflict that anyone unfamiliar was viewed with suspicion. Jamila worried that protective villagers might threaten us or, more likely, that Jumagul and Fahima would encounter repercussions for housing outsiders. She recalled that she had come here a couple of weeks prior with a cousin. Local girls, about thirteen years old, had chased them, throwing rocks and shouting obscenities, telling them to 'go back to Kabul'.

'Little did they know I came from America,' Jamila said.

o o o o o o o o o

To avoid disquieting the village, the family thought it was best that the three of us leave before nightfall. But even within that short time frame, this place and our hosts began to reveal themselves by afternoon. In the lull after a lunch of stewed beef and potatoes with rice – even for the relatively well-off, meat was eaten only a couple of times a week, since the lack of refrigeration made it impractical – I sat down with Fahima and Jumagul to talk. Jamila sat alongside, to interpret from Pashto. Fahima matter-of-factly described her daily routine, a 3.30am-to-10.30pm day of nonstop physical labour: milking the cow, pumping water, heating water, cooking, cleaning, washing clothes, patching the house's adobe walls, looking after the children, churning butter, baking bread. 'As soon as I go to bed, I fall asleep. I am exhausted, always,' she said, looking tired even uttering the words. 'But it is not the work that I mind. It is that my life is the same one day after another.' The flatness in her tone mirrored the unchanging landscape. 'I would have liked to go to school,' Fahima offered. 'I did, for a little while.'

But, she said, her father was killed by nomads and as the oldest child, she had to leave school to help her mother. Fahima, who had talked in a near-deadpan until now, stunned me with her sudden emotion. Her eyes welled up with tears. She sobbed. Jamila grew quieter as she conveyed her aunt's words to me. She lowered her head to compose herself, her face hidden in the looseness of her headscarf. Since I had arrived in Kabul a few days before, I had encountered the grief of Afghans in all forms. Nearly everyone had lost a loved one in the nation's quarter-century of war and chaos. But this was different. Fahima wasn't mourning just the loss of her father, but also the loss of opportunity. Every day of her life would continue to be the same. Such stultifying monotony was too painful for me to imagine.

Jumagul did not have it much easier, charged with taking care of the animals and crops, from the chickens and cattle to the vegetables and animal feed they grew themselves. For him, too, life was a mind-numbing routine laced with a bitter taste of what might have been. He had fled with the family to Pakistan during the Soviet invasion and had lived there for a decade with them. Three of his brothers had gone to the United

States, but because of his poor eyesight, they had asked him to return to the village and care for their parents and the family home. He had married Fahima soon after. The American family members often talked about bringing him to the United States for surgery that could fix his eyes. But post–11 September, getting a visa for an adult Afghan male was virtually impossible. Jumagul said he had liked Pakistan, the urban activity, the running water and the electricity. 'Unfortunately, I got stuck here. Why is everyone gone and I'm here?' he said. Unable to get a good look at his eyes behind his glasses, I wondered if there was irony or seriousness in his wry tone.

Our brief time in the village unfurled in a day of sharing tea, conversation, and food and exploring the local mosque and school, both of which had been primarily funded by the Shirzai family in the United States. As our time came to a close, we found ourselves in the same sitting room where we had begun, drinking more tea. As soon as any of our cups became less than half-full, Fahima or one of her children would quickly rush to refill it. In parting, Jumagul made a point of telling us about what Afghanistan was once like, before the wars and the drought started. He spoke of streams and trees, of people who were welcoming to, not afraid of, outsiders. Finally, he apologised for the state of his country, his dark-eyed gaze so piercing that this time I could make it out through the thick lenses. 'I fear you've found it a letdown,' he said softly. 'Please know that Afghanistan wasn't always like this.'

'I know,' I said.

'Have you ever seen a country in worse condition?'

'No, I haven't,' I replied.

o o o o o o o o o

Jumagul's blindness allowed him to see things only when he held them right in front of his glasses. We left Shilgar as a swirling dust storm engulfed the area. The sky and wind had manifested Jumagul and Fahima's myopic world. We couldn't see more than a few feet in front of us. As we drove past open fields, blankets of dust swept over herds of camels and sheep. Their nomadic keepers bent against the barrage just like the sparse, skinny trees. Our driver managed to stay on the roads, some with sheer drops into deep ditches on both sides, only by steering from memory, not sight. The storm subsided as we arrived in Ghazni. It was startling to have a clear view all of a sudden, like waking from a dream. Gone were the adobe buildings of the village. We were on the city's asphalt roads, driving past squat, cinderblock buildings.

I saw a US army Humvee roll by, full of soldiers. Their desert camouflage, blond buzz-cuts and sunburnt faces looked so out of place. With my scarf pulled over my mouth and nose in accordance with protocol, I caught a glimpse of their countenances. They looked so young and so lost. What did they see as they patrolled the city? The chaotic throngs of turbaned and bearded men walking, riding bicycles and driving cars must have seemed impenetrable and threatening. How would a soldier even begin to read a crowd like this? Their eyes lingered briefly, for no more than a second, on us three women in the back seat of the Toyota 4x4 at the gas station. Our Afghan driver and escort milled around outside of the car, in turbans and *shalwar kameez* like all the other men around them. In the midst of Ghazni's hubbub, we didn't warrant a second look. To the soldiers, only three sets of brown eyes looking out from our scarves were visible. They had no idea we were three fellow Americans.

I'm sure if we had met under other circumstances, we would have found common ground. Perhaps one of them was from Oregon. We might have seen the same movies, watched the same television shows or listened to the same music. At the very least, we might have been mutually relieved to find another fluent English speaker, and to converse without an interpreter.

'I know,' Jamila stage-whispered to me through her scarf. I could see from the crinkles at the corners of her eyes that she was grinning mischievously. 'We should roll down our window and yell as loud as we can, "Yo, American homeboys! United States is in da house!" Can you imagine the looks on their faces?'

I laughed, hard. For one deluded moment, it sounded like a grand idea – like a college prank that would have us cracking up for days afterwards. Then I imagined the startled soldiers open-firing on us, or the grizzled locals crowding around our truck, Kalashnikovs drawn. 'Uhh, I'm not sure that would be such a good idea,' I said, our eyes communicating smiles behind our scarves.

I had more in common with those soldiers than I did with Fahima, Jumagul, or any of the Afghans around us. Yet at that moment, I had assumed an appearance that kept me a world away from them. It was liberating and terrifying to float between two identities – between the one on my passport and a different one in the eyes of those soldiers.

I had found what I had longed for in 2001, when I stared at that picture of the village on the wall. By virtue of profession, opportunity, ethnicity and fate, I had landed on a threshold. From this vantage point, I could glimpse the United States and Afghanistan through the eyes of the other. And the view on either side was a lot like trying to see the world through a blinding dust storm. In some ways, I had come this far because I wanted to embrace that ambiguity instead of relying on easy assumptions. In other ways, the understanding I had gained by going to rural Afghanistan couldn't have been simpler and more human.

That picture of the village still hangs on the wall of the Shirzais' house in Portland. These days, I look at it fondly when

I stop by for dinner. I can't help thinking of a second picture whenever I see it. Stephanie took a candid photo of Fahima right after we had first arrived at her home. Fahima was leaning forward to pour tea, and the early-morning light had just streamed into the windows and through the excess fabric of her white scarf to backlight her striking, straight-nosed profile. Her lips were slightly parted; it was the unself-conscious expression of a woman who had hardly ever had her photograph taken, who didn't know to look up or pose when there was a lens pointed at her. She looks beautiful, sad and determined all at the same time.

Fahima has never seen the picture. She doesn't have email or a telephone. There isn't even mail delivery to Shilgar. But still, as America's view of the world has raced forward to other miseries and crises in Iraq, Madrid, the Indian Ocean and on our own Gulf coast, I have tried not to let that portrait of Fahima slip out of my mind. I imagine her in the village, toiling through her day, performing her daily prayers and regarding her four growing children, wondering what kind of Afghanistan they will inherit.

POL POT'S TOILET

BY CHRISTOPHER R COX

AFTER WE HAD been rattling around on rocky, rutted roads for four hours, the smooth track along the ridge of the Dangkrek Range came as a relief. Level and shaded by lush jungle from the dry-season sun, it prompted my driver to push his battered Nissan truck to nearly fifty kilometres per hour – warp speed for a byway in one of the most abject provinces in Cambodia. In the dappled midday light, he didn't see the studded, soda can–sized object in the middle of our route until it was too late to stop. No use swerving off the beaten path; red stakes jutting from the undergrowth meant the road's shoulders hadn't been de-mined. As the Chinese-made Type 58 fragmentation mine disappeared beneath the pick-up, I thought: it's only big enough to cripple, not kill.

Blame it on Pol Pot, the Khmer Rouge tyrant who took Cambodia to a dark place where as many as two million people were executed or died from disease, starvation and exhaustion. Those wretched excesses were now the stuff of memorials – complete with gift shops – that made this traumatised nation a global leader in holocaust tourism. It was a morbid niche market, for sure, but it annually attracted thousands of foreign visitors to Choeung Ek, a notorious Khmer Rouge killing field outside Phnom Penh, and Tuol Sleng, an old school in the capital that became their horrific torture centre. If the package tourists would pay to see a glass tower of bludgeoned skulls and rusted bed frames where prisoners bled to death, then why not Anlong Veng, where Pol Pot and his murderous henchmen made their final stand?

So it came to pass that Prime Minister Hun Sen designated a dismal district in a far corner of Cambodia for tourism development. The authoritarian leader (himself a Khmer Rouge officer in the 1970s) wanted to preserve the site – a thickly forested, heavily mined mountain range on the Thai border – as a vast Khmer Rouge theme park, presumably without club-wielding re-enactors or interactive self-criticism sessions. Of the hundreds of thousands of tourists who annually travelled to Siem Reap to see the ruins of Angkor Wat, there were bound to be half-baked world travellers who would tramp a further 140 kilometres north to visit Genocide World. See Pol Pot's villa! Marvel at his ash heap! Experience Year Zero today, in Anlong Veng!

And a few half-baked writers as well. I was sitting in the Ivy Bar, just off the Old Market in the revitalised colonial quarter of Siem Reap, nursing a happy-hour Angkor Beer and considering the drive up to Anlong Veng (bound to suck) and the destination itself (bound to suffer drug-resistant malaria). Perhaps I could convince my editor to take a travel story on the beach resort of Sihanoukville instead. The roads to the coast were excellent; the lobster dirt cheap. But something on the pub's wall caught my eye: a framed toilet seat. And not just any toilet seat. A small label proclaimed this to be Pol Pot's toilet seat, retrieved from Anlong Veng.

'The seat of power for many years', read the label. 'Even Pol Pot had shitty days.'

I ordered another Angkor Beer and tried to imagine Brother Number One copping a counter-revolutionary squat atop his

189.

bourgeois commode. This xenophobic despot had advocated the liquidation of anyone who spoke French, wore eyeglasses, or had technical training – let alone shat like a foreigner. That his Western-style porcelain throne might still be out there in the jungle was an irresistible notion; my Sihanoukville seafood dinner would have to wait. With the help of a Cambodian friend, Arn Chorn-Pond, I hired a driver desperate enough to subject his truck to the country's abusive rural roads. We left Siem Reap at dawn, with spare tyres and jerry cans of fuel piled in the truck bed; there would be no services ahead. After scattering a troop of macaque monkeys outside Angkor Wat, we bore northeast through paddy land that had been worked for more than a millennium.

The pavement ran out at Banteay Srei, a fairy-tale pink-sandstone temple nearly forty kilometres from Siem Reap. Our route skirted sacred mountains where Hindu deities had been carved into living river rock by ancient artisans, then soon devolved into a rutted trail through a thick forest teeming with butterflies. Arn remained pensive, staring out the truck's dusty windows at the dark wood. The bruising drive had conjured memories of his childhood, which I knew had been marred by hardship and horror. Raised by an aunt and unable to afford school, the boy had worked as a street vendor. When the Khmer Rouge seized power in 1975, he'd been consigned to a hard-labour brigade. The dawn-to-dusk work and starvation rations were a death sentence, so the clever youth volunteered to train as a musician. After five days of instruction, the guerrillas killed his master, then ordered Arn to play revolutionary anthems at public meetings and serenade evening gatherings for the leaders of Angka (the Organization). Arn also had more grisly duties: restraining prisoners while soldiers clubbed them to death inside a former Buddhist temple. The nightmare didn't end once the Vietnamese invaded Cambodia in late 1978. Arn was issued a carbine and sent to the front lines, part of a

cannon-fodder group of child-soldiers used by the Khmer
Rouge to draw enemy fire.

The fighting raged for months. Arn saw friends die. He held
alleged collaborators while other boys ran them through with
bayonets. Then he finally ran off, wandering through a forest
much like this, skirting skirmishes and avoiding mines while he
tracked monkeys in the canopy above, eating what they
dropped. Delirious with malaria, he eventually stumbled into a
squalid Thai refugee camp. There he had been adopted by an
American minister and taken to live on a New Hampshire farm.
He attended school for the first time and even graduated from
college; now his remarkable odyssey had brought him back to
Cambodia, to search for master musicians who had survived
the Khmer Rouge and could teach the classical repertoire to a
new generation of students.

Arn always knew he'd have to go home to confront his past.
Pol Pot's Anlong Veng seemed to be part of that journey.

'It's very hard to face your own ghosts,' he said. 'I want to try
to help rebuild Cambodia, but also rebuild my own life. There's
something missing there. I'm not sure if it's survivor's guilt…I
still have a lot of nightmares.'

The jungle gradually relented into a dry, open forest with
freshly cleared plots littered with blackened tree stumps. The
Khmer Rouge had remained operational here until 1998, and
Anlong Veng's district seat maintained an edgy, frontier feel.
Open-air barbershops, billiard halls and drink stalls lined the
main drag, which led to a dusty roundabout girdling a ludi-
crous monument that was decorated with concrete deer, cobras
and a very fat, white duck. Amputees lurched everywhere. The
most scenic spot in town was a bayou-like reservoir spiked
with drowned trees; it was built on orders of Ta Mok, the one-
legged Khmer Rouge military commander known as 'The
Butcher'.

'When I was a boy I heard his name all the time,' Arn said.

He'd fought west of here, in Beantey Meanchey province, as part of a strike-force of young boys that took its unit name – Trey Kanchoh – from a small fish that stunned its prey. Everyone else in Anlong Veng also seemed to have a Pol Pot pedigree – the district chief, a guesthouse owner, shopkeepers selling warm beer – but no-one wanted to discuss the past. A few months earlier, Angka's former Number Four, Ke Pauk, had died at his home here, peacefully and unpunished. Let bygones be bygones. Yet the gory history was palpable, visible. I saw it in the young, broken men. The skull-and-crossbones land mine signs. The silence and suspicion between strangers. Everyone here had been bloodied, or had blood on their hands. Nowhere else I've been – not East Timor, not Myanmar, not Uganda – ever felt as haunted, hellish, and unwhole to me as this bleak crossroads.

I was only too glad to leave Anlong Veng and head north for Kbal Ansoang, fourteen kilometres away in the Dangkrek Range, where the Khmer Rouge had imploded in a paroxysm of show trials and summary executions. In the foothills beyond a socialist-realist statue of a guerrilla carrying firewood, the road disintegrated into a steep, gullied track. We struggled to the ridgeline, just a few hundred metres from the Thai border, to find a Cambodian military checkpoint. We were allowed to pass only after hiring a local soldier for 'security'.

Min, the guard explained. It was a Khmer word I had heard a lot that day; it meant 'land mine'.

I paid the $5 and Jin Chal, a cherubic-looking thirty-five-year-old grunt, slid into the back seat between Arn and me. Jin wore camouflaged trousers, an olive-drab T-shirt, and the quiet fatalism of an army lifer. He'd been soldiering since he was ten years old; in this poor, violent place there was no dodging the draft.

'First I fight for Pol Pot,' he said in Khmer, while Arn translated. 'Now I fight for the government.'

A few days earlier, Jin had lost a friend from his outfit in the nearby forest. The man had gone out hunting, alone, and stepped on a mine. There was no-one to go for help, Jin related matter-of-factly, so his friend had bled to death.

'Life is always a risk,' Arn said.

After a few minutes' drive, we passed a charred field and Jin directed the driver to stop. We walked to a patchy clearing that held a squat, tin-roofed shelter covering a heap of grey-black ashes and bits of burned truck tyres. A clutch of half-empty plastic water bottles and a dirty glass holding fizzled joss sticks lay beneath one gable. A large, official-looking blue sign proclaimed, in both Khmer and English, 'Pol Pot Was Cremated Here'.

Pol Pot had died in his sleep, on 15 April 1998, during the Khmer Rouge's paranoid end-game. He was seventy-three years old. After allowing Thai forensic experts to take fingerprints and hair samples, his acolytes gave one of the twentieth century's greatest villains a low-rent Buddhist funeral atop a pile of rubbish. Bathed in wet heat and the wailing of a million cicadas, this utterly banal place was remarkable only for its very existence. What had kept enraged Cambodians from vandalising this site? What possessed people to leave offerings for this evil man's spirit? Respect or superstition? Fealty or fear?

'Now we go to Pol Pot's house,' Jin said.

We continued eastward along the ridge, crossing several rude log bridges. Soon, Arn and Jin were chatting like old schoolmates at a twenty-year reunion. The sun burned overhead, but big trees shaded the well-graded route as our driver accelerated. It was an oddly beautiful scene.

'I could have been here, like this guy,' said Arn, nodding at Jin, 'showing tourists around this place.'

There but for the grace of God, or karma, or just luck, I thought, just about the time the land mine appeared in the road. A sudden, collective silence filled the truck's cab as we passed over the ordnance. Then, nothing. We erupted in nervous, maniacal laughter.

'*Min?*' I asked, incredulous. Somehow the driver had straddled the explosive.

'*Min,*' Jin smiled sheepishly.

Shock swept like a cold wave through my guts. I might have to use that toilet if we ever made it alive to Pol Pot's villa. We passed Ta Mok's cinder-block house a few kilometres further, before the track ended at a clearing on the edge of a 300-metre precipice. Pol Pot had a beautiful setting from which to witness his movement's collapse – a nice brick dacha with rattan furniture, ceramic-tile floors, and a blue-porcelain shitter imported from Thailand. He would sit on his terrace, admire orchids blooming in coconut-shell planters, read *Paris-Match* magazine, or dote on his young daughter. Sometimes his secretary read him extracts from a Khmer-language edition of David Chandler's biography, *Brother Number One.*

The Khmer Rouge lords lived well compared to their dirt-poor subjects; some comrades were just more equal than others. By the mid-1990s, however, all but a handful of ardent followers had had enough deprivation. They surrendered, or deserted, and left the mountains to carve out a hard new life on the plains below. Meanwhile, in the echo chamber atop Kbal Ansoang, the Khmer Rouge devoured itself. Pol Pot accused his protégé of treason; the execution of Son Sen and fourteen family members was too much even for Ta Mok, who mutinied. Pol Pot was hauled before a kangaroo court and sentenced to life imprisonment. He died under house arrest just as government artillery came within range of this last bastion.

Aside from a graffiti-covered brick bunker, little remained of Pol Pot's villa. After his demise, the main residence had been almost totally scavenged for building materials. Only a few flourishes – the floor tiles and some shards of his famous toilet –

remained. Picking through the rubble, I found a sky-blue sliver of porcelain and slid it into my pocket.

Jin wandered to a nearby tree with sweet-smelling, lotus-like flowers, picked a handful of fruit, then offered some of the small, blood-coloured berries to me. They tasted like cherries.

'I planted the trees,' Jin said proudly. 'Pol Pot's orders. Are you hungry? Would you like to eat lunch?'

I didn't have much appetite, but we doubled back to a clearing near Ta Mok's old home. A Cambodian army officer appeared and bade us sit at a table beneath a recently erected thatched-roof pavilion at the edge of the escarpment. The restaurant, which had a million-dollar view of the Cambodian plains below, was decorated in Rustic Martial style, with orchids planted in rusting seventy-five-millimetre artillery casings. But now the fighting was finished and the major had plans – big plans – for this lonely place. Already, three or four visitors a week made it up the mountain; we were the first, and likely the last, guests this day. If the government only developed the park, more people would learn about the history of the Khmer Rouge, its leadership and their taste in expensive plumbing fixtures.

'It's an economy without smoke,' the major said brightly.

Except when those land mines exploded.

'I planted the bamboo, too,' said Jin, nodding towards a nearby decorative grove. 'Pol Pot's orders.'

I had to admit, the old monster had a fine eye for landscaping. Arn smiled, then strode purposefully towards the lush stand, where he quickly dug up several two-meter-tall sprays and loaded them into the truck's bed.

'Bamboo from hell,' he giggled.

Two days later, we replanted the infernal bamboo at Arn's small farm in southern Cambodia. This bit of Koh Kong province was far more pastoral than Anlong Veng: unmined and fertile, with a pond and orderly rows of pineapple bushes and

mango trees. Thunder rumbled in the nearby Elephant
Mountains, announcing the impending summer monsoon. For
Arn, the trip to the borderlands had been bittersweet, a
reminder of his own violent past – and a glimpse at the fate of
an old child-soldier who never made it to the refugee camps,
who stayed and fought, who went nowhere, yet who somehow
survived. Cambodia had a remarkable capacity for
perseverance.

'My soul feels less heavy,' my friend remarked.

I found I didn't feel anger as much as a profound sadness. A
thousand years ago this culture had been capable of
miraculous beauty, of monuments such as Angkor Wat, the
Bayon and Banteay Srei. But contemporary Khmer history was
a litany of ugliness and violence, a landscape of amputees, land
mines and pervasive corruption. Arn once told me that everyone
held both the Buddha and Pol Pot in his heart: the capacity for
loving kindness and, in some deep shadow, unblinking cruelty.
The despot was dead and gone, his ashes a shabby tourist
attraction, his old toilet broken and scattered. But his prized
bamboo would grow tall and strong on Arn's farm.

'It reminds me personally,' Arn said quietly as he patted
down dark earth around the root ball. 'I don't think anybody
else will notice it. But this bamboo is going to be beautiful to
look at.'

DEBAUCHED IN VALDAI

BY JEFFREY TAYLER

THROUGH THE FRIGID dark the wind blustered and the rain lashed down. My head lowered, I trudged across pavement carpeted with soggy sheathes of autumn leaves, my destination the restaurant Dar Valdaya, 'Gift of Valdai' – a shabby brick-and-glass behemoth visible through rippling curtains of fog as a row of sepia-lit picture windows glinting above the central square and its derelict shops, beyond the looming pink bulk of Trinity Cathedral. It was early December 2000, and in Valdai, a town of 20,000 deep in the birch and fir forests some 250 miles north of Moscow, there was nowhere else to go on a Friday night.

These were fabled forests and Valdai, a famous town, with a palace that had belonged to Empress Catherine the Great. During the tsarist centuries Valdai enjoyed acclaim as Gosudarevo Selo, the 'Sovereign's Village', for its popularity among royals enamoured of the surrounding region's sparkling lakes and piney breezes. After the Bolshevik revolution of 1917, Valdai deteriorated into a scattering of cabins and crumbling stucco hovels studded here and there with concrete Soviet monstrosities, but the countryside's reputation as an elite retreat never diminished. In its sylvan environs Stalin and

Brezhnev maintained dachas; Yeltsin loved to drink vodka; and President Putin relaxes, flying in from the Kremlin to his lakeside residence via helicopter, and passing so low that many Valdaians claim to have seen his face.

The woods around Valdai resemble the landscape of Russian fairy tales, but I had on my mind the for-adults-only words of Alexander Radishchev, the young Russian nobleman who, in 1796, penned the country's first revolutionary treatise-cum-travelogue, *A Journey from Saint Petersburg to Moscow*.

'Who does not know of the bread rolls and berouged maidens of Valdai?' he wrote. 'The brazen and shameless Valdai maidens stop every traveller passing through and attempt to ignite lust within him' – apparently by offering him bagel-like rolls sold with a kiss delivered through the hole in the middle. Such enticements, reproached Radischev, are designed 'to take advantage of his generosity at the expense of their chastity.' And should the traveller end up in one of Valdai's roadside bathhouses, the nobleman warned, he would suffer more maidens – and naked ones, at that – who would soap his limbs and, again, 'ignite within him the flame of lust…[so that] he would spend his night there, losing his money, health, and valuable travel time.' Though he doesn't say where, Radishchev admits that he himself lost 'valuable travel time' and picked up a *smradnaya bolezn* (stinking disease). He blamed it on Russian autocracy for allowing the spread of *rasputsvto mzdoimnoye,* or 'compensated debauchery'.

Inspired by the ideals of the Enlightenment, which Radishchev had imbibed during years of university study in Germany, *Journey* is a work of middling literary merit; its irreverent honesty, however, kindled the wrath of Catherine the Great. In its pages, in village after outback town, Radishchev, positioning himself as an advocate of Western-style Reform, Reason and Progress, fumes at Russian despotism and the morass of corruption it sheltered. The Empress had him exiled to Siberia for writing it. But, politics aside, I wondered: Could there have been any truth to his description of Valdai's 'maidens'? The bathhouses had long since vanished, but perhaps in the Dar Valdaya…

I hurried across the square and, opening a steel-and-glass door, climbed the steps up to the restaurant, a typically Soviet, cavernous and dusty, high-ceilinged hall with a chipped wooden dance floor and stage, and row after row of steel tables draped with tattered sheets. This was a shabby sight, to be sure, but after eight years in Russia, for me it meant dancing and drinking, meeting wan-eyed beautiful girls with creamy complexions and tragic, innate poise, and having soulful talks about love, loss, grief and fate. In Valdai, as in other hinterland towns, poverty was pervasive but generally bearable, and people did their best to dress as well as they could, approach life philosophically, and, at least one night a week, let off steam at a *p'yanka,* a traditional Russian booze-up.

I was almost the only patron, but most of the tables had been marked *zakazan* (reserved). Sure enough, within twenty minutes I was staring through the grimy windows at the drizzle-soaked square below, watching couples, raincoat hoods pulled tight over their heads, hurrying towards the restaurant door. The Dar Valdaya would be packed.

Most of those arriving turned out to be female. They left their fur hats and overcoats with the grumpy old lady at the checkroom and poured into the hall giggling and excited, ordering bottles of vodka, hors d'oeuvres of smoked meat and cheese, and entrées of pork and schnitzel. An hour or so later, the lights were low, the music blaring, and the dance floor crowded with young women who, depending on the song, either waltzed in loose embrace or bounced off each other in big band–style steps that gave them enormous pleasure and lots of sweaty contact. The few men present stood morosely at the bar, where they ordered carafes of vodka and plates of sausage.

I sipped my beer and wondered if I should take the very Russian step of picking up my beer and approaching the two young women sitting at the adjacent table to introduce myself, announcing, '*Devushki!* (Girls!) Mind if I join you?' This would in fact be more acceptable than asking straightaway for a dance. Then, also following Russian custom, I would offer to treat them to vodka and possibly their meals – in Russia, the man always pays. But as I was deliberating, one of the women turned to me, pulled out a chair and proffered the bottle of Posadskaya vodka that already stood between them.

'Please join us!' said Lida, who was short and dark, with flat Tatar cheeks and red pouty lips; her friend Ivetta was willowy and Slavic, her bouncy brown hair fashioned into a pageboy. Both were in their late twenties. Their pupils swam behind a thickening Posadskaya film.

201.

I got up and accepted gratefully, but said I'd stick to beer. Mixing beer and vodka makes for *yorsh*, or 'bristle brush' (one uses a *yorsh* to scrape clean the insides of bottles) – a state of violent, careening intoxication that I had experienced once and had no stomach for again.

'You, the man, will be drinking beer and we girls vodka?' answered Lida. 'Oh, that just isn't right, it's almost *indecent*. Please, drink vodka with us!'

I reconsidered. In Russia, it's an insult to refuse a drink, and generally people around one table share a bottle – and, consequently, levels of intoxication. Anyway, would just two beers and a shot of vodka give me a *yorsh*? Lida pushed the Posadskaya towards me (the man always serves) and I poured a round.

'*Za vstrechu!*' (To our meeting!) I said, raising my glass.

We downed the shots. Lida turned to me, shaking her head as the liquor sizzled down her throat. She asked if I was from Moscow. My being originally from the States drew puzzled smiles from both of them.

'You must be wondering where the men are, right?' she asked. 'Men're a dying breed here. They're drinking themselves to death all around us; they're no longer fit to be partners for women.'

By 'no longer fit' she was referring to the impotency brought on by alcoholism, which, as one Russian female friend of mine from a small town had told me, meant that 'our beautiful girls in the countryside are either going without sex or having sex with men who can't get it up enough to satisfy them.' Alcoholism is also largely responsible for the high male mortality rate that, in combination with a falling birth rate, may reduce Russia's population by a third in the next fifty years – a demographic calamity unparalleled in peacetime.

After deriding male drunkenness, Lida insisted on another toast. I poured us more shots, and she lifted her glass with an unsteady hand. 'To men, what few are left!'

We pounded back the booze. They told me their stories. Lida had two children but her husband had run off. Ivetta had no boyfriend but wanted one. Both hoped for family lives, companionship, a secure future. But there were few men in Valdai – time and again they repeated this. Now, at the evening's besotted peak, maybe one of four patrons in the restaurant was male.

Nevertheless, a man did stagger over. He was stout and drunk, and looked less than pleased to see me. Lida whispered, 'Uh-oh. That's a guy I used to go out with. He's a taxi driver. He's totally crazy!'

'Bug off!' she shouted, shoving him away. Staggering, he digested her words, gave me a menacing look, nodded and lurched back to the bar.

Half an hour and three shots later, we were all on the dance floor, I with Ivetta, Lida with the nutty driver. The men at the bar were slowly and deliberately counting out their roubles for more booze; women were embracing all around us, dancing slow and talking. No-one was sober but no-one was ashamed. At a Russian fête sobriety is considered an insult to one's friends. *Sobornost*, or 'collectivism', has the same proud ring in Russian as 'individualism' does in the West. Moreover, in Soviet times abstainers were regarded with suspicion, as potential informants eager to keep their heads clear for tomorrow's denunciation of the seditious utterings of tongues loosened by alcohol. The upshot is this: if one member of a group drinks, so do the others. That this contributes to a societal calamity goes unnoticed amid the revelry.

I don't recall when the *yorsh* began scrubbing through my ganglia, but scrub it did. After that dance, my memories dissolve into hazy snippets of toasts, pained confessions, professions of friendship and offers of hospitality.

The next morning I awoke woozy in my hotel room bed – alone – with no idea how I got there, but (as I quickly moved to check) with all my money and documents. No-one had approached me offering 'compensated debauchery' – that much I remembered. (In such a small town, I later learned, the risks of spoiling one's reputation would be too great.) Radishchev's words no longer held.

It was nine o'clock, raining and still dark outside. I sat up. My head spun, and I fell back and closed my eyes.

o o o o o o o o o

In the fall of 2005 I again found myself in Valdai, footloose on yet another wet Friday night. I had just reread Radishchev's *Journey*. I still shared his outrage over the succession of cruelties and humiliations that often pass for life in Russia. The country daily batters its residents with iniquities and injustices that most Russians endure fatalistically or try to ignore, but that I, as a Westerner, bristled at, as had Radishchev. I agreed with him that 'man's misfortunes result from his not looking squarely at the objects surrounding him' – an act accomplished better sober than not (and he was surely sober, for he proudly professed a distaste for vodka).

But now, having spent five more years in Moscow, I found Radishchev most of all a very non-Russian teetotalling prude who put naive faith in Reason and Progress as mankind's saviours. I felt I had good reason for changing my opinion: after all, since my first visit to Valdai, the West's exemplary Enlightenment state, the United States, had invaded Iraq and demonstrated to the world that neither Reason nor Progress prevail for long, even in a so-called democracy. Moreover, my wife and I had suffered several untimely deaths in our families. Our mortality was catching up to us. Would a sober assessment of the pain and annihilation to come help?

Baudelaire wrote, *'Pour ne pas sentir l'horrible fardeau du Temps qui brise vos épaules et vous penche vers la terre, il faut vous enivrer sans trêve. Mais de quoi? De vin, de poésie, ou de vertu, à votre guise. Mais enivrez-vous.'* (So as not to feel the terrible burden of Time that breaks your shoulders and bends you toward the earth, you must get drunk without respite. But drunk on what? On wine, on poetry, or on virtue, as you like. But get drunk.) He was right, and Radishchev, in his rational abstemiousness, wrong. The Russian *p'yanka,* I now saw, served to draw people together for commiseration, flights of sensual fancy and shared catharsis – about the only consolations one could count on before, possibly without warning, the heart stopped, the breath caught and the world went black.

So, tossing aside my Radishchev, I slipped through the entrance of the Hotel Valdai and out into the drizzling gloom, and made my way towards the restaurant along aspen-embowered lanes marked with puddles glinting like liquid amber from streetlights above. Windblown plastic brown empties of Tolstyak (Fat Man) beer bounced down the hilly sidewalks, keeping me company; from unseen quarters echoed the throaty cries of carousing youths, the playful shrieks of drunken girls. At the Dar Valdaya I found (not surprisingly) neither Lida nor Ivetta – nor practically anyone else. Since my first visit, the bartender told me, two new clubs had opened in town. The *krutyye* – the 'cool crowd' – now favoured the Café Uyezdnoye. So I went there.

The Uyezdnoye was a rustic boxcar of a building with ten or twelve rickety tables, all but three occupied by female partiers. As I surveyed the scene, cannonades of rain began rattling off the roof, but a disco ball spun a confetti of cheerful light over the dance floor.

At the bar I ordered a glass of wine. I paid, and a pallid female hand grabbed my arm.

'Please, join us!'

I turned to see Sonia, a young waitress who had served me at a restaurant earlier that day. She invited me to drink with her girlfriends, a barmaid and a cook who worked with her, who also recognised me. They were opening their third bottle of Moldovan red, but were sober compared to the burly threesomes of men, dressed in tracksuits and shaven-skulled, who were already lost to the *yorsh* and lolling groggy-headed behind nearby tables.

We took our seats. Sonia's lank brown curls fell astride a cheery moonface set with perky hazel eyes. She raised her wine for a toast *(Za vstrechu!)*, as did Masha, plumper and even paler, and Lena, whose mane of russet hair framed luminous green eyes and a red-lipped smile. Soon we clinked glasses and drank again, this time to Valdai, which they loved and said they would never leave.

'Oh, I adore this song!' said Sonia, jumping up with her girlfriends and pulling me onto the dance floor, where *yorsh*-mad thugs now lurched at lithe women who evaded their wobbly-footed advances. Lena and Masha slipped between

205.

grasping paws, admonishing their pursuers with curt cries of *'Ruki!'* (Watch your hands!). The thugs complied: men in Russia are used to obeying women, who, be they mothers, wives, guards or cashiers, tend to dominate everyday life.

The Soviet decades had famously dulled the blades of the sword side.

On the wall above the bar a plasma screen flickered music videos from Russian MTV: *popsa* – Russian pop – vignettes of sleek tanned bodies on tropical beaches, of Gangsta youths rapping in Moscow garages, of American superstars whose yearly income probably exceeded Valdai's GDP by a factor of five. As the wine soaked through our brains, our eyes returned to the screen seeking colour and light and joy in videos that, in warmer, more prosperous climes, I might have found a distraction. Well before midnight, as the rain pounded down outside and the fog gathered, the Uyezdnoye was resounding with squeals and laughter and sing-alongs and the clinking of glasses and the shouting of toasts.

Finally, the songs slowed. Tired, we slipped back to the table and sat down. Something darkened Lena's eyes.

'Is everything OK?' I asked.

No. She told me she had lost her parents in an accident and was married to a man whom, it turned out now, she didn't love. Masha teared up too, and said that her mother had recently died of cancer; the disease had come on swiftly, and caught the family unawares. Sonia dropped her gaze to her hands and her eyes watered. I hadn't the heart to ask her who in her family had passed away. (In Russia men who might be her father's age – in their early forties – begin dying of heart attacks brought on by cigarettes and alcohol.) My own mother had died suddenly eight months earlier, cutting my life into 'before' and 'after' halves, and leaving me with a pain I could not – and still cannot – imagine will ever vanish. But her death did one good thing for me: it made the grief of others as real as my own, or almost.

In the spangled gloom, we raised our glasses and toasted – silently this time, without clinking – to our lost relatives. So far north, this late October day had been short, ending around 3.30 in the afternoon; the cold and dark outside weighed on our moods; the rain lashing the windows besieged the café. We craved relief, and some measure, however small, of drink and debauchery offered it. There was no way to reason our way to 'closure', nothing any of us could say to ease the pain.

Pardoned in 1801, but unbalanced by years of exile, Radishchev returned to St Petersburg and put an end to his life. The revolutionary movement his *Journey* helped spark would culminate in the 1917 revolution that ushered in seven decades of bloodshed, terror and dispossession – a tyranny far worse than that of the tsars. But now that the Soviet Union is no more, the problems most Russians live with are, by and large, the fears and traumas that afflict most people, everywhere.

We grieve, but who among us will escape alive what Thomas Carlyle called this 'little gleam of Time between two eternities'? Whatever our country, we're all goners. The only paradise we're ever likely to know is the one offered by our senses, in the here and now, and the key to that paradise is élan and daring, love and madness, song and drink!

The song changed to 'Chornyye Glaza', a fast-paced *popsa* tune, and our eyes lit up.

'Let's dance!' I said.

We drank our wine to the dregs, and jumped up to join the revellers.

STRANGER IN PARADISE
BY ALEX SHESHUNOFF

TEN DAYS SPENT on a freighter not so much threatened by
rust as held together by it convinced me it was time to pick an
island, any island. So I picked Pig. Part travel agent calendar
and part *Far Side* cartoon, the island of Pig was a destination
so familiar I wondered why I had bothered coming at all. Short,
stunted palm trees grew on Pig's windward tip, their trunks
permanently bent backward by the constant breeze. Fluffy
thunderheads marched across the horizon.

As the dark blue of the open ocean turned to the turquoise
clarity of the shallows, I asked myself perhaps sincerely for the
first time in my life, 'Why am I here?' It is easy to say in New
York City that you want to move to a thirty-acre island located
4480 miles southwest of Hawaii, but I was about to actually do
it. Was it the isolation that I sought? The dispossession? The
loneliness? I realised I was equally pulled by the idyllic sway of
island life ahead and pushed from behind by the aggregate of
my years in New York. I hoped to reduce the number of vari-
ables in my life and see which were making the largest
contribution towards my happiness, take away friends and
electricity and see which one I missed more…that kind of
thing.

As at the Polynesian Pavilion at Epcot Center, the men's house on Pig was set back from the beach in a dense grove of palm trees. It was made of thatch and peaked in a ridge that ran its length, about three fishing boats long, while the bottom was open to the elements. I hunched under the thatch roof to enter. The open-air interior was classic Skipper's Fish House: shark fins, tangled nets and Japanese glass fishing buoys dangled from every joist.

Twenty-five men and a dozen children sat on the woven-mat floor, forming a loose ring around a central clutch of plump chiefs lying on their sides or their elbows. Though hardly hot enough to need it, one of the chiefs waved a small, hand-woven fan. Another rolled on to his stomach, the palm of his foot facing skyward, occasionally twitching at a passing fly.

Except for their digital watches, pink flowers in their hair, and wispy loin cloths known as *thu*, everyone was naked. The men's skin, slightly fairer than that of the women, was a dark bronze. And there was a lot of it – the men's bellies and boobs were slowly colliding like tectonic plates, the former oozing into some dark subduction zone as the latter gradually formed a new layer over the top. I couldn't help but feel self-conscious in my own clumsily tied *thu* revealing its own vast swaths of pasty skin .

'Hello, my name is Paul,' one of the chiefs said, holding out large fleshy fingers. 'Welcome to Pig.'

'Good to be here, Paul,' I said, weaving my way through.

'Welcome,' he said again, rising awkwardly with a tangle of children clinging to his arms, neck and legs. He was six feet tall with a broad, flat nose, greying hair and a beard no longer than a pencil eraser. His short hair and short beard gave him one of those faces that would look the same if turned upside-down.

'Are you Eric? We heard you were coming.' He smiled, forcing his cheeks upward and his eyelids into narrow slits, momentarily hiding his small but alert brown eyes.

'Umm, it's Alex. Yes, I was coming. I mean, I am coming. I'm here.' He tilted his head to the side and gave me a look of concern. Not knowing what to do, I just smiled. He smiled back. Then the whole room smiled back. Silence. What now?

Gifts. I took four packs of Lucky Strikes I had been carrying in a clear plastic bag and handed them to Chief Paul. 'I brought you these.'

He looked in his hands without speaking. All stared. Perhaps I was making a frightful mistake, not just in timing but in kind? I realised I wasn't sure where cigarettes fell in that confusing continuum of things the people of Pig wanted and didn't want – gasoline engines were OK, but not T-shirts; electricity but not air-conditioning; fishing hooks, but not fishing reels.

Chief Paul's eyes moved down towards his hands and then up at me. 'Wonderful!' he said. 'We ran out of cigarettes six months ago.' He distributed the cigarettes to the adults in the room and said, 'We haven't seen Lucky Strikes since the American GI's brought them in the war.'

I walked down to the beach. A swarm of about two dozen children were gathering in a tightening circle around me. 'What are we going to do with him now?' their eyes seemed to be plotting. Apparently they sensed my fear because as I turned my back to walk towards the men's house, a coconut whizzed past my head. 'This is it,' I thought. 'They are going to break my spectacles and turn me into taro soup like Piggy in *Lord of the Flies*. Best case, my head will end up on a stake to warn others.'

I spun around. Several were laughing. I had no choice but to throw a coconut back at the smallest of them. Only harder and with better aim. That's just a joke. Instead I did all that anyone would do under such trying circumstances: introduce the dizzy-bat game with palm fronds.

It was a hit and we played for a few hours before someone told me it was time for dinner. I ate some leftover fish and went to sleep in an empty thatch hut. The following morning Chief

Paul greeted me with a question that had been nagging him. 'We heard that communism ended,' he said as I walked into the men's house. 'Is that something the Americans did?'

'Good morning,' I said. The chiefs, anxious for an answer, just nodded. 'Well,' I began, 'the Americans would like to think it is something that they did, but communism probably ended communism.' I sat down on a piece of matting and said, 'With no incentive to work, people just rely on others.'

'Here everyone contributes,' Chief Paul said. He looked skyward and clapped his hands three times. Within a minute most of the island – maybe a hundred people – had scampered to the men's house. 'Today will be a community day,' he announced broadly. 'We will clean the church.'

Chief Paul turned towards me with a grin: though a big fish in perhaps the world's smallest pond, it was good to be chief. And it seemed like a pleasant pond as well. As I dusted the louvres on the windows, I noticed this sign:

DANCE! – NEXT FRIDAY
We will be having a dance: you can do the church dance
or any dance that will make people laugh.

Soon life settled into a little groove – over the next few weeks I learned how to spear fish, make fish traps and herd reef fish into nets. One afternoon an older chief named Vincent pulled me aside. 'Do you have any news magazines?' he said in a hushed tone. 'You know, like *Time* or *Business Week*?'

I told him I didn't but a few steps later I remembered I did have an old *Newsweek*. I paused while I weighed whether or not to give it to him. This was really straight out of *The Gods Must Be Crazy:* I potentially could be contributing to the slow erosion of one of the least visited cultures left on earth. But on the way to my hut I realised I was being arrogant. It was not my choice to make. If they were going to preserve their culture, it was going to be an active decision on their part, not an accident of ignorance or geography. Anyway global warming and rising seas would destroy their culture long before any magazine would. I gave Vincent the *Newsweek*. He nodded thanks and stood under a nearby coconut palm to read it.

A few minutes later a crowd of perhaps thirty had encircled Vincent. I shuffled over and stood on tiptoes to see the object of their awe. It was not the Chinese rattling the Taiwanese. It wasn't celebrity gossip. It was an advertisement for a Chevy Tahoe, a two-page spread featuring a sparkling, silver SUV on top of a snow-capped mountain. They gawked at the magazine and I gawked at them gawking. Between the sport utility vehicle, the snow and the jagged peaks, it was hard to imagine anything more foreign to the people of Pig. Nor anything more foreign to me than their wonder.

o o o o o o o o

The day before the boat was to return, all the men gathered in their house.

'Chief Paul, how you are feeling?' I asked.

'Alone,' he said, staring at the ground. If there is one thing you don't feel on a thirty-acre island with a hundred people, it's alone. He smiled so broadly his eyes closed.

Except for us talking, the place was silent. All just gazed out to sea, picked their nails or flicked away flies. I jimmied a board against a post and leaned against it. Despite my insect bites, coral-scraped legs and a mysterious rash developing on my left arm, I felt I could have been in heaven. Chief Paul nudged my shoulder and whispered, 'Eric, forget the boat. Why don't you stay on our island? You can live with my family. Meet my daughters.'

'Oh, it's Alex.'

'Pig is very beautiful. You will like it here.'

'Chief Paul, I don't know. I do like it here but…' I must have grimaced. 'Can I tell you tomorrow, before the boat comes?' Though charmed by the invitation to live on Pig, I was immediately disappointed with myself. When faced with the real thing – move to a small island in the Pacific as the guest of a chief with a reasonable chance of marrying his daughter and spending the rest of my days watching giggling grandchildren play in the surf – I had hesitated. And decisions that big shouldn't involve hesitation.

'While you think about it,' he said, 'why don't we check the fish traps?'

We waddled to the beach and climbed into a dugout canoe, and kneeling, started to paddle. Hand-hewn, elegant and smooth, it sliced through the placid lagoon. The temperature was about seventy-five degrees Fahrenheit, and the sun, having just broken through the clouds, was shining on our backs. The only sounds were the distant crashing of waves and the nearby dribbling of water off our wooden paddles.

In theory this was the Delta Dream Vacation–brochure life I had imagined. But did I really want to live the rest of my life here? I thought about the outer island Peace Corps volunteer who, I'd been told when first starting to plan this escape, had jumped out of a palm tree so that he would break his legs and have to be evacuated home. What did he know that I didn't? How long would it actually be before I succumbed to sunstroke, boredom or a health care system that sent people to church rather than a hospital?

As Chief Paul slid overboard to check the traps, I felt like a wimp for not wanting to end my days among the people of Pig. Wouldn't Tony Robbins toss a fist in the air and say, 'Just do it!'? Probably, but for seventeen days, I hadn't sat in a chair. That, I realised, was what I missed most: chairs.

People in the outer islands of Yap squat. They squat on their heels. They squat on coconut shells. But they never sit in a chair. It's not that they don't have the money for chairs or the skill to make them, they just don't think about wanting them. I had sat on many chairs in my life and could imagine sitting on them in the future – nothing like seventeen days spent squatting on a coconut to make one not want to spend an eighteenth.

o o o o o o o o o

'We're going to watch the video,' Chief Paul said when we got back to shore.

'There's only one?'

'You'll love it,' he said. I later learned that the French foreign ministry had donated fifty solar panels to Pig about a year earlier to help 'reduce greenhouse emissions.' But no-one had bothered to tell the people of Pig that the panels were on the way.

'Ah,' I imagined a chief saying, 'someone sent us a gift. Wonder what it is?'

'And look!' someone else had said. 'There's a card!'

Figuring that electricity is useless without television, the American government had donated a television and VCR. The result was a real-life slumber party stumper: if you lived on a remote Pacific island and could have just one video, which one would it be? Turns out, the folks on Pig had the answer: *Gas-Attack Training Made Simple*.

Though grainy and low-budget, this cinematic gem made by the US army featured men in fatigues running into a cinder-block building filled with some sort of smoky-looking gas. The camera follows them inside where we watch each soldier cough, put on a gas mask and run out again. For twenty long, long minutes, soldier after soldier runs into the building, coughs, puts on a gas mask, and runs out again while a deep and stern narrator intones:

> *The poison gas is uncomfortable.*
> *Duty. Honour. Country.*

The entire island was in attendance. All were riveted. 'Chief Paul, where did you get this creepy video?'

'It's from my son. He's in the army. Stationed in Texas,' he said without removing his eyes from the screen. 'Isn't it great?'

'Yes, yes, it is,' I said. I stumbled through a question to Chief Paul about the cultural future of Pig.

'We must work hard,' he said without turning away from the television, 'to balance the old ways with the new ways. Young people who don't like the old ways can leave. As long as we have enough people to sustain our population we will be OK.'

I then did the only humane thing I could and asked for his address so that others might forward a few videos. He swears this address will actually work:

Chief Paul

Pig Island

Yap, FSM

'And you're sure people should send videos?' I asked.

> *The poison gas is uncomfortable.*
> *Duty. Honour. Country.*

'Yes, Alex,' he said. 'I think that would be a good thing.'

THE LIVING MUSEUM OF NOWHERE & EVERYWHERE

BY ROLF POTTS

HAVING JUST JOURNEYED to the remote corners of Asia as part of a life-altering two-year sojourn, I'll admit I wasn't expecting much when I returned to the United States and joined my sister on a weekend antique-shopping excursion to Minneapolis, Kansas.

Kristin, a city girl who'd recently moved with her husband and young sons to a farm in a neighbouring county, sensed my lagging interest as we strolled the main drag of the small prairie town. 'If you're not into shopping,' she suggested, 'there's a little museum here you might want to check out.'

I considered her suggestion, my mind wandering back to Asia. One month before, in Myanmar, I'd bought a $40 bicycle with the goal of pedalling into the middle of nowhere. I'd hoped to find an experience as far from the tourist trail as that rickety one-speed bike could take me, and I felt I'd succeeded admirably. Rolling over dusty Burmese roads for three weeks, I'd feasted on two-cent mangoes, explored obscure caves, slept in out-of-the-way Buddhist monasteries, dodged secret police informants and met plenty of warm and fascinating people.

Now that I was in Kansas visiting family, however – strolling around a town where I didn't look much different from the locals – I felt somehow more isolated than in any place I'd discovered in the hinterland of Myanmar. Admittedly, the town of Minneapolis (not to be confused with the major city in Minnesota) wasn't Timbuktu; it was a pleasant community of 2000 people, not far from a major interstate highway, and home to a small newspaper, a grain elevator, a car dealership, a Pizza Hut, a couple of banks, a bar and (thanks to its aging population) a handful of antique stores.

Still, in terms of international travel, Minneapolis, Kansas, was nowhere – a geographical nonentity, neither exotic nor familiar enough to tickle a wanderer's imagination. It was, I'd presumed, just another nondescript Great Plains community, one of many that had been slowly dwindling in size for half a century, each year losing a few more of its young people to places like Wichita and Denver and Kansas City. The few outsiders who strayed into this part of the United States came wearing smirks, looking for Middle American kitsch – record-setting balls of twine, Elvis impersonators, deranged religious zealots – but Minneapolis hosted no such oddities. Indeed, on paper, this part of Kansas was off-the-beaten-path in the least appealing sense of the word; I'd met plenty of fellow travellers who'd be happy to get lost on the nameless backroads of Myanmar, but none who viewed this flat, grassy stretch of America as anything more than flyover country.

Thus, faced with an afternoon of antiques and post-Asia ennui, I decided to try to prove my assumptions wrong about Minneapolis, Kansas. Even if it didn't promise the sublime wonders of backcountry Myanmar, I reasoned I could at least find something distinctive and telling about the place.

'I'm not in the mood for a museum,' I told Kristin. 'I think I'll just go get some coffee.'

In truth, I was never much in the mood for museums, anywhere. Having lived in Asia and Europe, I'd come to regard museums as soulless cultural trophy cases, devoid of charm or

217.

surprise or epiphany. For me, an afternoon spent eyeing pretty girls in the Jardin des Tuileries was far more rewarding than squinting at baroque maidens in the Louvre, and I'd found that people-watching in the foodstalls off Bangkok's Sukhumvit Road was more culturally revealing than anything in the palatial galleries of Thailand's National Museum. Even Cairo's Egyptian Museum, in all its cluttered, mouldering frumpiness, wasn't half as charming as an evening of playing backgammon and smoking apple tobacco in a noisy Arab café a few blocks away.

Hence, I was confident that thirty minutes in a local coffee joint would show me more of small-town Kansas than an entire afternoon in the local museum.

When I arrived at the café, I noticed a thin, elderly man easing his way out of a white sedan parked out front. I knew I had to introduce myself the instant I saw the vanity tag on his front bumper. It read: World War II Veteran: China * Burma * India.

'I couldn't help but notice your bumper tag,' I said to him. 'How long has it been since you were in Burma?'

The old fellow cocked an eyebrow. 'Since never,' he said. 'I served in India. On an airfield near Calcutta.'

'How was it?'

'If you're looking for war stories, you're outta luck,' he said. 'I was never in combat.'

'That's OK. I'm just curious to know what you thought of Asia.'

The man thought for a moment, absently scratching under the brim of his ball cap ('D&M Body Shop', the cap read, 'You Bend 'Em, We'll Mend 'Em'). 'What I remember most about India was how poor it was,' he said finally. 'You had to be careful when you took your shower, because kids from the town would sneak up and steal your soap. Even the officers in the Indian army didn't have much money. One time I gave an Indian commander a pack of cigarettes and he made his whole company bow down and worship me.' He chuckled at the memory.

'Didn't that make you feel uncomfortable?'

'Oh, not really. I was too busy taking their photo. Wish I knew what happened to that one. Got some nice shots in Egypt, too, but they all got lost over the years.'

'When did you go to Egypt?'

'About the same time. Egypt was full of military, and the Ay-rabs knew we had money. Ask some fella on the street corner where the pyramids were, and pretty soon there were two dozen Egyptians fighting over who was gonna be your tour guide. I ended up hiring a couple fellas for next to nothing; they put me up on a camel, and took me all over Giza. When it was all done, they chopped off a chunk of the Great Pyramid of Cheops and gave it to me as a souvenir.'

'Wow. I was in Egypt a couple years ago, and they kept a tight rein on that kind of thing.'

The old war veteran sized me up. 'You know, if you're interested in international stuff, you should see our museum. They've got a little bit of everything in there.'

'I'm not too keen on museums,' I said. 'Your little chunk of pyramid would be far more interesting to me than anything I'd find in a museum.'

'Well then it looks like we've got a problem,' he said. 'Because that little chunk of pyramid is sitting in the museum right now.'

Trumped, I followed the man down a side street. He told me his name was Kirk Ottland, and that he'd graduated from high school in Minneapolis back in 1931. 'My family lived way out in the country,' he said. 'In the winter I lived in a boarding house so I wouldn't have to walk all that way in bad weather.'

From the outside, the Ottawa County Museum looked like a glorified machine-shed – modern and functional, like something you might see in an industrial park. Inside, the museum was more like a carefully ordered attic, with narrow rows of period clothing, tools, army uniforms, sports trophies, souvenir plates, dolls, fossils, war medals, books, framed letters and railroad equipment twisting maze-like from wall to wall under fluorescent lights. A vintage fire engine shared space with mammoth tusks and a collection of walking canes.

Kirk took me to a glassed-in display case, where his white-tan chunk of the Great Pyramid sat alongside arrowheads, fossilised leaves and small meteorites. 'Kind of hard to look at that little rock and imagine the rest of the pyramid,' he said. 'It's a little like showing you a mountain oyster and asking you to imagine the bull, I guess.' He paused for a chuckle. 'But that's where it came from.'

Scanning the room, I noticed that the back corner of the museum was dedicated to George Washington Carver, the famed African American botanist. 'Did Carver live in Kansas?' I asked Kirk.

'For a while,' he replied, 'when he was a teenager.' Kirk took me back to the Carver exhibit and showed me pictures and letters from the late nineteenth century, when the great science prodigy was a star student at Minneapolis High School. A wall display showed how, while at the Tuskegee Institute in Alabama, Carver had processed peanuts into instant coffee, margarine, mock oysters, rubbing oil, laxatives, shampoo, shaving cream, gasoline, plastics, glue, insecticide, and perhaps most famously, peanut butter.

'Not many black families left in Minneapolis these days,' Kirk told me. 'But I went to high school with some black kids.'

'Was there much racism back then?'

'Oh, I'd reckon there was. We had a kid on the football team, by the name of Cooper. A good kid and a great athlete, but he always had to drink last from the water bottle. We didn't even think that was strange at the time; that's just the way it was.'

Kirk and I moved on to a display of fossils. A sign over a set of sturdy dinosaur bones read 'Silvisaurus Condrayi'.

'Apart from the George Washington Carver stuff, I'd reckon those dinosaur bones are the most popular display here,' he said. 'I'll go get Jettie Condray, and he can tell you more about them.'

'Who's Jettie Condray?' I asked.

'He's the curator. And it was his daddy who found those dinosaur bones.'

Kirk ambled off to the museum office and came back with a powerfully built, kind-faced man who sported a greying flat-top haircut. Jettie Condray looked more like a farmer than a museum curator – and it turned out he'd been both. 'I've been a teacher, too,' Jettie said. 'But I've been interested in museums ever since my dad found that dinosaur out on our land.'

'How'd that happen?'

'Well, he was just riding his horse across the property, and he saw some white material sticking out of a ravine. Turned out to be the skeleton of a twelve-foot armoured dinosaur that had never been identified by science.'

'What did he do with it?'

'He called some officials from the University of Kansas, who came and dug it up and took it to the museum in Lawrence. Our display is just a plaster cast of the original bones, but they named the dinosaur after my dad. It shows up from time to time in dinosaur encyclopaedias and kids books. It's not as well known as the more popular dinosaurs, like the T-Rex or the triceratops, but we're proud to have found it.'

By this point, any resistance I had to the museum had vanished. I asked Jettie if he could show me around the exhibits; he took a laser pointer from his pocket and went to work, speaking with pride and enthusiasm about every display in the room. In addition to the Carver exhibit and the Silvisaurus Condrayi bones, the marquee museum exhibits included a set of letters written to Abraham Lincoln by Ottawa County resident Grace Bedell Billings (who, at age eleven, reputedly convinced Lincoln to grow a beard), and a restored 1917 Fordson tractor that had once appeared in a 1984 issue of *National Geographic*.

Compared to the Louvre or the Smithsonian or the Hermitage, of course, the Ottawa County Museum was just a shed full of provincial miscellany. But unlike in any of those world-famous galleries, it was easy to feel the human energy behind the displays in the little museum, and – on occasion – to meet the people whose lives were transformed by those objects. The regal, well-endowed international museums that had disappointed me in the past were the stuff of erudition and empire; this place was a haven of connection and continuity – a window through which a small town looked out at the world, and by which the world was brought home and held up for display by the people who lived there. Minneapolis, Kansas, may have been 'nowhere', in a certain sense, but this building, in its own, humble way, was a living museum of everywhere.

Later, when I met up with my sister, she was somewhat apologetic about keeping me waiting. 'This place isn't exactly Myanmar, is it?' she said.

I thought back to Myanmar, and the pride I'd felt in straying off the beaten path there. Somehow, the thrill of that journey contained a hint of narcissism – an egoistic desire to see myself, vivid and unique, in the reflection of a land so unlike my own. Minneapolis, Kansas, offered no such temptation; it had only offered itself, in all its understated and charming reality.

'You're right,' I told her. 'Myanmar it's not.'

A VISIT TO KANASANKATAN
BY JASON ELLIOT

AT THE END of a long journey in the Middle East, I received a message from an English friend I hadn't seen for years. Would I like to visit him on my way back home? He was now living, as he put it, at the point where the Arab and African worlds meet, and promised it would be worth the detour. 'Come to Kanasankatan,' he said. 'It's not at all what you would expect.'

A follow-up phone call piqued my curiosity. The capital was said to have originated as a remote outpost of the Roman Empire, and its terrible climate had made it the least favourite of its imperial occupiers. Centuries ago, its seafaring natives had achieved notoriety for their pugnacity, greed and nautical prowess. By the sound of it, things hadn't changed all that much: in the area where my friend lived, the only form of law had, until very recently, been enforced by rival gangs. Even the police hadn't dared to appear there until a few years ago; this was said to be a particular source of local pride.

I agreed to visit, knowing it would be my last glimpse of the East for a good while. Diverting my journey home, I called on arrival at the airport. A combination of train and bus would bring me to the right part of the city, explained my friend. But his directions were disconcertingly vague. 'Just ask for the

"Tower of Terror",' he quipped, explaining that, at thirty stories, the apartment block where he lived was nothing short of a national landmark. 'Used to be the most popular place for suicides. Murders too. Try to get here before dark, and use your Arabic if you need to.'

It was the end of summer; people looked weary and sapped by the heat. In the late afternoon, a Somali bus driver with a terrifying disregard for pedestrian life dropped me at a crossroads in the capital. A trio of veiled women, each cradling a sleeping infant, descended with me, speaking a language I had never before heard. I followed a street named after a thousand-year-old saint, and asked directions from passersby. Two men spoke no English; a third was a deaf-mute, and didn't speak at all. On a cobbled side-street lined with stunted acacia, the air shook with the noise of a pneumatic drill. A truck was being loaded with bits of road, and a hopelessly inefficient team of workmen were excavating broken pipes in water-filled craters. I felt a pang of pity for the residents, and marvelled at the natives' indifference to dust and noise.

Further on, I could hear the cackle of seagulls from over-head. There was the smell of rotting fish, and a street sign which, translated, read 'Port of Beauty'. To the north, a long, straight road ran towards railway tracks and a filthy canal. Century-old brick buildings rose on either side, their neglected window-frames and lintels all slightly askew. The shops beneath them bore signs in quaintly misspelled English, or in Arabic letters that I could just decipher as I walked along: Thobani Chemist, Halal butcher, Ka-na-san-ka-tan Mosque. All the smells of the East seemed to be represented there: turmeric-laden vapours from ill-lit kitchens, the oily smoke of grilling kebabs, the occasional whiff of marijuana and, from a tiny stall where a turbaned man was selling Korans, rose-scented incense. The entire street was lined with stalls selling secondhand clothes and used furniture, broken radios,

225.

fifty-pound sacks of rice, and pyramids of fruits and vegetables that I couldn't identify.

I wondered what I might learn about a nation from a single street? It was always hard to know. I felt the gaze of watchful men who looked as though they spent the entire day puffing silently at their water-pipes. I wondered if I could detect hostility in their eyes; perhaps it was no more than weary indifference at the sight of an outsider. I felt pale and con-spicuous. Arabic, several African languages, and Portuguese were being spoken all around me. There were dark-skinned men in striped cloaks and slippers, and women in gowns and veils of various kinds. One woman's veil – an ancestral memory, perhaps, of the days when the Arabs had fought their way across the untamed portions of Africa – was hemmed in imi-tation leopard-skin. Another, but for the dark eyes behind an opening like an arrow-slit, concealed all. Crouched in anony-mous doorways, beggars and the dispossessed muttered pleas for loose change.

For a private challenge, I decided to buy a joint of meat and present it to my friend. The butcher was a big, bearded man with a crater-like scar in the centre of his forehead. I explained I wanted lamb. He disappeared and returned with a split-open carcass over his shoulder, sharpening his knife as I pointed to the leg.

He asked what country I was from, and whether I were a Muslim. 'You would make a good Muslim,' he chuckled, as he cut into the meat.

What was life like here? I asked. He shook his head gently and, between sighs, recounted the ills of the nation. Its leader was deeply unpopular but refused to relinquish power; worse, there was no-one fit to replace him. His compatriots were dying in an unpopular war financed by international criminals; the economy was out of control; and not long ago, suicide bombs had killed a score of people in the capital.

Handing over a fraction of what I would have paid in central London, I thanked him and left, suddenly remembering the colloquial expression of appreciation.

'*Che zmayt!*'

'*Che zmayt!*' he beamed back.

Further along, a couple of teenage boys were standing beside the entrance to a mosque.

'*As-salaamu aleikum.*'

'*Wa aleikum salaam.*'

Wanting directions, I asked the elder boy if he spoke Arabic.

'*Akurs afakindo.*' This was an affirmation, in the local dialect. I asked if he knew the whereabouts of the 'Tower of Terror'.

'*Yakan faki n'missit kanya,*' he said, waving an arm in the direction of the ancient iron railway bridge. He was right: beyond the tracks, unmistakably, rose the tower. It was a brutal-looking rectangle of brown concrete, peaked with a sheaf of bristling antennae. In scale it had the starkness of a Cold War military headquarters. A desultory geometry of washing lines, strung up and down its balconies, gave it a look of moth-eaten patchwork. It was a relic of the years when Soviet influence had been at its height in the region; yet the locals were said to be as proud of it as Parisians of the Eiffel Tower.

It was a grim-looking setting. To the east stretched long identical rows of government housing, wedged at their far end under a section of elevated highway. There was a squeal and rattle of train as I crossed the bridge and, just there, amid the graffiti and peeling posters, the wind-blown refuse and architecture devoid of even the memory of beauty, I felt a stab of resentment for the people who had allowed their culture to be claimed by the anonymity of such ugliness. It was a depressing revelation – that four-and-a-half billion years of terrestrial evolution had come to this. But it was a scene

replicated in cities all over the world; I had seen so many
others like it, where the sum of human endeavour seems so
hideously overrated, and where life seems likely to survive any
catastrophe virtually unchanged, as cockroaches have been
predicted to do. Proof, in short – if it were one day confirmed
that there was indeed a divine scheme behind the existence of
humanity – that the scheme had gone definitively awry. I had
been to this place in a thousand other places; I was in all of
them now, and they were no different. I was nowhere.

The tower loomed up; I reached the entrance and, over a
faulty intercom, began a frustrating negotiation with the
African guard who spoke only a few words of English.
Eventually I heard my friend's voice, was buzzed inside, and
headed towards the twentieth floor in the single functioning
lift. I found his apartment at the end of a long corridor, passing,
at every doorway, the unidentifiable fragrance of an evening
meal in preparation.

My friend greeted me with a smile and a glass of chilled
Sancerre. I felt deeply relieved. 'Welcome to the Tower,' he said.
'Let's go onto the balcony. It'll help you to get your bearings.'

Far below, I could make out the mosque I had earlier caught
sight of, where the evening light now struck a band of tiled
calligraphy on its roof, and an ant-like procession of men were
filing towards the entrance. I felt a long way from home. We
gazed over the panorama beyond, and my friend pointed out the
city's monuments.

'Look,' he said, pointing to a slender spike on the horizon.
'You can just see Big Ben.'

It was true. His outstretched hand led my eye in a sweeping
arc above the river Thames, resting for a few moments in turn
on Westminster Abbey, the pyramidal glow of Vauxhall Cross,
and the pale and hollow towers of Battersea power station.

'People don't believe me when I tell them this is Kensington,'
he said gloomily.

'But this is W.10,' I said. 'Strictly speaking, it's North Kensington.'

He waved away this distinction with a look of disdain, and refilled my glass.

'Next time, don't come via Portobello Road,' he advised me. 'Get the bus from Victoria Station. It stops outside the door, just where it says "Trellick Tower".'

My friend was quite right: it was not what I had expected. For a few minutes we watched the planes sinking towards eye level on their final approach towards Heathrow airport, and then, as it grew cooler, moved back indoors.

THAILAND DREAMING

BY JIM BENNING

IT WAS HOT and humid when I set out for dinner in the small
southern Thailand city of Hat Yai, and I felt the world
expanding and shrinking around me, depending on which road
I walked down. On one rutted old street, two men led a
wrinkled grey elephant down the sidewalk, pausing in front of
a shark-fin soup restaurant to read the menu. Around the
corner, as though in a parallel universe, a well-lit 7-Eleven
convenience store illuminated the road, and a couple of young
women in blue jeans chatted behind street stalls, their tables
lined with the latest in knock-off Oakley sunglasses and World
Wrestling Federation T-shirts.

I had just stepped off the train from Malaysia and was
hungry. I had been dreaming of my arrival in Thailand, and of
eating the fragrant coconut-seasoned dishes I had enjoyed at
Thai restaurants back home in Los Angeles. But here in
southern Thailand, I wasn't finding much. I'd passed Chinese
restaurants and a few kitchens serving the same Malaysian-
style curry I'd been eating for weeks. Then I spotted the Sizzler,
with its familiar red and green sign: 'Steaks, Seafood, Salad'.

I couldn't believe it. All sorts of Western chains had made
inroads into Asian capitals like Bangkok and Kathmandu, but

I'd never seen a Sizzler abroad, and I certainly never expected to find one in a small city like Hat Yai. I wanted to head back towards the elephant.

When I began my five months of travel in Asia, I made an earnest pledge to try to avoid chain restaurants, which I saw as contributing to cultural homogenisation. Instead, I told myself, I would dine only in local establishments, exasperating waiters as I butchered their native language, struggling valiantly to pronounce dishes like *moo goo gai pan*. As many travellers like to point out, the word 'travel' is rooted in the French word *'travail'*. It's work. You get out of it what you put into it, and it shouldn't be too easy.

But after I'd walked several more blocks and still hadn't found a restaurant serving anything new, the promise of crispy fresh vegetables from a salad bar, something I hadn't come across in months on the road, sounded alluring. I headed for the Sizzler and put my cultural travels on hold. At least that's what I assumed.

The Sizzler, it turned out, was packed with people. Well-dressed locals – men in slacks and button-down shirts, women in stylish skirts and blouses – sat on benches, waiting for tables. Soft-spoken Thai dinner conversations spilled out the front door, along with the buttery aroma of baked potatoes. I added my name to a waiting list. Those around me carefully studied menus on display, pointing to glossy photographs of chicken sandwiches and fries. They turned the menu pages slowly, as though leafing through an exotic wisdom text. Their eyes gleamed. I'd never seen such quiet anticipation at a Sizzler, a decidedly middle-of-the-road American chain. After a short wait, a slight young woman opened the front door and carefully enunciated my name: 'Mr Jim?'

Once inside, I was surprised to find myself surrounded by pastoral images of California, my home state. Colourful wall-sized murals depicted sight after familiar sight. In one, the

Golden Gate Bridge spanned the blue waters of San Francisco Bay, giving way to Marin County's rolling hills. In another, Santa Barbara's whitewashed Spanish-style courthouse looked out over the city's inviting red-tile roofs. Yet another wall featured the famous Hollywood sign beaming forth from the Santa Monica Mountains. The scenes brought back warm memories, but they also struck me in a way I wouldn't have expected. How dry and desert-like California looked, how brown and dusty and sun-scorched, through the prism of the lush, green Southeast Asian countryside I'd been travelling in for weeks.

A visit to the Sizzler in Thailand was more complicated than I had imagined. I was seeing the familiar as deliciously exotic, and the exotic as oddly familiar. In a way, the Sizzler offered the perfect chance to see America, or at least one idealised version of America, through Thai eyes.

A waiter smiled and handed me an English-language menu, and I studied my options: steaks, fried shrimp, salads. One item in particular, the Malibu Chicken Supreme, caught my eye. The menu lovingly described the dish's features, raving that it was 'a favourite of the stars'. A favourite of the stars? The message to these Thai diners was clear: thousands of miles away, in the shadow of the real Hollywood sign, Tom Cruise himself probably stopped by the local Sizzler for a bite of Malibu Chicken after a long day at the studio lot. Even more seductively, the description seemed to imply that anyone, anywhere in the world, even in a small town in southern Thailand, could enjoy the sweet taste of Hollywood stardom, or at least a glimmer of celebrity glamour, by ordering the Malibu Chicken.

As I devoured a plateful of salad (I passed on the celebrity chicken), I looked at the diners around me, sitting in booths, sipping Cokes and munching burgers, surrounded by California scenes. They were devouring a vision of the American dream.

Did they know that their chances of spotting Tom Cruise at a Hollywood Sizzler were about the same as mine were of meeting the Buddha in a Bangkok nightclub? Did they care? I suspected not.

I could relate to them. Back home, I hadn't eaten at a Sizzler in at least a decade. But I drove right by one each week to eat at my favourite Thai restaurant, a delicious hole-in-the-wall in the middle of a Thai immigrant neighbourhood. How often I had sat inside, filling myself with panang curry and coconut soup, studying the black-and-white photographs of wild-looking Buddhist temples and Thai markets hung on the walls, nursing my dream of one day sampling my favourite dishes in their Thai homeland. Now, here I was, in just that place, surrounded by Thais eating my native food, surrounded by images of California, perhaps dreaming the same dream I had been, only in reverse.

What drives us to jet off to a foreign country where we know not a soul and can't begin to speak the language? At least in my case, it can be something as simple as a photograph in a magazine, an exotic song whose lyrics I can't begin to understand, or a savoury dish served up at a local ethnic restaurant. These images and sounds and flavours, however innocuous they may at first appear, plant seeds in our imaginations. Sometimes, days or months or even years later, those seeds take root in our dreams. When they do, we find ourselves on wide-bodied jets, crossing oceans or continents, burning to explore the world on the other side.

But the best part of the adventure is that when we finally arrive in that other place, we rarely find just what we had expected. The world is far more complex, and people are far more complicated, than most of our imaginations can accommodate. Never would I have imagined, sitting back home in my favourite Thai café, that I'd spend my first night in Thailand searching in vain for panang curry but settling for a

Sizzler. My dream never would have tolerated that. And I never would have guessed that I'd actually enjoy it.

After dinner, I walked back onto the steamy streets of Hat Yai, and I saw the traditional Thailand I had dreamed of back in Los Angeles. It was visible in the ancient buildings plastered with squiggly Thai writing, in a dark, musty shop selling bee products, and in that same wrinkled elephant still making its way silently down the road. Yet I also saw a distinctly more modern Thailand, one that I hadn't fully envisioned at home. It was embodied on a nearby street corner, not far from the 7-Eleven. There, a band of young, long-haired Thai musicians plugged a guitar, bass and microphone into an amplifier. Counting off a few beats, they launched into the Eagles' rock classic, 'Hotel California'. It was an anthem from another place and another time, resurrected here for a new generation of dreamers nurturing their own visions of a faraway land.

ANIMALS, THE LOT OF US

BY ALANA SEMUELS

THE VACATION BROCHURES featured glossy pictures of
brilliant sunsets over vast African plains, gangly giraffes
drinking glistening water next to friendly elephants, and rustic
huts on the edge of peaceful estuaries. From the haven of our
comfortable home, my mother pored over the information,
trying to convince me to join her on an African vacation. I was
already planning to spend the summer living in Botswana, but
she wanted to meet up with me in the Okavango Delta and go
on a safari.

The word 'safari' for me conjured images of Englishmen in
tan hats and brown loafers tracking lions through the jungle,
and from the way my mother described it, this was exactly
what she desired. She adored the idea of spending time with me
in the middle of nowhere, and booked the arrangements before
I even had a chance to say 'amoebic dysentery'. And so I was
snared.

As the time drew near, I began to have serious apprehensions
about the impending trip. Don't get me wrong – I was excited,
enthralled even, about the prospect of travelling through the
wilds of Botswana with my mother and immersing myself in
the bush. She and I get along as well as the next mother-

daughter pair. I was not intimidated by the idea of roughing it, and do not have any problems with animals, provided they are not crawling into my tent and gnawing at my appendages. Yet the three things – roughing it, my mother and the wild animals – seemed a bit much when mixed together and tossed into the middle of Africa.

A few weeks before I met my mother in the Delta, I was walking down a street in Gaborone, Botswana, when a headline from a local newspaper caught my eye. In bold font, it screamed out: 'Boy Mauled to Death by Hyenas in Okavango Delta'. I bought the paper and read it with terror growing in my heart. The story began: A young boy was dragged from his tent last week as he slept, and carried off by a pack of hyenas. His parents chased after the animals, but by the time they caught up to them, the boy was dead. I suddenly felt like a deer about to be shipped to Wisconsin in the middle of hunting season. If a bony young boy could be dragged from his tent while sleeping in an established tent site and devoured in a few short minutes, what horrors would befall my none-too-thin body in the middle of the Delta?

○ ○ ○ ○ ○ ○ ○ ○

After two months of living in Gaborone, Botswana's poky capital city, I have mixed feelings about venturing farther out into the wilderness. But when I meet my mother at the Maun airport, she is armed with guidebooks, binoculars, and even some rations – whether for bait or sustenance I cannot tell. She's more than ready for an adventure.

I on the other hand balk when I catch sight of the propeller plane that will take us on the next leg of our journey, deep into the heart of the Okavango Delta, away from pretty much everything but the waiting hyenas. It looks like an early discarded attempt by the Wright brothers.

The brazen Australian pilot, Mike, who smells of rum, throws my duffel bag into the luggage compartment, and proceeds to toss in the large bags of the other passengers, three crates of oranges, a few jugs of water, a rusty rifle, and two very bulky mysterious bundles. I nervously ask Mike how much weight the plane can hold and still fly, and he responds with a wink, 'Well, love, guess we'll just have to wait and see.' I do not find that amusing. My mother takes a picture.

Sputtering and tilting, the plane takes off and ploughs through the sky, clamorous in its trajectory over the limitless plains. As we fly over the Delta, I peer down over the channels and passageways of water that join and divide at various junctions, forming veins in the soggy land. I sit quietly hoping I will not get motion sick. My mother leans over and loudly asks me if I am getting motion sick. I roll my eyes and turn away. I marvel with the other five passengers at the beauty of the land – we yell over the chugging plane and agree that the Delta is indeed very nice. The German man who is tightly holding his newlywed bride and sitting almost upon my lap turns around and bellows how remote and exotic the Delta is. The other passengers concur. The plane jolts unexpectedly and I think: no escape.

When we disembark and are led to the main base camp for all of the adventurous travellers heading out into the Delta, an old Englishman in a tan hat and brown loafers meets us. He explains that he is required by law to give us a safety talk about the dangers of travelling into the bush. Feeling like I am back in summer camp, I glance at my mother. She leans over and points at the cluster of tents raised on platforms overlooking the water.

'Just like in the brochures,' she says.

The man explains that we will be travelling into the perilous wilderness in small motorless boats, surrounded on all sides by such dangerous wildlife as crocodiles and hippos. He fails to mention a way to avert potential confrontations. A Danish tourist asks if our guides carry guns, and the old Englishman replies that they carry spears, gesturing to one leaning on the wall behind him. I take one glance at said spear, which looks like a remnant from the last millennium, and wish that I had brought a gun of my own.

The next morning we meet the guide who will take us away from the relative safety and running water of base camp into the bush for three nights. He is tall, dark and muscular, and introduces himself, in broken English, as Baseki. The promised spear – about as intimidating as an oversized toothpick – is held tightly in his hand. He leads us to a very small and brittle canoe, and from the look in my mother's eyes, I suspect that it too was in the brochure. He loads our small bags into it, as well as the tent equipment, a small stove, and three coolers of food, one of which contains only raw hamburger meat. He motions for me to climb in. I raise my eyebrow. '*Mokoro,*' he explains, as if knowing the word for this kind of vessel will quell all my fears. Taking a deep breath, I climb in and sit down. My mother takes a picture.

The three of us glide away into the channels of the Delta. Baseki stands in the back pushing us through the water with a long pole, I sit in the front holding on for dear life, and my mother attempts to begin a conversation about the fauna of the Delta. Sometimes the channel gets narrow, and Baseki steers us through the weeds, creating a new path. My front row seat gives me the opportunity to help break a new path through the weeds with my face. As I spit out the spider webs, I turn and politely ask Baseki where we are going. He grins mischievously.

'I have a special island. Away from other tourists. Many animals there.' My mother chirrups with excitement, and I grind my teeth into the closest thing to a grin that I can muster.

Baseki paddles on all morning, through thick weeds and boundless expanses of open water. I sit back and relax, rolling

239.

up my sleeves and hoping the African sun will beat down on me
and tan my skin so I can camouflage with the surroundings. I
close my eyes and listen to Baseki's grunts as he pushes the
heavy load onward. My mother pokes me.

'Don't close your eyes,' she urges. 'We might see some
animals!'

I close them with spite. After an hour, she has seen three
white birds, a log that she insisted was a crocodile, and a
stork's nest. I open my eyes and amuse myself by playing with
the zoom lens on our high-tech camera. Zoom in. Zoom out.
Zoom in. And out.

I am half-asleep and drooling on my burnt arm when we pull
out of the weeds into a large pond of water. Suddenly there are
animals everywhere. My mother pulls out her safari guide, and
identifies the animals as impala, lechwe, blue wildebeest and
zebra. The names sound foreign rolling off her tongue, like an
incantation in a different language. The animals look at us,
shrug and return to their grazing. Clearly they are accustomed
to the peculiar sight we make: a tall guide leading two white
women through the crocodile-infested waters. They do not look
very afraid of his spear.

Baseki pulls up to an island across from where the majority
of animals are grazing and announces proudly, 'Here! Baseki
Island.' As he begins to unload the supplies, I climb out of the
boat and survey our surroundings. Two acacia trees stretch up
from the flat plain, above a small area where the grass has been
trampled. I look around. Flies cluster around fresh animal
dung. The grasses surrounding the campsite sway mockingly,
reminding me of the animals lurking in their midst. A small
white bone lies complacently in the shallow grass. 'Human?' I
ask Baseki. He giggles but does not answer. Here we set
up camp.

At the pleading of my mother, and against my protests,
Baseki takes us on a short nature walk around the island, and I

step gingerly around the piles of impala bones and elephant dung that seem to pop up at every turn. While he identifies the various animal tracks and dung piles, I keep my eyes peeled for any lurking predators and try to avoid the scrutinising lens of my mother's camera. When she insists that I pose squatting by an animal's rotting skull, I again roll my eyes and walk away.

Baseki holds up his hand suddenly and quiets my mother's question about the dung colour of female elephants. The bushes sway in front of us and I am convinced that I have reached the end of my short life. Baseki grips his spear. The camera in my mother's hand zooms.

The bushes part and a yellow flash darts out fifty feet in front of us and scampers away. All I see are its bared teeth. It is followed a few seconds later by another whir that looks like a dog. And with that, they are gone. I stand shaking, feeling very much like prey.

Baseki laughs. 'Spotted hyena and wild dog. They fight over dead impala.'

My mother grins triumphantly. 'I think I got a pretty good camera angle.'

With pursed lips, I ask Baseki if I can carry the spear.

We spend the rest of the day setting up the campsite and watching the animals graze. Baseki wanders off into the bush, and my mother and I sit alone on the banks of the Delta, watching the sun set. It slowly disappears behind the palm trees of the opposing bank, leaving pink and orange remnants in its wake. We ravage through the supplies and find crackers and jelly and hamburger meat.

Before I even notice, it is very dark and we are sitting vulnerable as grazing animals beneath the acacia trees, the tempting smell of jelly wafting out over the water. As my mother changes her film, I wonder why Baseki wandered off and left us alone in the bush, and if he perhaps inadvertently (or maybe even on purpose) stumbled into our earlier acquaintances, the hyena and the dog. The darkness around us glitters with the eyes of hungry predators lurking in wait.

As the night deepens, and the predators creep closer, I am all for climbing into our hyena-proofed tent and hiding out there until morning. My mother wants to chat. I admire her strategy; at home I can usually escape her attempts by wandering off into another room or insisting that I have work to do. Now I have nowhere to wander but into the bush. When she asks me if I've met any nice Jewish boys in Africa, I decide that a hungry lion might at that moment be a more pleasant companion.

When Baseki returns from his wanderings, he announces that the animals are out on the prowl. I take this as my cue to climb into our tent and lie waiting for sleep. A low cry like the sound of a sly baby pierces the night.

'Hyena,' Baseki explains from his tent.

My mother has to ask, 'How close?'

'Close.' More cries join in and the voices whoop and holler, ascending and descending through the night air. 'Now closer.'

I lie in the tent remembering the carcasses that we passed on our nature walk that very day. I had rolled my eyes when my mother commented on how vulnerable we were walking through the bush. But relieved as I am to have made it through the day without seeking refuge in a pile of fresh zebra dung, I am not sure that I will live to tell about it. The possibility is humbling. I think back to the little boy who had been dragged from his tent just a few weeks earlier and against my instincts, reach out and grab my mother's hand. For once, she is silent. I am suddenly ashamed for my behaviour, and wonder if all daughters are so snide. From the sound of the hyenas outside our tent, I don't doubt it. Animals, the lot of us, stuck together under one African sky.

PRIMAVERA

BY ART BUSSE

WE'VE CAUGHT TUSCANY in its last day of winter, prolonged by a late cold spell. At the end of dormancy, the countryside is still wearing its reserved palette of dark colours – rust, red, brown and black – with the occasional patch of snow still clinging to the sheltered indentations of ground.

It is a poignant moment in this year's cycle of seasons, but there have been so many years. We are immersed in something old here, very old. There is a dignity, a solemnity, a sense that things were settled here long ago. It is not the overbearing obligation of tradition, just the comfort and resolve that come from knowing how things are. After centuries of strife, Tuscany has achieved an angle of repose requiring no further adjustments. Life goes on, but without the questioning, and without the need to challenge the basic assumptions. There is change, but it is cyclical and comes around of its own accord. Here one is free, as the olive trees are, to grow, to bear fruit and, eventually, to die.

The weather turned on the day we arrived, but the earth has not yet responded, nor have the people. A warm and sunny afternoon on the piazza in the town of Greve finds the locals in winter coats, scarves and boots, with looks that speak of waiting. It will take more than one warm afternoon to change a long winter's habits.

Mira and I have been together for two years now and have reached that difficult moment in a relationship where the wind begins to go out of its sails. We've tracked down our crucial differences and wonder if they might be irreconcilable. The heat of passion is giving way to the heat of friction. We love each other still, and don't want to give up, but can't help feeling dispirited and tired. Our clear line of sight into the future has disappeared around a bend and the loss of forward momentum is dragging us down. Secretly, we have been hoping for intervention.

A month ago, as if on cue, our friends Christian and Roberta Parma unexpectedly invited us to join them for Easter at their Tuscan estate. Three weeks in Italy seemed like a very good idea. We jumped at the offer. Now, jet-lagged and disoriented, staring at the barren Tuscan countryside, something barely discernible is beginning to shift.

Halfway between Siena and Florence, in the middle of the Chianti region, the small town of Greve sits astride a river at the bottom of a natural bowl of rolling hills. Up the east slope of that bowl, past the cleared and terraced hillsides of olive groves, vineyards, and the occasional almond tree, through the late winter haze from fires set to burn off the trimmings of olive branches, at a natural vantage point, the Parmas' 1000-year-old estate commands the Greve Valley.

Mira, herself a writer, had me take up the *English Patient* as we packed for the trip, thinking that Michael Ondaatje's writing would be a good place to go from Don DeLillo's, whose *Underworld* I had just finished and loved. Neither of us remembered that it is largely set here in Tuscany at an old villa just over the olive-strewn hills from the Parmas' estate.

So when I've had enough of the hills and villas and people of Tuscany, I retreat to a quiet corner of our *castellare* and read about the same hills and villas populated by the ghost-like people who survived the winding down of the last great war. I float with them through their reveries of life and death and love and beauty and pain cast out over a nightmarish landscape nearly as dark as the one our medieval stronghold was meant to survive.

Beauty and pain, love and suffering, over and over again, appearing in that form then and this form now, and countless times in countless forms in between. Always recognisable in the way they seize us, cast us out of the tower, then lift up our battered souls on gentle wings.

All are well represented here. Beauty can be found in abundance at the Parmas' dinner parties. There are heiresses, countesses, and Milanese models all preening to the strains of Christian's acclaim. Effusive and enthusiastic, he is set off by the beauty he has surrounded himself with and rolls out a steady and entertaining stream of stories about his hundreds of conquests on three continents. Replete with spontaneous conversions and chivalrous saves, the landscape of his persona has more saints, sinners and miracles than the Church he so lovingly denounces.

Pain, too, it seems, has a place at the table, as each reference to the towering beauties and the playboy antics of our host digs deeper into the soul of my smouldering, suffering Mira. Beautiful in her own right, but darker, warmer, softer and smarter, she can excite and enlighten a room with her sensuous insinuation and fresh ideas the way trade in spices brought on the Renaissance. But alas, her virtues, though fully appreciated around the table, are of no comfort to her when she feels passed over for the long legs and blond hair of her competitors.

The following day we have reserved tickets to the Uffizi, Florence's premier art museum, and find that Renaissance painting is the perfect vehicle for processing the previous

evening's joys and abuses, bringing us to a deeper and ever
more abrasive understanding of what we are as a couple.

I make the mistake of pointing out the resemblance between
Botticelli's Venus and one of the dinner guests. Later we come
to a painting featuring a sumptuously endowed Florentine
matron holding a bowl of ripe fruit just below her exposed
breasts as a starving man looks on and drools. Mira, similarly
endowed, remarks that it is a perfect rendition of my complaint
about her – that she is a little too free in the care and feeding of
the other men in our group of friends. When I agree, she lashes
out at me for assigning her the matron with the unpleasing face
while reserving Venus for the enemy. Then, as we are about to
leave, she becomes enraptured with a painting of three women
slitting a man's throat, the only painting in the museum done
by a woman.

Meanwhile, the only painting in the place that speaks to me
is a diptych of Adam and Eve circa 1500. There is something
unnerving in Eve's willing engagement with God's separation of
the sexes. It's as if she's saying, 'If this is why we are here in
these opposing forms, then let's get on with it. Give me that
apple. Armed with the knowledge of good and evil, with my feet
firmly on the ground and this serpent whispering advice in my
ear, I'll make this thing happen!' I am reminded of serious-
minded thirteen-year-old girls poring over the how-to articles
in *Seventeen* magazine.

Adam, on the other hand, with his dreamy, wistful looks,
seems a little clueless, a little innocent, a little more connected
still to the unformed spirit within. I envy women their grounded
nature, their solid connection with the earth, with their bodies. I
worry about men. We seem too vulnerable, like deer in the headlights of these practical and determined women.

A band strikes up a song at the outdoor trattoria on the
piazza where we lunch after the museum, snapping me out of
my reverie and drawing my attention to the musicians: a

guitarist, a saxophonist and a violinist, all mature, robust Italian men, and all sharing a look that says their pride is at stake. It's as if they expect to not be taken seriously, to receive no respect for their musical talents. They play beautifully anyway and suffer.

In the days that follow we are encouraged to visit this town and that, but it is the country that keeps calling. So we pack picnics of prosciutto and bread and cheese and local wines and do our best to lose ourselves down the back roads, looking for the right spots to breathe as deeply as we can of this place, and of each other. They are easily found in the hillside groves and vineyards, and the soft embrace of nature leads easily to our own soft embraces.

But looking up from our lovemaking, we can't help but notice the looming, sombre architecture. It is one of bastion and siege. The high ground has all been taken. On it stand impenetrable castles, ramparts, and towers made of stone pulled from the hillsides and river beds. No doubt there were other architectures from other eras, but that of the Dark Ages was built to withstand all onslaughts, including that of time. So here it stands today, a monument to security, while in the monument's shadow lurks the uneasy implication of the threat that commissioned it.

There is no escaping the symbolism and once again we are reminded of what's troubling our relationship. No sooner do we open, soft and vulnerable, to love, than fear demands we surround it with walls, and what provides safety for one, imprisons the other. Is love a flower that must be protected to grow, or a flame that needs air to burn? These are the questions we travel with. Where are the answers to be found?

Sleep is deep in our medieval keep, but with the body safe from harm, the unconscious is emboldened, producing dreams like dark underground rivers with currents more powerful than the dreamers who loosed them. At the end of winter, with no

248.

clear direction forward, no sense of what comes next, no real belief in renewal, Tuscany waits, waits as it has every year, for something in the dirt to stir and take it by surprise. We lie down at the end of our days and are taken by our dreams.

Mira battles sea creatures and snakes, while I follow the elusive glow of a lantern as it recedes just out of sight down around the curve of a stair in a dark castle turret, carried by an ephemeral young woman. And we are not alone in our nocturnal journeys. Dreams fill the *castellare*. Roberta, our hostess, who by day is surrounded by the most innocent and endearing light, is ferocious in dreams by night. She is a Jungian therapist and our casual breakfasts are the stomping grounds for her carnal archetypes as she recounts her heroic battles with the beasts and horrors of the night before. We join her, pouring out our souls over coffee, fruit, bread and cheese. She shares her arcane books on psychology and mythology, and the three of us forge ahead through our fears. With our time here in Tuscany drawing to a close, it seems that something important is almost within our grasp.

After breakfast on our last day with the Parmas we pull on our boots, head off to explore the land surrounding their estate – and find something extraordinary. Along an ancient Roman road, built over an even older Etruscan path, running beside a tributary creek as it cuts deeper and higher into the hillside skirting the estate's northern boundary, into the woods on the south slope of the narrowing canyon, past the two dogs that come down from the ramshackle compound of stone farm houses above, one all bravado but missing a leg, the other unable to conceal even from strangers her need to be loved, past the old woman in the apron busy gathering wood to fire her *forno* for the morning bread she is baking, through the compound and down behind it, past the roosts of roosters and hens, to where the trail returns to the creek, up high now, in deep, far away from the town, where memory is outdistanced, and history asserts itself, at the top of the canyon, at the end of the world, spanning the creek and leading to nowhere – there is a bridge.

It would be easy to miss it, as no doubt many have before, for the trail continues past it, following the creek back down on its return leg to town. The creekside brush has grown close in around it and centuries of decomposing leaves have covered its upper surface in a thick layer of earth that has its own growth. From the trail upstream it looks almost as if the creek bed narrows at a certain point and the forest floors on either side reach for and find each other.

Summoning up a little courage, we chance the crossing, let ourselves slowly down the steep creek embankment and, standing downstream at the edge of the water, turn around and look. It's 2000 years old, natural as the forest that provided its stones, perfectly simple, perfectly functional, and perfectly formed in the classic, gravity-defying arch that bears Rome's name, holding the sweet spot between nature, invention, survival and beauty.

Standing together, alone in the woods, in the presence of something so right, puts much to rest. That we are capable of such simple perfection. That what deserves to, endures, while the rest falls away. That there is justice in time. What began to shift within us on our arrival now comes back around fully formed. Dark times, like Dark Ages, come and go, alternating with periods of light. Barren fields will grow again. Summer's bounty will fade. Lovers turn towards and away from each other, in and out of love, on a spinning planet circling a flaming sun hurtling through space.

We relax against each other, like the dry-fitted stones of the old bridge, holding each other up with a force exactly equal to what wants to bring us down. We begin to imagine that, even with nothing more to bind us than the shape of our association, we too may endure. Everything falls into place.

Primavera

It's Easter, and time to return to Rome for our flight home. All around us on the drive south the Italian countryside, first dormant, then tentative, now bursts into life filling the air with a rush of renewal. Suddenly, it's easy to believe.

IN THE CAULDRON WITH BEETHOVEN

BY JAMES HAMILTON

CAME A TIME in my life, with two kids in out-of-state universities and my writing career in a lean and hungry place, when I went to Hollywood looking for relief. I knew the terrain fairly well, having done a rewrite on a screenplay that led to a credit on a feature production. That experience had been carried out more or less on my terms, and I didn't have to leave my own backyard in Northern California. But in the time frame I'm speaking of here, I was camping out on their turf, living the precarious life that goes with being under contract to independent producers even hungrier than I was.

I had been contracted to write two original screenplays on a 'spec' basis, with no assurance that either would be produced. These binding agreements were known back then in the business as step-deals: two drafts and a rewrite, then a final polish, with payment doled out at each step, in percentages. The money, at Writer's Guild minimums, was modest, and the big chunk was to be paid on the beginning of 'principal photography' – that storied Hollywood euphemism for the pot of gold at the end of the rainbow, when they actually put film in the camera and start shooting the picture. The rule of thumb with this kind of story-mining operation was roughly eight to two: that is, put ten projects into the hopper, maybe two would get produced.

But it was the money on the table at the end of each step that I was after, so that I could make tuition or arrange plane fare from distant colleges back to California for the holidays or summer break for my son and daughter. This was blood money, no question about it. Submitting an entire draft of a script was infinitely easier and less stressful than doing it in four parts, having it picked over in front of the man who was signing the cheques and whose eye never wavered from the whims of the box office. Story conferences could be harrowing, the scalpel in the producer's hand always out, the writer maddened by the sight of it. My strategy was to pretend to fight hard for scenes I didn't particularly like anyway, thus saving the real battle for others that were indispensable to the story.

In six months I was frazzled by the process, obsessed with protecting my themes, but most of all, exhausted from fighting off a producer's addiction to expository scenes that I knew would be deadly in the mouths of actors. It got so bad I'd lie awake at night and hear voices in my ear that were like voice-overs from old film noir movies: Bogart as the psychotic writer in *In a Lonely Place* or William Holden in *Sunset Boulevard* as the screenwriter whose despair over his career leads him into the spidery clutches of Gloria Swanson. It all reached a climax on completion of the final draft of the second project, when the producer, whose wife was active in women's liberation circles in west Los Angeles, suggested politicising the female lead role, conforming to his wife's 'hobby', as he disingenuously called it.

This was a preposterous suggestion, given what the script was all about, and I stormed out of the office, saying I'd be out of town for a couple of weeks, hoping for better results when I returned. I drove to my apartment, threw some things together, made a couple of getaway phone calls, then headed east on Highway 10 with no destination in mind. It was the dead of

253.

summer, I wanted no part of a crowded coastline, and I wanted to avoid an alpine setting of structured fun and family scenes and clogged mountain roads. All I knew was that I had to get out of Los Angeles, had to shed my skin somewhere, anywhere. I headed east, vaguely in the direction of Las Vegas, where a good friend lived, crossing the boiling Mojave in mid-afternoon.

I stopped in Victorville, a town I had always liked for its hardscrabble, gritty desert feel. I checked into a motel, then later went into the roughest bar I could find along the main drag. It was a Friday night payday and the place was packed with construction workers and desert folks, a species of eccentric humanity I've always felt comfortable around. I drank at the bar for a while in the furious din, then somehow fell in with a group of men at a large round table, where we drank and shook dice for round after round.

At the table was a short, powerfully built, white-haired Mexican bricklayer as wide as he was tall, and somehow he challenged me to an arm-wrestle. He looked to be at least twice my age; in fact, he looked like somebody's kindly grandfather. A tall Indian, quite young, with a long thick braid down his back, stood behind him. A crowd suddenly gathered around our table; bets were made, money was on the table, including my own. There was no way out. The Indian never took his eyes off me.

I won the best two out of three from the Mexican. But as I reached for my winnings, a chant went up from the crowd: 'Double or nothing! Double or nothing!' My opponent smiled and said, 'And with the left arm, amigo.'

'The left!' I exclaimed, as the crowd got quiet. *'La izquerida?'*

'Si,' said the Mexican. *'La izquerida.'*

With great dispatch the powerful mason nearly tore my left arm out of the socket, and he threw in a gentle smile to boot.

The next morning, thirsty and hungover, my left arm hanging lifelessly at my side, I headed out of town, still not sure where I was going. At a north–east junction stop sign I came across the same tall Indian who had witnessed my defeat. He wore a straw cowboy hat down low over his eyes and had his thumb out in the northerly direction. On an impulse I stopped and motioned for him to get in. He said his name was Tall Tommy and he was Shoshone Indian, on his way to Death Valley, where he worked for the Park Service. Was I going that far? If so, he would tell me many funny stories along the way.

And so he did, and the miles flew by, and before I knew it we were at the entrance to Death Valley. Tall Tommy told me to pull over and stop the car. He looked at me for a moment, and said, 'You sure you want to do this?' I wasn't sure; in fact, I had no idea what he was talking about.

'It's the middle of July, man,' he said. 'A hunnert and twenty degrees. You'll be all alone out there.'

I nodded my head. On his instructions we drove to park headquarters and went inside, where he outfitted me with several brochures and reference booklets on the history of Death Valley. Then he told me to go open the trunk of my car, he'd be right out. In a few minutes he came out carrying a sack with four half-gallon jugs of water in it, which he put in the trunk. He said, 'You watch yourself out there. Stay indoors afternoons; always drink lots of water. If your car breaks down, stay with it.' Then he took off his hat and said, 'You're gonna need this,' and set it on my head; it fit perfectly and I thanked him. I asked where I could get the best view of the valley; I needed to get my bearings. 'Dante's View', he said, and gave me directions. Then we shook hands and said maybe we'd run into each other again while I was in the park.

Dante's View is a tourist overlook roughly 5000 feet above sea level, appropriately named after the great Italian poet and his hellish vision of the inferno. One of the historical markers told me that many of the attractions and sites associated with Death Valley are malignant and dark, obsessed with foreboding: Coffin Peak, Dry Bone Canyon, the Funeral Mountains. The

Devil himself, too, has always been a featured attraction here:
There's the Devil's Golf Course, the Devil's Cornfield, Devil's
Hole, Hell's Gate, and so on, a litany of nightmares christened
by some of the Forty-Niner wagon parties who crossed this
fiery hell on the way to the gold fields of the Sierra, and had
reason to know what they were talking about.

I looked around at multiple mountain ranges, then stared
into the abyss below; the heat rose up from the valley floor as if
from a gigantic anvil. The valley swings northward for 140
miles but appeared to be no more than ten or fifteen miles
wide. The salt etchings hold the eye far into the distance; the
bitter, eroded hills assault the senses with geologic upheaval.
The colours as far as I could see in the shimmering heat were a
spectrum of every conceivable variation of brown and tan and
beige, blowtorched into the broken hills as if by hand, leaving
here and there splotches of white.

'Christ!' I thought. 'What went on here?' The marker said that
I was staring at four billion years of geologic time, but to my
eye the tumult and chaos looked like it had taken place a week
ago, acted out on a stage created by the violent foldings and
faultings and upliftings of old moody earth, raving and ranting.
Suddenly, the elation I had felt at getting out of Los Angeles and
away from my personal problems, along with the excitement of
being on the open road and the hell-raising nonsense of the
night before, vanished; by accident, I had stumbled onto a
serious place, a place to be reckoned with.

I drove down into the bottom of the valley to a place called
Badwater, almost 300 feet below sea level, the hottest, driest,
lowest place in the western hemisphere. I parked on the side of
the road and wandered out across the salt flats. There was not
another human being in sight; the isolation was itself an
experience. The sun beating down from above was not one I had
ever seen or been blistered by. This sun was a bleached-out
white thing made ugly and shapeless by its own light, and it

was pitiless. I thought of those wretched gold-diggers making their way across this abandoned lake bed.

After a while I stopped walking and stood very still, scarcely breathing. I wouldn't know until later that I had discovered another of the great wonders of Death Valley: its silence. The silence here, like the summer heat, is a force unto itself. It is so profound it made me want to listen to it, to behold it, and it drove me to do a strange thing.

I walked back to my car and drank deeply from one of the jugs of water, then opened a small bag of tape cassettes I had grabbed at random when I left my apartment. There were two Mozart symphonies and three Beethoven pieces, including the ninth symphony, along with some jazz. I picked out the C Minor Piano Concerto of Beethoven and put it on, opened all four doors of the car, then turned the speakers on full blast.

It was as if I had set off ten sticks of dynamite. Beethoven exploded into the air. I laughed out loud, giddy from the sound. The acoustical dynamics of the walled valley, with mountains rising straight up on all sides and as high as 11,000 feet, had created a perfect amphitheatre. I walked back out onto the desert and paced back and forth, 'conducting' the orchestra myself, waving my baton. The concerto poured up and into and across the valley, and the fusion of the triumphant, combative music with the forbidding landscape left me shaken.

For the next three days I surrendered to this strange environment. It was like having a museum all to myself. I obeyed Tall Tommy's orders and took refuge in my motel room during the afternoons. The temperature was averaging around 120 degrees Fahrenheit and up, and the ground temperature was said to be forty or fifty degrees hotter. I moved about carefully, respectfully, in the kiln-dried air, in a state of surprising equanimity, and yet it was strangely invigorating. I would go out to explore the desert by first light, climbing the narrow canyons or hiking the fascinating alluvial fans that grace the entrances to them.

The light at that hour is exquisite, and gives these rents in the earth a hushed clarity, a sense of precarious solitude. Seen from Dante's View that first day these hills had looked bitter and forbidding, but when I was among them, I felt enfolded within them in a strangely secretive way. The canyons also revealed in full measure the remorseless effects of erosion. Because the hills are impermeable and unclothed, the runoff from even a mild cloudburst is prodigious, and sometimes calamitous, and accounts for the smoothed sculptured walls and the occasional mosaic arrangement of small stones and pebbles laid in as if by hand, a permanent matrix of whites, a variety of soft greens and browns, warm and smooth to the touch.

At night I used the desert as my private music hall and, with miraculous luck, it was bathed in an immense full moon. I did Mozart one night at a different location, and the final night I spent out on the Sand Dunes, one of the Valley's most popular attractions by day – in winter, that is. I had hiked the dunes that morning early, hoping I might see a coyote, or at least the tracks of one. I have a thing about coyotes: the last one I'd seen was loping down a street at dawn in a posh section of Beverly Hills, not far from where I was living; surely I'd find one in Death Valley.

I went back to the Dunes around midnight, in a delicate dry breeze and eighty-nine degrees of temperature. Once again I opened all four doors of the car and for this farewell occasion I fired up Beethoven's Ninth Symphony full blast. Near where I had parked the car were a couple of old weather-beaten picnic tables. I climbed on one of them and lay back on the pillow I had brought along for the occasion and looked up at the stars.

The night before, Mozart had filled the valley with the grace and sweet perfection of the Jupiter Symphony, his last symphonic work. But Beethoven in this setting tore through the heavens, reordered the stars. It was a colossal, celestial marriage of Art and Nature. I knew the work well and had seen it performed, but on this night I heard music that was boundless in a setting equally as boundless. The massive architecture of the symphony had found its equal in this ancient place. I had always heard music critics throw around the words 'affirmation' and 'adoration' when describing this monumental work, but in the famous final choral movement that night it became clear what Beethoven was saying from within his deafness, his raging silence: adore the spirit, affirm the journey.

I awoke at dawn and headed out of the dunes. My tracks from the night before were clearly visible. But what a freeway I was on! Beside my prints were a myriad of other tracks, critters of all sorts who live in the mesquite villages – kangaroo rats, lizards, beetles, the tiny, dainty paws of the kit fox and the goofy meanderings of the sidewinder snake. It was as if a convention had taken place while I slept. Then my eye caught the tracks of a coyote coming up the slope of a dune ten feet from where I was standing. They crossed directly over my footprints and kept going, heading southeast. I bent down and matched them up with those in my guidebook.

259.

I'd found my coyote. Time to go, I said to myself.

I packed my gear, then dropped Tall Tommy's hat off at park headquarters, with a note inside thanking him for the chance meeting, and also telling him that now I knew where to find him. Then I high-tailed it out of the park west up into the Panamint Mountains to an overlook I'd read about, Mahogany Flats, at an elevation of 8130 feet. The air was now startlingly thin and fragrant with the smell of pine cones. From here I was able to take a farewell look at Death Valley. I could see the whole immense panorama: west to the Inyo and White Mountains, Mt Whitney and the Sierra, south to the San Bernardino range, east to the glowering Funerals, with the Amargosa Range beyond; and finally the immaculate museum below, cursed by its name, born out of terrible violence and chaos into a place of order and unadorned beauty.

And it didn't need a rewrite.

BREAKDOWN
THE AFRICAN WAY

BY DON MEREDITH

A DUSTY RED road reaches into vistas of umbrella thorn. Once this country teemed with buffalo, rhino, elephant, lion. This morning a lilac-breasted roller keeps me company. Tawny brown and pale purple splashed with blue and aqua, he rides a branch of whistling thorn. An hour after sunrise and Nanyuki lies five miles behind me at the base of 17,000-foot Mt Kenya, the second highest mountain in Africa, a glacier-capped equatorial Matterhorn rising above the upland sweep of the Laikipia Plain.

Another hour's walking brings me to a Maasai village, a lonely cluster of plank houses, women, small children, a few toothless elders loitering in the shade. I attempt a few words of Maa. *'Na kitok! Takuenya!'*

'Iko!'

'Ashe naleng!'

Seeking jobs, the men have gone to Nairobi, while older boys follow herds of Boran and long-horned Ankole cattle in search of forage. The women stare boldly but speak little. The children begin a plaintive chant: 'Pen! Pen! Pen!' I have no pens, but no-one seems to mind. I'm nothing but a small diversion in an otherwise eventless day. I walk on, a covey of small boys

tagging along until they drift back to the village, melt into
the bush.

By mid-morning the mountain stands behind pearly curtains
of cloud. The road, stretching into the distance, parallels the
equator, varying no more than a hundred yards on either side of
the imaginary line. Pied barbets gossip endlessly in the bush as
finches, bush shrikes, rollers and carmine bee-eaters race
among the acacias, and buffalo weavers plait lion-coloured
grass into untidy nests. For a few breathless moments, buffalo
on my mind, I search for their black murderous hulls moored
among the trees.

A Land Rover passes, a pair of pink faces gazing dead ahead,
expats travelling to one of the ranches on this road that ends
seventy-five miles away at Thomson's Falls. Neither driver nor
passenger glances in my direction.

Soon another vehicle rattles up, a battered pickup that slows
to a dusty stop. A figure in blue coveralls vaults from the
driver's seat and hurtles towards me.

A slim, soft-spoken Kikuyu, Herbert Wahome, proprietor of
Nanyuki's New Mount Kenya Garage, was once my companion
on a safari to see the sitatunga, the rare marsh antelope of
Saiwa Swamp. It's two years since we last met. After excited
greetings in the empty road, I ask Herbert where he's going.

A *matatu*, he tells me, a Mitsubishi half-bus, has broken
down in a village along the northwestern flank of the Aberdare
Mountains. With his brother Peter to lend a hand and a couple
of friends to give moral support, Herbert intends to dismantle
the ailing motor and haul it back to Nanyuki for repair. He's in
a hurry. The lights on his pickup are on the blink and he must
be back before dark.

When Herbert asks me to join them, it takes just seconds to
decide. He bounds behind the wheel as I scale the rear bumper
into the pickup bed to join two men who quickly make room
and introduce themselves: Kamau and Waweru. We're still

261.

shaking hands when Herbert lets out the clutch and we jolt away.

A timelessness reigns on this high plateau, an endless expanse of nyika, thorn tree scrub that runs forever. With the sun at its zenith, the little pickup, dwarfed by the immensity of the plain, clatters over the hard places, slithers across patches of sand. After a few miles the engine's drone suddenly ceases and we coast to a stop.

Herbert leaps out. 'Wiring!' he shouts, poking his head under the hood. As he begins tinkering, the rest of us climb down to stretch in the empty road. It's hot and still, the air spiced with the fragrance of upland scrub like the dry, winy smell of California chaparral or the herby maquis of the Mediterranean. Suddenly, Kamau touches my shoulder. 'Just there,' he whispers, pointing to a shallow swale thirty yards off the road where fever trees have tapped water. A dozen giraffes browse on the high foliage. One turns to examine us, flicks an ear and elegantly ambles off.

Wiring repaired, a push-start has us underway. The nyika shimmers blankly under the heat haze. Soon a zebra holds his ground at the road's edge while his harem wheels and gallops away across a sweep of coppery grassland. Then nothing but the road and the pickup trailing a scarf of red dust.

At last we turn from the Thomson's Falls road and follow a series of complicated detours, expedient homemade byways through the bush that avoid the most punishing depredations of the deplorable track. After crossing the Ewaso Nyiro River over a flimsy bridge, we mount a rise and park among ragtag structures, an architectural miscellany of boards, straw, mud-and-wattle, plastic, rock and tin. This is Ngobit, as close to nowhere as you're likely to come. In a place of honour at the village centre, scruffy residents in hand-me-down attire gather around the broken Mitsubishi, paying mute tribute to this doleful monument of halted progress.

Equipped with socket sets, assorted screwdrivers, ball-peen hammers and sundry angled extensions, Herbert and Peter go to work as I drift off towards the river. Surveying the ailing bus and the two small men attempting to eviscerate it, I'm overcome with a sinking feeling that this could take a very long time. Before it's over, Ngobit might become all too familiar. I recall Graham Greene's *The Lawless Roads*: 'It is curious how the most dismal place after twenty-four hours begins to seem like home…You get accustomed in a few weeks to the idea of living or dying in the most bizarre surroundings.'

I doze for an hour in the shade along the river, a broad muddy stream flowing between grassy banks. When I wake I'm in the thick of a collection of gaunt cows navigating towards water. Two herd boys, dark eyes narrowed in mocha faces, lean perilously over the bridge's railing, staring down at me.

'*Jambo, rafiki!*' I shout. Hello, friends!

The boys dash for safety, terrified by my white skin. Then, slowly, dark eyes peer over the railing and shy rejoinders of '*Jambo*' come weakly down to me, thin voices ragged with fear.

I follow the timorous herd boys Juma and Esa, and their forty lowing, dewlapped cattle up the hill into Ngobit. As the cows dawdle among a scant cluster of homespun buildings, I lead the boys into a *duka*, a shop whose exterior is a screaming blue and vibrant yellow billboard trumpeting 'Blue Band Good Start Margarine at Very Cheap Prices!' Inside, dim shelves hold forlorn packets of Omo laundry soap, a pound of muddy potatoes, and eleven minuscule cans of tomato paste. After a lengthy search, the proprietor, a tubercular man with malarial eyes, comes up with two bottles of Fanta. They're warm, of course. No electricity in Ngobit. I pop the tops and hand the sodas to the boys who examine them warily, uncertain if Fanta is *dawa* (medicine), or something to rub in their hair. I watch them trailing after the cows, the Fantas clutched in their small fists like graven idols.

Across the dusty track, in a cinder-block shelter heralding 'Sportsman – The True Flavour of Kenya' painted in fire-engine red and grief-stricken black, a cheerful young woman in khakis and a porkpie hat sells me two packs of Sportsman cigarettes that I take to Herbert and Peter. To my surprise, I discover the Mitsubishi nearly dismantled. While Herbert draws bolts from oily crevices and impossible crannies, Peter cleans and sorts parts, systematically storing them in a nearby shed. As I bend over the *matatu*'s grease-sodden innards, Peter lifts out the radiator and sponges off the gunk. Remarkably, it appears we won't live and die in Ngobit after all.

Following a brief break for a smoke, Herbert crawls under to drain the oil and unbolt the pan, and I excuse myself to head for Endangered Species Drinks Garden, Ngobit's only saloon, a dim, cement-floored establishment whose scarred tables bear the stains of countless beer bottles. I add another, a warm Tusker, then buy beers for the cook and waitress, twin sisters sporting matching Minnie Mouse T-shirts, and two more for Kamau and Waweru, my companions from the pickup who have taken up residence at a corner table. As I join them, villagers wander in. Word is out that a *mzungu* is in town, standing drinks for the populace.

When and where they slaughter the goats and put them on the grill is anybody's guess. After another round of Tuskers, the smoky aroma of grilled meat fills the Endangered Species. At our corner table Waweru's brother Simon and a contingent of villagers join us. The conversation turns to Shakespeare. Did he exist? Was he more than a ham actor? Did Francis Bacon write the plays? Simon, a lean, scholarly thirty-five-year-old, is a Baconian, while the younger Waweru sticks by the Bard. When not arguing the finer points of Elizabethan literature, these two are partners in the Mitsubishi under repair. While Herbert and Peter struggle with nuts and bolts, and the denizens of the Endangered Species wolf savoury grilled goat and drink more beer while I pick up the tab, Waweru recites reams from *Hamlet* and *King Lear* and Simon discourses on Bacon's theory of inductive reasoning. It is curious how, in a few hours, you grow used to the most bizarre surroundings.

Late afternoon. With a throng of villagers waving goodbye, Juma, Esa and their dewlapped cows among them, we pull out of Ngobit, this nowhere that willy-nilly has become somewhere. Huddled in the pickup's bed around the oil-gummed motor like tired but contented warriors gathered over the carcass of some great African beast felled after a day's hard hunting, we drive down the slope, cross the bridge over the river, and pick our way through the puzzle of improvised bush-tracks before turning east on the road to Nanyuki.

A dying sun fires the thin blue of the paling sky and, in the distance, opalescent clouds part and Mt Kenya's snows glitter a pink colour. The giraffes are not far from where we left them. As evening comes on, one pair stands side-by-side twining their long, serpentine necks in the slow arabesques of a ritual dance. Around their heads go, necks intertwined as though tying knots or knitting. The pickup slides to a stop and we silently watch this elegant cotillion. 'They are in love,' Kamau whispers.

'The Italians have a term for it,' I answer. '*Il stagione di amore.*'

The zebras appear further on, the stallion and harem browsing on the roadside, paying no attention as we pass. Then Kamau grips my arm and Waweru drums on the roof of the cab. Herbert skids to a stop and instantly we're milling in the road.

'What is it? What's happened?'

'There,' Kamau says. '*Tembo*, a big one – look!'

Off to the west, deep in a scruff of thorn, a bull elephant stands silhouetted against the setting sun. Slowly, he reaches out with his trunk, wrapping it around the limb of a tree. A shriek of splintering wood rends the air as he rips it clear.

It's late. With no headlights, the road has grown harder to follow. Herbert herds us into the pickup and we set off, leaving the elephant imprinted against the fiery sunset like a grey ship at anchor in the deep ocean of the nyika.

We pass the Maasai village, dim lights glimmering through chinks in the planks – homemade kerosene lamps, rope wicks dipped in discarded soda cans. The Maasai slip behind; Nanyuki lies a half-hour ahead. We're silent. Nothing left to say. We all feel it – the tranquil end to a perfect day settling over us like a rug woven from the velvet colours of the approaching night.

Then like mythic beasts blazoned on a coat of arms, a pair of cheetahs stand against the vanishing tropical twilight. On the road's edge, impassive, they gaze as we pass, thin as string, their pale coats ghostly in the dimness. We don't slow. No-one speaks. As suddenly as they appear, the cheetahs are gone. But in the battered pickup careening blindly through the enveloping darkness, they are, like Ngobit itself, an after-image that will stay forever.

UPRIVER
BY STANLEY STEWART

IN BORNEO THERE were only two destinations: upriver
and down.

Downriver were the sorry towns of Chinese shop-houses, the
shuttered government offices and the anxious people of the
coast. Upriver was the interior, a world of forests and fat brown
streams, of head-hunters and disappointed missionaries, of
blowpipes and all-night raves in longhouses decorated with
human skulls. Upriver took you to places the roads couldn't
reach. It was not merely a destination. In Borneo it was what
people were: *hulu* – upriver.

I was feeling kind of *hulu* myself. Perhaps I had been
travelling for too long. I wanted some place untroubled by
arrivals and departures. I had the notion that upriver might
offer stillness, some kind of permanence, after the transient
feeling of the towns. Perhaps I toyed with ideas of innocence. I
was soon aware that such perceptions were not widely shared
in the towns where people tended to think of upriver as a
barbarian darkness. Yet they did their best to reassure me. They
said the missionaries had done a great deal to persuade the
upriver tribes to give up the old habit of decapitating the house
guests.

Down at the dock the river clawed at the rotting pylons. The boats looked like aeroplane fuselages that had lost their wings in some nasty incident. Inside the passengers sat in rows of broken seats, mesmerised by the onboard entertainment, a relentless diet of kung fu videos. I took my place between an enormous bald Iban in the terminal stages of emphysema and a boy with a lapful of roosters. A cloud of diesel fumes signalled our departure.

We swung upriver through wide river bends. The water was the colour of wet clay, its swollen surface disturbed by sinister eddies and half-submerged logs. Dark forest pressed down to the water's edge. From time to time the trees parted to reveal the longhouses of the Kayan and the Kenyah tribes. They looked like elongated Appalachian shacks, elevated on stilts, built of timber off-cuts, thatch and corrugated metal. Each longhouse was a communal village of many families, all sharing the same roof, the same veranda and the same problems with noisy neighbours.

Then the trees closed again, and the river was swamped with green reflections. Above us was a wilderness of clouds. As the afternoon wore on, the clouds sank into the treetops, and a melancholy rain came on, pockmarking the smooth surface of the water.

I stayed the night at Long Panai. It wasn't a scheduled stop. The fuselage made a slow fly-past, and I leapt ashore with a triple jump that would have astonished my old gym teacher. Long Panai was a substantial place; the longhouse ran along the riverbank for a quarter of a mile and contained 120 families. People sat outside on the covered veranda sifting rice and gossip. The young people looked like sober suburban kids, with their baseball caps turned backwards, while their parents looked like New Age freaks: a confusion of wild tattoos, pierced body parts, dangling ear lobes, patchwork clothing and funny-looking cigarettes.

269.

I was staying with Thomas, who was a minor royal. His reception room was the model of aristocratic taste, imported from downriver: furnished with purple arm chairs and a lime-green sofa encased in plastic. On the walls, among the ceremonial swords, the hornbill beaks, and the stretched skin of a flying squirrel, was a painting of Jesus and a picture of Bon Jovi torn from a magazine. Jesus and Bon Jovi were both very big in Sarawak.

Both of Thomas' grandfathers had been chiefs, though on opposite sides of a tribal war. His parents' marriage had been part of the peace treaty. Through Thomas' childhood political tensions had masqueraded as domestic strife.

'The old religion gave my family many powers,' Thomas was saying. He was a slow, thoughtful man with a stretched shiny face. 'It was a big responsibility. My paternal grandfather, for instance, could cure the sick by spitting on them. Also he was bulletproof.'

I said it was a wonder they had taken up Christianity when they already had such a useful faith.

'Who needs bulletproofing these days?' he said. 'Like you, we want to be in Paradise with the Holy Ghost. We want Eternal Life.'

After dinner – a rabbit – we sat outside on the veranda, drinking bowls of *tuak*, a homemade rice wine with a donkey's kick. Liana vines, climbing the stilts beneath the longhouse, curled round our feet. The evening was spread out across the surface of the river. From the depths of the forest at our backs came a discourse of animal shrieks. An old branch fell from a tree near the house with an echoing crash.

'We are rotting here,' Thomas sighed. 'Nothing survives in these forests. The damp, the termites, the vegetation, they overwhelm everything. If we fell asleep on these chairs, vines would be climbing our legs when we woke in the morning.'

Night fell, and the fireflies began to dance.

'When I was young I longed for life downriver. I felt claustrophobic here. I wanted someplace with possibilities. Here nothing changes.'

A chorus of frogs rose from the reed-beds below the house. Beyond, the river was a sheet of polished blackness, its movement invisible.

'What do you hope to find in Sarawak?' he asked.

I mumbled something about the drama of the river and virgin forests. I would have felt foolish talking to him about stillness, the quality he longed to escape.

'There is nothing here. Only trees and more trees. It is all the same. There is nowhere to go.'

The next morning I found a boatman with a *prau*, a dugout canoe, to take me further upriver. After an hour or so on the river we turned into a tributary where the narrow stream was cluttered with fallen trees. Hornbills shrieked from the forest canopy. The forest trailed leafy fingers in the current, and we slipped through cool chambers of shade beneath the strangler figs. An escarpment reared on our right, packed with giant hardwoods.

In the early afternoon an Iban longhouse, surrounded by black pigs and stands of maize, appeared on the left bank of the river. It was a ramshackle affair elevated on a rickety wilderness of stilts. Laundry and children dangled from the railings. The chief was away in the fields and we were received by his mother, a tiny octogenarian. Her lips and teeth were crimson with betel nut. Blue tattoos swarmed up her arms and across her bare breasts, and her elongated ear lobes hung down to her shoulders. She served us *tuak* for afternoon tea. It had a faint taste of sticking plasters. Sitting in the front parlour on straw mats, I checked the rafters for skulls, and was disappointed to find there weren't any.

With the boatman as translator, I asked about head-hunting. The woman was old enough to remember its heyday.

'The heads protected us,' she said, her gaze lingering on my cranium as she shifted a vast wad of betel nut from one side of her mouth to the other. 'They made the longhouse safe.'

In the old days, after a head-hunting expedition, the heads were skinned and smoked over a fire before being hung from the rafters in rattan nets. Properly appeased and respected, the heads brought blessings to the longhouse, from warding off evil spirits to producing rain. The magical powers of the heads waned with time so fresh goods were always in demand. Without fresh heads, the old woman said, longhouses are vulnerable. Now we have nothing to protect us.

In the evening we partied. After a rather murky dinner of fish and rice, more *tuak* was produced, and we moved outside to the passageway that acted as the village square. The neighbours began to gather. Music was provided by an erratic cassette player. After a few drinks the dancing began. Young girls arrived wearing sarongs and straw bonnets decorated with hornbill feathers. They turned slowly on the balls of their feet, gesturing with their long-fingered hands.

I asked if it was a dance of courtship. 'A war dance,' the chief cried merrily, throwing back another bowl of *tuak*. The chief was everything his mother was not: big, boisterous and coarse. As the drinking progressed, the entertainment grew a little ragged. A barrel-shaped man in a torn sarong sang 'Oh God Our Help in Ages Past'. He made it sound like a drinking song.

The chief's mother, a stickler for cultural traditions, was unimpressed with such innovation. She disappeared for a time, and when she returned she was wearing a blue silk gown. She had tied her hair in a bun and put kohl around her eyes. The girls and the men fell away and the old woman took centre stage. She danced exquisitely. Her face had the quality of a mask, austere and aloof, while her long delicate hands were full of expression. She was the Margot Fonteyn of Sarawak. Her performance was the highlight of the evening.

Or so, naively, I thought. In fact the entertainment thus far was merely a prelude to the star turn: me. On the wrong side of my tenth bowl of *tuak* I suddenly noticed that the assembled Ibans were waving at me. Closer inspection revealed they were waving me to my feet.

I demurred, but it was too late. A press gang of young women was bearing down on me. Someone put a straw bonnet on my head. Strong arms were lifting me. Through a veil of hornbill feathers, I suddenly found myself standing before the entire longhouse: a sea of expectant upturned faces. 'Make the Dance of England,' bellowed the chief.

In a *tuak*-inspired moment, I decided against such narrow nationalism and opted instead for the Dance of Europe. It seemed to offer more scope.

I began with the flamenco, a stirring rendition of heel-clicking and finger-snapping. I moved on to a Bohemian polka, interspersing this with bits of an Alpine jig of my own invention. Dizziness cut short the Irish reel and I passed groggily on to a high-kicking Cossack number which I ascribed to the Poles. When I tried a bit of Morris dancing, it came out like a storm troopers' rally.

My audience went wild. They held their sides and hooted. They beat the ground and howled. Even the chief's mother was amused. She clung to a post, dabbing at her eyes.

My performance marked the end of the evening, for which I was grateful. I felt I had been dancing on the *Titanic*. The longhouse seemed to be pitching in heavy seas. I made my way to a corner of the chief's front parlour and was asleep before I had finished unrolling my mat. At dawn I was awoken by the routine longhouse cacophony: crowing roosters, howling dogs and people quarrelling over breakfast five households away.

My performance of the previous evening had earned me a reputation as a comic turn. Crowds now gathered to watch me eat breakfast in the hope that I might do something funny. I was unable to oblige unless a minor bout of retching over the grilled chicken feet counted as fun. Perhaps understandably, my audience seemed to believe it did.

We pressed onwards, following the trail of rivers further into the interior. Herons patrolled the banks, lifting their feet primly from the water with each step. Brilliant kingfishers, blue and orange, flashed among the overhanging boughs. A monitor lizard, as still and gnarled as driftwood, watched us from a sandbank. A tribe of gibbons passed through the treetops on our right, hooting as they went. Fish eagles rose from their perches at our approach, and flew away upriver, disappearing around the bend ahead. Through that whole afternoon, as we bore upriver, we were preceded by eagles.

In the early evening we came to the last longhouse on the river. Women were washing in the shallows, and their voices and soft laughter drifted across the water. We moored the canoe and followed them up a mud path. The stairway, leading up to the longhouse platform, was a log carved in the form of a woman. Steps had been notched up the sides of her thighs and ribs. A few people sat outside their doors in the wide passageway that ran the length of the house. Tiny oil lamps burned at their feet, throwing tall shadows across the walls above their heads.

In the twilight fireflies swooned above the water like errant stars, and the pigs snuffled beneath the house.

I called in on the headman, and fell into another discussion about religion. Like Thomas he was an enthusiast for Christianity. It might have knocked head-hunting on the head, but in other respects he reckoned it was a good thing. His chief worry was backsliders. The Baptists used to operate in these regions, he explained, but the pastor, who was based on the coast, was no longer able to make the journey upriver. In the absence of the Baptists, things were getting out of hand, and the chief hoped the Anglicans might take an interest.

'Harvest festival is a bad time for backsliding,' the chief said. 'So much drinking and playing with the girls. The girls become so frisky, and the boys get too virile.'

I tried to look disapproving. I had heard about the harvest festivals. It was a time of carousing and licentiousness. In the party atmosphere, women strapped large phalluses round their waist, and taunted their menfolk. I cursed myself for travelling at the wrong season.

'I am thinking the Anglicans could sort us out once and for all,' he said. 'Do you know any Anglicans?'

'A few,' I said. 'Not overly virile.'

'I think it is time for the Anglicans.'

'I shall mention it to them. It sounds like an Anglican kind of thing.'

In the morning the longhouse was wrapped in a cloud, and the river was a tunnel of mist beneath dripping branches. After breakfast I set off for a walk through the forests. Among a tangle of orchids, I came upon the tomb of a local dignitary. In the riot of vegetation it looked like a garden shed overwhelmed by its garden. The boatman explained that the former chief had been a key figure in the War of the Penises, a notorious altercation that had neighbouring tribes trading insults to one another's manhood.

The great man had been buried with his belongings, which were littered about the sarcophagus inside the shed: a few clothes, an old wireless, a favourite rattan chair, some pillows, his shield and two swords. Thirty years had made them look like garden shed junk, rusty, cobwebbed, moth-eaten and mouldy. In another thirty years, they would be jungle. I thought of Thomas: nothing survives in these forests.

We walked on, cutting back towards the river where a canoe from the longhouse was waiting. Two boatmen poled me upriver over shallow rapids. Their shins were tattooed with fish hooks, a talisman for fisherman's luck. The longhouses all lay behind us now. The river narrowed to a green aisle beneath the leafy vaults of the forest. Giant hardwoods rose from beds of tiny unfurled ferns. The water was clear as air, running over smooth amber boulders. A long curve brought us to a waterfall. Beyond, the river was too shallow for boats. This place, miles above the last longhouse, was as far upriver as men ever came.

We drew the boat onto the sand bank and the boatmen made a fire and cooked lunch: chicken flavoured with lemon grass and ginger, baked inside bamboo. I swam in the sheltered pool beneath the waterfall. The forest tilted above me, overhanging the water, trailing vines like long stout ropes. The air was full of butterflies, iridescent green and lemon yellow. The boatmen sharpened their swords on the rocks, smoked palm-leaf roll-ups and watched the tree tops, cradling their blowpipes. Some sweet stillness was suspended on the liquid notes of birds.

I asked the boatmen the name of this place. They shrugged. It has no name, they said.

Eden, it occurred to me, must have been like this: a river, a sandbank, dappled sunlight, birdsong, the close embrace of forests. It was a virginal world. There was nothing to disturb this place. Only ourselves.

LISA ALPINE

Curiosity about what and who is around the next bend or beyond the curve of the horizon has fuelled Lisa Alpine's voyaging since she left home at eighteen to live in Paris. She has owned an import company, published a newspaper and, for the last two decades, woven writing and dance into her travel passion. The travel columnist for the *Pacific Sun* in Marin County, California, Lisa is a member of the Wild Writing Women group and teaches dance and writing workshops around the globe. Visit www .lisaalpine.com and www.danceweaver.com for more on her writing and dancing activities and offerings.

JIM BENNING

Jim Benning is a writer based in Southern California. His stories have appeared in *National Geographic Adventure, Outside, Men's Journal,* the *Washington Post* and the *Los Angeles Times*. He cofounded and coedits the online travel magazine WorldHum.com.

ART BUSSE

Art Busse was born and raised in Chicago, studied social theory at Princeton and Stanford universities, and has lived and worked in the San Francisco Bay area for the past three decades. He has developed a specialty in expressive architecture evoking strong emotions in response to place. His latest project, 'Cambio', has received wide media attention and thousands of visitors.

TIM CAHILL

Tim Cahill has won multiple awards for his travel and outdoor writing over the last thirty years. He is the author of nine books, literally hundreds of magazine articles, and is the co-author of three Imax screenplays, two of which were nominated for Academy Awards. He lives in Montana with his wife, Linnea.

ANGIE CHUANG

Angie Chuang is a journalist and writer in Portland, Oregon. She writes newspaper and magazine articles, literary nonfiction and poetry about the intersections of cultures in today's ever-shrinking world. Her work as a staff writer for the *Oregonian* has been recognised by the Columbia University School of Journalism, the Society of American Travel Writers and the Pacific Northwest Newspapers Association. 'A Picture of a Village' is based on a 2004 trip to Afghanistan. She is working on a book that further explores that journey, and the people and places at its heart.

JOSHUA CLARK

Joshua Clark, founder of Light of New Orleans Publishing, edited an award-winning and best-selling anthology, *French Quarter Fiction: The Newest Stories of America's Oldest Bohemia,* as well as Judy Conner's *Southern Fried Divorce,* and other books. He regularly contributes fiction, travel writing and photography to various national publications, from the *Los Angeles Times* to the *Miami Herald,* and has covered New Orleans for Salon.com and NPR.

CHRIS COLIN

Chris Colin is a former Salon.com editor and the author of *What Really Happened to the Class of '93*. He lives in San Francisco, New York and Ljubljana. If you've been lowered down a mysterious hole in the earth, don't be a stranger: chris@chriscolin.com.

CHRISTOPHER R COX

Christopher R Cox is a recovering newspaper journalist of nearly twenty years who has embarked on a full-time regimen of freelance writing, Larium and Third World travel. He is the author of the adventure-travel book *Chasing the Dragon: Into the Heart of the Golden Triangle*, about Myanmar's narco-warlords, and a contributor to *Men's Journal, Outside, Travel + Leisure, Reader's Digest* and *Destin-Asian*, among other magazines. He exacted his revenge on Cambodia's boat transport in the previous Lonely Planet anthology, *By the Seat of My Pants*. When not flying coach class, he lives in Acton, Massachusetts.

JASON ELLIOT

Jason Elliot's first book, *An Unexpected Light: Travels in Afghanistan*, won the Thomas Cook/ Daily Telegraph Travel Book award and was a *New York Times* bestseller. His new book is *Mirrors of the Unseen: Journeys in Iran*. He lives in London.

BILL FINK

Bill Fink's tales of global foolishness have appeared in a number of travel writing anthologies, including *Best Travel Writing 2006* and *By the Seat of My Pants,* and in the *San Francisco Chronicle*, where he is a regular contributor. For his latest, check out www.geocities.com/billfink2004.

ROSE GEORGE

Rose George is a freelance writer based in London. Previously senior editor of *Colors*, she is now executive features editor of *Tank* magazine. Her travels have taken in Saddam Hussein's birthday party; the alternative world soccer final in Thimphu, between Bhutan and Montserrat; and beauty salons in Afghanistan. Her first book, *A Life Removed: Hunting for Refuge in the Modern World,* is about refugees in Liberia and Cote d'Ivoire. She is currently working on a book about human waste.

CONOR GRENNAN

Conor Grennan is an Irish American who spent eight years working in international public policy in Prague and Brussels before realising he didn't have anything interesting to say at parties; he recently spent a year and a half travelling the world trying to change that. His work can also be found in the anthology *What Color is Your Jockstrap?* and online at www.conorgrennan.com. Please feel free to invite him to your next party.

Author Biographies

JAMES HAMILTON

James Hamilton has written for the *Village Voice, Men's Journal, Poets & Writers, San Francisco Focus, Sports Illustrated, California Magazine, South Dakota Review, Westways* and other magazines. He is also a screenwriter. He lives in the Bay Area.

PAM HOUSTON

Pam Houston is the author of four books, including *Cowboys Are My Weakness*, which won the 1993 Western States Book Award and has been translated into nine languages; *Waltzing the Cat*, which won the WILLA Award for Contemporary Fiction; and, most recently, *Sight Hound*. Her stories have been selected for the O Henry Awards and the Pushcart Prize, and have appeared in *The Best American Short Stories* and *The Best American Short Stories of the Century*. A former river-running and dall sheep–hunting guide, she is currently the director of creative writing at the University of California, Davis, and lives at 9000 feet above sea level near the headwaters of the Rio Grand.

PICO IYER

Pico Iyer has made a habit of going nowhere, travelling from Paraguay to Bhutan, North Korea to Iceland. For many years now, he has divided his time between an anonymous apartment in a nowhere suburb in Japan and a Benedictine hermitage in California. His books describing such journeys include *Video Night in Kathmandu, The Lady and the Monk, The Global Soul*, and, most recently, *Sun After Dark*.

KERRY LORIMER

Kerry Lorimer had never really sailed before she took an unpaid job as delivery crew aboard a twenty-metre yacht and sailed across the Atlantic Ocean. She's since sailed numerous laps of the Caribbean and United States east coast, completed a Pacific crossing and various shorter trips – and on the South Georgia voyage, sailed around Cape Horn. Kerry has worked and travelled in over one hundred countries on all seven continents and now runs a Sydney-based communications consultancy that specialises in nature-based tourism. Her photos are widely published, including in many Lonely Planet guides. Her travel articles have been published in magazines and newspapers and she is the coordinating author of Lonely Planet's book on responsible tourism, *Code Green: Experiences of a Lifetime*.

DON MEREDITH

A native Californian, Don Meredith has journeyed to Nowhere on five continents and survived to tell his tales in numerous journals, among them *Poets & Writers*, *The Texas Review*, Salon.com, *Image* and several anthologies, including Lonely Planet's *The Kindness of Strangers*. A confirmed expatriate, Meredith has lived on a Dalmatian island, a Tuscan farm, and, for the past dozen years, on an island off the Kenya coast. His most recent book is *Where the Tigers Were: Travels through Literary Landscapes*.

ROLF POTTS

Rolf Potts is the author of *Vagabonding: An Uncommon Guide to the Art of Long-Term World Travel*. His travel essays have appeared in dozens of major publications around the world, including *National Geographic Traveler*, *Conde Nast Traveler*, Salon.com, National Public Radio, *The Best American Travel Writing 2000* and several Lonely Planet anthologies. Though he keeps no permanent residence, Potts feels somewhat at home in Bangkok, Cairo, Paris, New Orleans, and north-central Kansas, where he recently renovated a small farmhouse one mile away from his sister's farm. His virtual home is http://rolfpotts.com.

LAURA RESAU

Laura Resau is an author, anthropologist, teacher and contributor to numerous anthologies and magazines. Her young adult novels, *What the Moon Saw* and *Red Glass*, are set in Oaxaca, Mexico, where she worked for two years. She now lives in Colorado, and stays busy dreaming up excuses to hop on the next plane to southern Mexico. Visit her website at www.lauraresau.com.

MICHELLE RICHMOND

Michelle Richmond's first novel, *Dream of the Blue Room*, is set in China. Her other books are *The Girl in the Fall-Away Dress* and the forthcoming novel *Ocean Beach*. Her stories and essays have appeared in *Glimmer Train*, *Playboy*, the *San Francisco Chronicle* and elsewhere. She lives in San Francisco, where she teaches creative writing and publishes the online literary journal *Fiction Attic*.

ANTHONY SATTIN

Anthony Sattin is a writer and broadcaster with a love of literature, travel, North Africa and the Middle East, particularly Egypt, where he lived for some years. A Fellow of the Royal Geographical Society, he has travelled widely and is a specialist in the history of travel in the Middle East and North Africa. He is the author of several critically acclaimed books, including *The Pharaoh's Shadow: Travels in Ancient and Modern Egypt* and *The Gates of Africa: Death, Discovery and the Search for Timbuktu.* Anthony coedited Lonely Planet's *A House Somewhere: Tales of Life Abroad* and his writings have appeared in several other Lonely Planet titles. He is based in London, where he is a regular contributor of both travel features and book reviews to the *Sunday Times*.

ALANA SEMUELS

Alana Semuels is originally from Boston, but currently lives in London where she works as a freelance journalist. She is a regular contributor to the *Boston Globe*, among other publications. She has lived in Greece, Guatemala and Botswana, and has travelled throughout the world in search of a good story. She hopes her mother will still speak to her after the publication of this one.

ALEX SHESHUNOFF

After graduating from college, Alex Sheshunoff started and ran an online lifestyle magazine about New York City called *New York Now*. When the Internet bubble burst, he spent his meagre savings on a one-way ticket to Yap and packed the hundred books he was most embarrassed not to have read during college. During his two years in the western Pacific, Alex would finish his books, meet the woman who would become his wife, and build a bungalow with fourteen friends on a remote island. His work has appeared in the *Austin American Statesman, the Arizona Republic* and *ABC World News Now*. Originally from Austin, Texas, Alex is pursuing an MFA in creative writing from the University of Iowa, where he is also a Museum writer-in-residence. He is currently finishing a book about the western Pacific.

STANLEY STEWART

Stanley Stewart is the author of three books on travel: *Old Serpent Nile* chronicles a journey from the mouth to the source of the White Nile; *Frontiers of Heaven* records his travels in China along the Silk Road; and *In the Empire of Genghis Khan* is an account of a thousand-mile ride across Mongolia. The last two books both won the Thomas Cook/Daily Telegraph Travel Book award in the UK, and have been translated into a dozen languages. When not travelling, Stanley divides his time between Dorset and Rome.

KARL TARO GREENFELD

Karl Taro Greenfeld is the author of three books about Asia, including, most recently, *China Syndrome: The True Story of the 21st Century's First Great Epidemic*. A longtime writer and editor for *Time* and *Sports Illustrated*, Karl has written travel stories for *Conde Nast Traveler*, Salon.com, *The Paris Review*, *Men's Journal*, *Outside* and other publications.

JEFFREY TAYLER

Jeffrey Tayler is a correspondent for the *Atlantic Monthly* and a contributor to *Conde Nast Traveler*, *National Geographic* and *Harper's*. He has published five travel books, including *Facing the Congo* and *Angry Wind: Through Muslim Black Africa by Truck, Bus, Boat and Camel*. His most recent book is *River of No Reprieve: Descending Siberia's Waterway of Exile, Death, and Destiny*.

JUDY TIERNEY

After taking a year-long sabbatical to travel through Africa, India, Southeast Asia, Australia and New Zealand, Judy Tierney left corporate America to work as a freelance marketing consultant. She continues to explore the world and write about her adventures. Her work has appeared in numerous publications, including Lonely Planet's *By the Seat of My Pants*, the *Dallas Morning News*, the *Denver Post* and on www.travelerstales.com. A Texas native, she now resides in San Francisco.

DAVI WALDERS

Davi Walders' poetry and prose have appeared in more than 150 anthologies and journals, including *The American Scholar, JAMA, Seneca Review, Crab Orchard Review, Ms* and *Washington Woman.* Her awards include a Maryland State Artist's Grant in Poetry, Hadassah of Greater Washington's Myrtle Wreath Award, a Time Out for Women Writing Grant from the Association for Religion and Intellectual Life, an Alden B Dow Creativity Fellowship, and fellowships at Ragdale Foundation, Blue Mountain Center, and Virginia Center for the Creative Arts. She developed and directs the Vital Signs Writing Project at the National Institutes of Health in Bethesda, Maryland, which helps patients and families who want to write and share their stories. Her work has been choreographed by the Gottlob/Oka Dance Co of Cleveland and read by Garrison Keillor on *Writer's Almanac.*

DANNY WALLACE

Danny Wallace is a writer and television presenter based in London. His books include *Join Me* (in which he started his own cult) and *Yes Man* (in which he said 'yes'...to *everything*). Both are currently being developed for film. He recently became King Danny I after founding his own nation, in the BBC2 series *How to Start Your Own Country.* His website is at www.dannywallace.com.